The Politics of
the Western Indian
Ocean Islands

edited by
John M. Ostheimer

The Politics of the Western Indian Ocean Islands

PRAEGER SPECIAL STUDIES IN INTERNATIONAL POLITICS AND GOVERNMENT

Praeger Publishers New York Washington London

Library of Congress Cataloging in Publication Data
Main entry under title:

The Politics of the western Indian Ocean islands.

(Praeger special studies in international politics and
government)
    Bibliography: p.
    Includes index.
    1. Madagascar—Politics and government. 2. Comoro
Islands—Politics and government.   3. Maldive Islands—
Politics and government.   4. Reunion—Politics and
government.   5. Seychelles—Politics and government.
I. Ostheimer, John M.
JQ3466. P64   320. 9'69   73-19447
ISBN 0-275-28839-0

320.969
P769

76- 5629   PRAEGER PUBLISHERS
        111 Fourth Avenue, New York, N.Y. 10003, U.S.A.

Published in the United States of America in 1975
by Praeger Publishers, Inc.

Printed in the United States of America

Dedicated to
Ellen, Gibson, and Bill
whose patience and inspiration are
both abundant

ACKNOWLEDGMENTS

The idea for this book came originally from my having lived for two years in Dar es Salaam, longing for a chance to explore and study the islands I knew were over the horizon, connected to Africa in so many ways, but still so distant. In 1973, a Fulbright-Hayes Research Fellowship provided the opportunity to experience the islands firsthand.

I am indebted to the Fulbright-Hayes program, the Research Fellowship Program of the Cultural Affairs Office of Southeast Asia Treaty Organization, the Transition Foundation, and Northern Arizona University for their support in money and time that made the trip possible. Also, I owe a debt to the many people in the region, both officials and private citizens, who shared with me what they knew of island politics (though I am, of course, responsible for any cases in which I may have misinterpreted the facts). I also thank my colleagues who took up whatever slack was created by my absence from the university.

My coauthors deserve praise for their patience with the dilemmas of long-distance communications, and I have profited from the research assistance and critical readings of many people, but I must mention the research help of Ann Slobodchikoff in particular.

In Chapters 4 and 7, I have used materials that were published in my articles on Seychelles in the Journal of Commonwealth and Comparative Politics (London) and on Comoros in The African Review (Dar es Salaam), and I wish to thank the editors of those journals for their permission to do so.

My thanks to Karen Oftedahl for an admirable typing job, and particularly to my wife, Nancy, for her continual help from start to finish of the project and then the book.

CONTENTS

LIST OF TABLES, MAPS, AND FIGURES

The Politics of
the Western Indian
Ocean Islands

1

INTRODUCTION
John M. Ostheimer

The "forgotten islands" of the Western Indian Ocean have always been synonymous for "seclusion." Most of these sleepy islands could be reached only by boat until the late 1960s, even then only by people with time and funds to burn. The Islands languished in a distant corner of the world, as safe from the self-serving strategies of the new world superpowers as they were from the feeble "development efforts" of their own tired colonial masters. Then change began, first in the 1950s as Qantas and Air France started commercial air routes to Madagascar and Australia with stops in the major islands of the Mascarenes chain (Mauritius and Réunion). For the more adventurous, Air France and its subsidiary, Air Madagascar, added service to the Comoros. In the early 1970s an ancient DC-4 on the Tananarive-Dar es Salaam route was stopping there twice a week: Comoros was still obscure. Seychelles had no commercial air service until 1971, and Maldives still had none in 1974.

The 20th century may have had more than its share of political turmoil, but as these sluggish travel developments imply, rarely was the Indian Ocean affected. Only a decade ago, Comoros and Réunion were reliably ensconced in the French fold, and although formally independent, the Malagasy Republic (Madagascar) was still France's firm ally. Maldives and Seychelles were gradually stirring from status as colonies, while qualms in the minds of Anglo-American geostrategy planners about the impact of coming independence (1968) in unstable Mauritius were offset by plans for the overtly strategic British Indian Ocean Territory (BIOT), a huge sector of the Western Indian Ocean marked off by Britain in 1965.

BIOT and particularly the intense recent discussion of a possible U.S. sea and air base at Diego Garcia atoll indicate that the region has the potential to become the stuff of world confrontations; but not

MAP 1.1

Western Indian Ocean

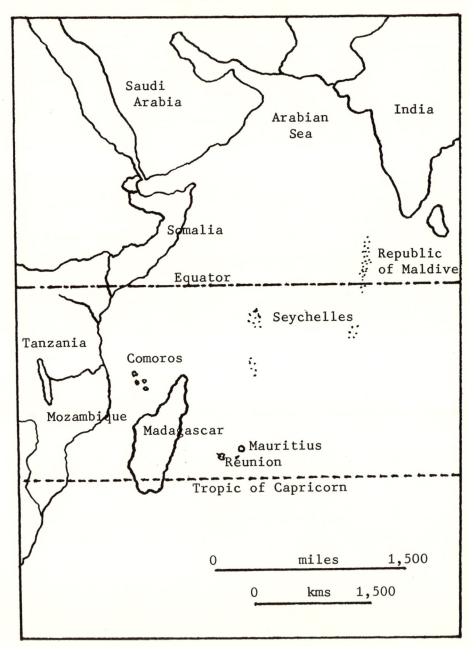

MAP 1.2

British Indian Ocean Territory

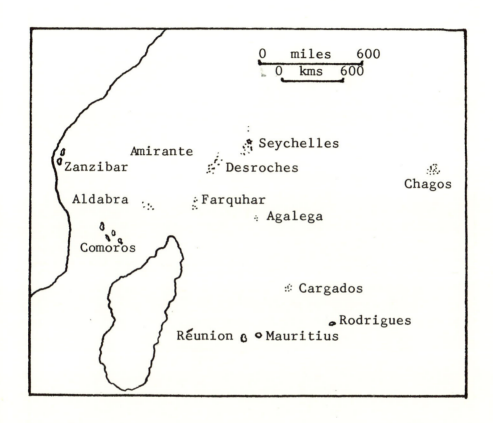

Note: Islands included in BIOT: Chagos Archipelago (formerly under British colonial governor in Mauritius); Desroches Archipelago, Farquhar, and Aldabra (formerly under British colonial governor in Seychelles).

nearly enough is known about this remote yet increasingly significant
part of the globe. This book tries to fill that gap. Its main purpose is
to explore, in detail, the politics of the region's six major islands.
But, as preliminaries, the introductory chapter outlines first the
Western Indian Ocean's importance to the states located on its periphery and, in return, the special nature that that impressive variety
of states gives to the region. Chapter 1 also places the region into
context from the broader perspective of world politics. The chapter
concentrates on the period since 1971, as the development of the
region's role in world politics before then has been covered elsewhere. [1]

For purposes of retaining manageability over the subject matter,
the geographic scope was confined to oceanic rather than coastal
islands and restricted to the western sector of the world's third
largest ocean, resulting from an imaginary line drawn south from
the tip of the Indian subcontinent. This practice is less defensible
objectively than it is for the subjective purposes of manageability.
Socioethnic influences from the Eastern Indian Ocean have reached
to the East African coast. Also, it is hard to discuss the contemporary
geostrategic problems of trade and military supply routes without
bringing the Eastern Indian Ocean, as well as the Mediterranean,
Atlantic, and Pacific into the discussion as well. But some limiting
of scope was necessary.

The Western Indian Ocean has earned a newfound importance in
world politics partly because of fundamental instabilities in the international power system. The traditional "peacemakers" have been in
retreat for some time. Great Britain, despite the ebb and flow of
remnants of imperial sentiment, as Tory and Labour Governments
succeeded each other, has withdrawn its forces almost completely
east of Suez. If any further strategic-purpose developments were to
occur in British-owned terrain there, the United States would have to
be responsible, or at least would pay the bill. Soon after BIOT was
created, in November 1965, the controversy over whether to develop
a base on Aldabra island demonstrated that British employment of
the BIOT would confront a variety of serious obstacles. During the
heyday of empire, Sir Tufton Beamish's Royal Society for the Protection of Birds would not have been much of a threat to the development of Aldabra as a "stepping stone" to the Far east. But by
November 1967, the Royal Society had overpowered British defense
planners. [2] Besides flightless rails, giant tortoises, pink-footed
boobies, and frigate birds, Beamish's allies included the devaluation
of the pound and a Labour Government uncommited to such remnants
of empire as island bases. Prime Minister Harold Wilson decreed
that the general idea of developing the young BIOT as a staging area
be shelved. Soon thereafter, in January 1968, the Wilson government
announced an escalated plan for military withdrawal "East of Suez"

that left the Singapore and Malaysia governments gasping; they had
been counting on a more leisurely seven-year period in which to
develop their own defense forces to a level of self-sufficiency.[3] After
the Conservatives took over, in June 1971, their election promises
of restoring a more gradual approach to withdrawal soon had to be
drastically scaled down. The Hong Kong post, the small base at Gan
in Maldives, and Singapore would be staffed, but with a far less significant force than Heath's party had promised. England's last heavy
cruiser, Belfast, was decommissioned in 1971, as was the last carrier,
Ark Royal, in 1972; the slow development of the "through-deck aircraft cruisers" completed the picture of Britain's declining ability
to intervene in Indian Ocean politics, or to be a factor in international
power balance in the area.[4] In December 1974, the Wilson government announced finally that the last British forces would withdraw
west of Suez.

     It took longer for France to admit the necessity of "belt-tighten-
ing," and the causes derived less from internal economic problems
than in Britain's case. For Britain, trade with the Far East had long
ago turned the Indian Ocean into a "stepping stone," rather than an
end in itself. The French owned fewer "uninhabited" islands and installed bases on those very territories that provided the rationale for
extending military force in the area. Deprived of the more significant
East Asian holdings by Napoleon's failure, the French had located
themselves on the periphery: French Polynesia and New Caledonia
to the east; Réunion, Comoros, Madagascar, and TFAI (French Territory of Afars and Issas, formerly Djibouti) to the west. Therefore,
loss of French bases, located on the soil of the last three territories,
would mean a loss of control in a more direct sense than Britain had
faced. Political change in Madagascar, an independent country that
had agreed, until 1972, to a continuing French military presence,
brought a retrenchment onto Réunion and, at least temporarily,
Comoros.

     A third colonial power, Portugal, found its power position
drastically altered during the fateful year of 1974: Mozambique had
been ruled by Portugal for 450 years, but Portuguese influence had
eroded since the start of the Front for the Liberation of Mozambique
(FRELIMO) insurrection in 1964 and Mozambique had become independent under a black government as 1974 ended.[5]

     In place of the historic remnants of Western European empires
appeared the world's superpowers of the 1970s: the United States,
USSR, China, and, at least in economic terms, Japan. The growing
influence of these countries must be studied in the context of the
possibilities the region's unstable political setting opens up to them.
The communist nations have long been interested in the area. One
reason is the historic concern of the Soviets with warm-water ports
for access to the wider world. Both the Soviets and the Chinese have

established diplomatic contacts in the Western Indian Ocean area. [6]
The Indo-Pakistani conflict and the birth of Bangladesh heightened
big-power awareness, but the region's significance has been hammered
home most dramatically by the sequence of events that began with the
"six-day war" and the Suez Canal's closure in 1967 and concluded
(temporarily?) with renewed war and oil boycott in 1973-74. Super-
tankers introduced after 1967 (which may still prevail after the reopening of Suez in late 1974 because of their cost-cutting potential)
brought the crucial transportation routes southward along the East
Coast of Africa for the first time since the canal had opened more
than a century before. Yuan-li Wu has argued that it would not be
wise in any case for Western countries to redevelop dependence on
Suez. "The most fundamental question from the defense point of view
is whether it pays to substitute for a longer route what may be a more
vulnerable one." [7]

Economic factors were, then, at least partly responsible for
the growing great-power competition in the Indian Ocean. By 1975 a
"mini-race" was in progress as Americans and Soviet strategists
vied to see which country could best lay claim to the Indian Ocean
(without being a disruptive presence there). Circular reasoning prevailed on both sides: President Gerald Ford, Admirals Elmo Zumwalt
and Thomas Moorer, and others argued that the United States should
spend millions to develop an air base on Diego Garcia, an island
leased for 50 years from the BIOT, so that Soviet presence should
not exceed the American in the region: Advocates of a base on Diego
Garcia argued that the Soviets had already installed bases on Socotra,
at Berbera, Somalia, and perhaps elsewhere and had cajoled the
governments of Aden, Singapore, and Mauritius into providing port
facilities. Conversely, Senators Stuart Symington, Claiborne Pell,
Charles Percy, as well as Chester Bowles, and others, argued that
development of the Diego Garcia facility would only trigger an expensive and useless new Soviet presence. [8] It was literally true, as
the diverse reaction to a May 1974 United Nations report demonstrated,
that people's perceptions of the area differed: Three experts com-
missioned by the United Nations had reported that China maintained
"bases" in Tanzania, Sri Lanka, and Pakistan. In the ensuing squabble,
it was obvious that one's definition of a "base" was an essential aspect
of the disagreement. [9]

The Indian Ocean's strategic importance for the world's great
powers may be guaranteed by the very remoteness and vastness of
the area. Depending on the progress (or lack of it) of the SALT
negotiations during the second half of the decade, and on the technological advances in subsurface missilery, the world's third largest
ocean may fit the label of "a vast launching pad for missile-firing
submarines . . . [which] with its 28,350,000 square miles of blue
water in which to get lost—becomes increasingly important in the
'balance of terror'." [10]

In discussing the Western Indian Ocean's contemporary importance one must also consider the nature of the political systems located there. Obviously a wide variety of states and territories touch the Indian Ocean, but some generalizations are possible. These political units are, by and large, politically unstable as well as terribly poor. The Indian subcontinent offers little support, as far as basic resources are concerned, for its three states, countries that have proven their mettle as political hot-spots since 1971. Few ventured to predict that the April 1974 negotiations (to clear up prisoner exchange and other holdover problems from the 1971 war) would result in genuine, long-term détente; the underlying problems facing the 700 million people of India, Bangladesh, and Pakistan were too severe. Starvation was already a grim reality on the subcontinent by the mid 1970s.[11]

The volatile politics of the Arabian peninsula involves fewer people directly, but the indirect effects are perhaps even more important for the industrial Western countries than are fireworks generated by the Indian subcontinent simply because the fate of the Arabians has direct bearing on 90 percent of the world's oil exports. The resurgent nationalism of the Shah's Iran and the inherent instability of the Arab Emirates on the east side of the peninsula and of Yemen on the West, as well as the revolutionary motives of the South Yemen regime, has assured the world that peninsular politics will not lack future excitement. [12]

As though not to be outdone, the Horn of Africa also remains volatile. As one scholar wrote, "Given the competing priorities, limited resources, and the heritage of the past, the prospects for smooth progress toward a modern society are not good."[13] Somali nationalism is one major upsetting force, for the Somalis overflow into the surrounding countries. Added to the difficulty Coptic Christian Ethiopia has had in controlling the Muslim rebellion in its northern provinces is, once again, the haunting specter of famine.

Kenya presents a rare picture of apparent stability, but the inevitable departure of "Mzee" (the old wise one) Jomo Kenyatta may bring the hidden tensions of intertribal resentment to the surface. Further South, Zanzibar, officially a part of Tanzania, has retreated into isolation during the decade since its bloody 1964 revolution, and mainland Tanzania has been genuinely occupied with its own political and socioeconomic experimentation. While not capable or desirous of causing trouble for outside influences in their part of the world, The Tanzanians have been outspoken advocates of the "zone of peace" concept for the Indian Ocean, and have been critics of Western influence there. [14] Mozambique's FRELIMO government, at this writing, seemed unlikely to be sympathetic to heavy U.S. influence in the region, while the South African Republic's possible contribution to Western Indian Ocean affairs depended heavily on one's interpretation:

Its strong economy and "western"-oriented government made the country a "bastion of anticommunist stability" to some, while to others South African racial policies and inequalities meant the continent's southern tip held an inherent promise of future chaos.

Encircled by this overall context, frequently volatile, sometimes explosive, are the six island systems discussed in this volume. Even within the region as a whole, one would never list these six societies at the top ranks of importance. But they are unquestionably important enough not to be completely lost in the shuffle. That has been their fate thus far. The only two works to have examined Indian Ocean Islands in a detailed, comparative treatment were quite dated by the time of this study. [15]

In the mid-1970s, whether independent or tied to England or France, the islands were undergoing significant political changes. Five years after political independence, Mauritius's complex, culturally divided society was still moving towards an expression of its own identity. That Mauritius had hosted the annual conference of the Afro-Malagasy-Mauritian Common Organization (OCAM), and had given attention to Senegal's president-poet Léopold Sedar Senghor, the "patron saint of Negritude," indicated the developing nonwhite consciousness of the island's peoples and government. Although Mauritius remained friendly with nearly every country, the influence of Western democracies was not enhanced by the war in Bangladesh. Mauritius maintained a polite silence although Sir Seewoosagur Ramgoolam's pro-Indian government could not have appreciated the sympathy shown by some countries (especially the United States) for Pakistan during that conflict. Anglo-American development at Diego Garcia, being discussed openly during 1973-74, drew strident comments from several Indo-Pacific nations. Mauritius was undoubtedly under pressure to take a stand that would jeopardize its "friends with all" posture in the face of what Australia, New Zealand, Madagascar, and India have already termed a threat to the Indian Ocean "zone of peace." [16]

In Madagascar, anti-French trends after the coup of 1972 pointed even more vigorously in the same direction. France no longer had influence on the island: Personnel were withdrawn from her Ivato and Diego Suarez bases, and France could no longer rely on them for effective staging of forceful interventions. The new political climate of the island republic ended this capability conclusively. In a sense, the Malagasy have staged a "second independence revolution," moving from French-dominated "formal independence" (1960-72) to a more complete psychological, economic, and institutional rupture: a recovery of an authentic national identity long buried under French colonial and post colonial domination. The impact of these events on world powers' presence in the area may have been previewed by the sudden decision, in December 1973, to deny docking space to four U.S. destroyers. [17]

In the Maldives, the redirection in 1974 of foreign policy ties towards India might indicate a desire to broaden contacts, and the results may produce greater involvement by that republic in the political pressures of the region.

Politicians in the remaining islands, which are still dependencies, sought guidance from currents of opinion elsewhere, and they began searching first in their own "backyard." In the Comoro Islands, although events were moving toward independence from France, the autonomy advocates faced a ticklish prospect of bargaining with the leaders of the southernmost of the four islands, Mayotte. Comorian politicians were therefore divided on the future of their islands.

Seychelles, whose formal relationship with the administering authority is similar to that of Comoros, was even more suddenly pressing for independence. Since the mid 1960s an autonomy movement, the Seychelles People's United Party (the minority party in the islands' legislature) had hammered constantly at the "evils" of British colonialism. By 1974, the governing party also desired more autonomy, partly in order to "deal" with the opposition.

Finally, in Réunion, which had appeared "safe" as an integral part of France, a combination of growing Creole cultural consciousness and increasingly successful political organization by the independence-oriented parties, especially the Communist Party of Réunion, may someday force a change in status for the island. French departure from Madagascar again clouded the issue, for rent and price increases resulting from the burgeoning forces stationed in Saint Denis were adding to the economic woes of many Réunionnais.

In these six island systems, it would appear that just as the Western countries became politically aware of the strategic Indian Ocean vacuum, political awakening in the area seriously threatened external influence. Ten years have seen remarkable change. "Great powers keep out of our ocean!" was a new sentiment that could be heard in significant and vocal segments of opinion in all six islands, and it pervaded the leaderships of the littoral states from Sri Lanka to the new black government that dominates Mozambique. Yet the islanders faced a dilemma in their very smallness. The variety of outside forces that seemed large enough to overwhelm them must have appeared bewildering. Japan's fishing fleets cruised along their shores and her goods flooded the less tariff-protected of Indian Ocean markets. The Organization of African Unity (OAU) and littoral African states loomed as powerful "meddlers" in internal island politics. The islanders were increasingly caught in the Francophonic-Anglophonic cultural war. Soviet, American, and Chinese presence looked most ominous of all. The Western Indian Ocean islands are small, and they need friends, but the choices in the mid-1970s were complex ones.

This volume is designed to pull together studies of internal political development in each of the islands. The Indian Ocean is not a widely known area, and most readers will probably find the current information function of the book to be the most useful of its intentions. Chapter 3, by Professor Allen, presents political developments in Madagascar. This is followed by studies of the other Francophonic islands, the Comoros and Réunion. The focus then changes to the islands that were, or are, under British influence.

A second purpose also exists: As social scientists, we wish to examine these Western Indian Ocean islands for qualitative differences between such societies and the larger, more familiar, nation-states. The stresses within small, isolated political systems in process of opening up to the outside world present new opportunities for social science. The pressures of intensified modern activity are an ideal laboratory in which to observe the response to such stress. In Chapter 2, some of the literature on the uniqueness of island politics, in the generic sense, is reviewed and, in some cases, tested by data collected by the principal author. Readers less interested in these more theoretical aspects of the study may wish to proceed directly to Chapter 3.

NOTES

1. A. J. Cottrell and R. M. Burrell, The Indian Ocean: Its Political, Economic and Military Importance (New York: Praeger Publishers, 1972); U.S. Congress, House Committee on Foreign Affairs, Subcommittee on National Security Policy and Scientific Developments, The Indian Ocean: Political and Strategic Future, 92d Cong. 2d Sess. Hearings of May, June, and August 1972 (Washington, D.C.: Government Printing Office, September 1971).

2. New York Times (February 25, March 5, August 15, November 23, 1967); Times of London (November 2 and 17, 1967).

3. New York Times (January 17, 1968); Time (January 19, 1968).

4. New York Times (October 29, 1970); A. J. R. Groom, "British Defence Policy under the Conservatives," Round Table 252 (1973): 483-505; B. Vivekanandan, "Heath Government's Policy for South Asia," India Quarterly 29, 3 (1973): 211-55. For developments in British Naval forces, see New York Times (July 20, 1971).

5. C. L. Sulzberger, "Hatching Dinosaur Eggs," New York Times (May 20, 1974).

6. Hanson W. Baldwin, "The Indian Ocean Contest: The Soviet Union's Increasing Interest," New York Times (March 20, 1972); Russell Brines, "Geopolitics in the Indian Ocean," Christian Science Monitor (October 30, 1974); New York Times (December 6, 1973);

William J. Barnds, "Arms Race or Arms Control in the Indian Ocean?" America (October 14, 1972): 280-82.

7. Raw Material Supply in a Multipolar World (New York: Crane Russak-National Strategy Information Center, 1973), p. 43. See also pp. 28-29.

8. Warren Unna, "Whom Do You Trust: Justifying Diego Garcia," New Republic (August 31, 1974); W. Unna, "Diego Garcia," New Republic (March 9, 1974); New York Times (January 22, 1974; March 13, 1974; March 21, 1974; May 9, 1974; August 2, 1974; and September 1, 1974); Chester Bowles, "A Considerable Speck," New York Times (May 13, 1974); National Review (July 6, 1973); Jurg Meister, "Diego Garcia: Outpost in the Indian Ocean," Swiss Review of World Affairs (April 1974): 6, 7; Bernard Weintraub, "The Value of Diego Garcia," New York Times (June 2, 1974); Richard J. Levine, "The Debate over Diego Garcia," Wall Street Journal (April 4, 1974); "Atoll Trouble," Time (April 1, 1974); U S. Congressional Record, 93d Cong., 2d Sess., Senate Debates 120, 62 (April 3, 1974 and May 6, 1974).

9. Economist (May 25, 1974); New York Times (May 19, 1974).

10. Baldwin, op. cit. See also George H. Quester, ed., Sea Power in the 1970s (New York: Dunnellen, Kennikat, 1974); Rear Adm. E. M. Eller, The Soviet Sea Challenge (Chicago: Regnery, 1972); T. B. Millar, Soviet Policies in the Indian Ocean Area (Canberra: Australian National University Press, 1972).

11. New York Times (April 10, 1974); K. P. Misra, "Trilateralism in South Asia," Asia Survey 14, 7 (1974): 627-36; Economist (July 6, 1974); Robert Jackson, "The Great Powers and the Indian Sub-Continent," International Affairs 49, 1 (1973): 35-50.

12. For example, see Stanley Karnow's analysis of Omani Politics in "Confrontation in the Persian Gulf," New Republic (May 4, 1974); J. Bowyer Bell, "South Arabia: Violence and Revolt," Conflict Studies 40 (November 1973); on Yemen, New York Times (June 14, 1974). See also M. A. Saleem Khan, "Oil Politics in the Persian Gulf Region," India Quarterly 30, 1 (1974): 25-41. On Iran, New York Times (September 28, 1974); Sepehr Zabih, "Iran Today," Current History 66, 390 (1974): 66-69.

13. J. Bowyer Bell, The Horn of Africa: Strategic Magnet in the Seventies (New York: Crane Russak-National Strategy Information Center, 1973), p. 47.

14. Christian Science Monitor (November 5, 1973).

15. Theodore L. Stoddard, et al., Area Handbook for the Indian Ocean Territories (Washington, D.C.: Government Printing Office, 1971); Philip M. Allen, "Self-Determination in the Western Indian Ocean," International Conciliation 560 (November 1966).

16. New York Times (April 10, 1974; October 1, 1974).

    17. New York _Times_ (December 1, 1972; December 27, 1973); J. C. de L'Estrac, "Océan Indien, Zone de Paix; Les Appétits et les Intérêts Derrière un Slogan," _Lumière_ (Tananarive) March 25, 1973.

2

ARE ISLANDERS
DIFFERENT?
A SURVEY OF
THEORETICAL IDEAS
John M. Ostheimer

The Western Indian Ocean islands offer a unique chance to observe the interaction of several conditions, each of which affects political systems elsewhere in the world, but which in combination may give some uniqueness to the area. First, they are all islands, and the distance between them and the world centers of activity and power are great. Second, most of the systems involved are extremely small; even Madagascar is "small" in some ways. Third, most of the societies concerned are racially mixed. This chapter will deal with each of these conditions separately, then discuss their collective impact on the politics of the islands. The chapter will also refer to some of the major differences between these islands: Each is unique in many ways.

THE POLITICAL EFFECTS OF GEOGRAPHICAL ISOLATION

Isolation is a relative thing. In some ways Nairobi is less "isolated" from London than is a hamlet in Devon. Also, isolation's effects may vary with the type of relationship an isolated spot has developed with the outside world. Réunion and Mauritius share a mutual degree of geographic remoteness; but for most Réunionnais political isolation would mean interruption of contact with France, while Mauritians are equally concerned with events and attitudes in several parts of the world. In spite of these difficulties of defining isolation, we may generalize somewhat about Indian Ocean islands because in all cases the extent of their world involvement is relatively recent. Stanley de Smith, who has lived on islands while advising their leadership on constitutional structures, has written: "The inhabitants of inaccessible islands usually have a parochial outlook, and they are seldom influenced by the prevailing currents of world opinion."[1]

If lack of information and parochial outlook are problems islanders face, how can the degree of their parochialism be measured? During March 1973, the author attempted, through a survey of politically related attitudes, to provide some test of the effects of isolation. For Seychelles, where the survey was carried out, results from the political information sections of the questionnaire seem at first to substantiate de Smith's view. Seychelles College (secondary school) students, a cluster sample of future elites, were tested on the names of world leaders and the heads of the British Conservative and Labour parties. They scored very low on this part of the questionnaire.

Cross-cultural equivalence is certainly a problem in tests of this type, and without the funds to carry out simultaneous scientific sample surveys in the manner of the Civic Culture study, or Patterns of Human Concerns, inferences cannot be strongly asserted. Nonetheless, one comparison with American data is possible. Using Survey Research Center data, Jennings found that American high school seniors (also the modal age of the Seychelles College respondents) were more concerned with "cosmopolitan" affairs than with local. The most persistent pattern of salience to emerge from their expressed interest in, knowledge of, and trust in various levels of government (from highest to lowest) was 1) international, 2) national, 3) state, 4) local. Compare this ranking with the results in Table 2.1; For Seychelles College students, a very different picture emerged. Not surprisingly, they demonstrated detailed knowledge of the political personnel of their island. They were "under a spell" of local politics and had little time for the rest of the world. De Smith has offered some explanation for such parochialism among islanders:

> This may be attributed to preoccupation with the
> means of subsistence, partly to lack of incentives
> to diversify their talents, partly to social and religious
> pressures toward conformity, partly to the irrelevance
> of ideologies and the importance of dominant individuals,
> and partly to the poverty of the informative media.[2]

What possible effects might such concentration on local affairs have? It would not be surprising to find (although difficult to prove) that isolation limits the ability of a society to draw on experiences outside

TABLE 2.1

Measure of Political Knowledge, Seychelles

(number of leaders of the British and Seychelles political parties, and of selected world countries, identified correctly by Seychelles secondary school students)[a]

Number of Leaders Named by Respondents	British Labour Party	British Conservative Party	Seychelles Peoples' United Party	Seychelles Democratic Party	Leaders of World Countries
None	214	203	17	13	61
One	67	60	3	2	15
Two	10	22	9	1	10
Three	1	6	21	16	22
Four	0	1	47	27	34
Five	0	0	195	232	150[b]
Total	292	292	292	292	292

[a]Countries listed were USSR, Philippines, Canada, England, France, United States, Greece, China, West Germany, Nigeria, India, Chile, Mauritius, Kenya, Malagasy Republic, and Tanzania.

[b]These respondents were able to name five or more world leaders.

Source: Compiled by the author.

its boundaries. The potential to base decisions on a range of options
would therefore be restricted. Even when islanders come to realize
that their fate is inextricably tied to events elsewhere, the adjust-
ment to a more flexible, outward-looking response comes slowly.
A decade ago, Philip Allen commented on the general results of
isolation in the Western Indian Ocean:

> Eager to acquire what they know of modernity, advance-
> ment, and institutional maturity, the islanders remain
> plunged in chronic poverty and in the residue of centuries
> of isolation from international main currents . . . leaders
> cling . . . to their own insular rock. They are diffident,
> often aloof, and fearful of being overwhelmed by the power
> of a foreign world. [3]

How interesting to know (and how difficult to measure) what effects
the fast-moving 1960-74 period, with increased communications and
travel links between Indian Ocean islands and the outside world, have
had on the leadership and masses of the relevant societies. It is
tempting to extend the effects of isolation into the following hypothesis:
The more isolated an island society, the more likely that people will
assume they cannot stand on their own; distance varies inversely with
demand for independence. According to this theory, dependence need
is bolstered by the sense of feebleness experienced at the fringes of
an interconnected and dynamic world. The people of Pitcairn, for
example, have shown that they do not want to live in bustling England,
but they willingly accept English constitutional rule. Contrarily, one
can find in the sparse theoretical literature on islands, a stated direct
relationship between insularity and demand for separate political autonomy. According to the UN Institute for Training and Research
(UNITAR) study, "The most obvious factor [explaining claims to
separate international identity] is physical, geographical isolation.
This element is particularly strong in the case of islands, especially
remote ones."[4]

Though the Indian Ocean fails to provide an adequate data base
for any kind of statistical test of the relationship between remoteness
and the desire for autonomy, its islands do provide some generalizations on the subject: One of the more remote island systems, Maldives,
became independent and joined the United Nations in 1968. Social
change, communications with the outside world, and psychological
independence have lagged. (The Maldives did not challenge the British
base at Gan.) Mauritius, independent the same year, has served as
a landing point in a cross-ocean air route for years. A multipolar
ethnicity continues to develop with its tensions barely below the surface, while the Ramgoolam government, at least until the recent
ouster of the Creole leader Gaetan Duval from the coalition, continued

to establish complex economic and cultural relationships with many countries. Réunion, with nearly the same relatively high access to world communications, eschewed independence. Obviously the tenacity of French control was the determining factor. Until recently, the Comoros also resisted independence. But like Seychelles, Comoros shares the Maldivian degree of geographical isolation.

No pattern emerges from this, although it can be said that all three of the more remote areas (Maldives, Seychelles, and Comoros) are either independent, nearly so, or arguing out the case. The Seychelles survey respondents dealt ambivalently with the issue of independence. Table 2.2 Column B indicates a list of issues rated as "important concerns" when they were pointed out as possible choices to a sampling of 300 Seychellois. But in an open-ended question before the choices were offered, Column A, other issues more frequently received ratings of "important." These data might indicate that independence was a frequent but superficial concern during 1973 for Seychellois. Consistent with the data on political information presented in Table 2.2, the Seychellois respondents cared deeply about local affairs, proportionately more so, I shall argue, than citizens of small communities within large countries.

To summarize, de Smith and the UNITAR authors are not upheld by the results of our introductory examination of Western Indian Ocean islands. Intervening factors confuse any clear relationship between geographic isolation and political self-sufficiency as expressed by demands for independence.

ISOLATION AND ISLAND CULTURES

Students of island societies have discussed possible psychological effects of isolation on cultural development. According to Stanley de Smith, island societies are more clearly distinguished from their neighbors than are cultures that share a land border. This is difficult to prove when comparisons are limited to older countries, where boundaries evolved "nationally." But when islands are compared with the frequently undefined borders separating new countries of Africa, de Smith's contention is self-evident. Even so, de Smith argues that a paradox exists: If subcultures are present on the same island mutual hostility may be unusually intense. According to de Smith, these two principles interact as follows:

Islands have clearly defined boundaries. Save where an island is divided into alien political units or is psychologically dominated by communal affiliations, its inhabitants tend to have a strong sense of "belonging" to a distinct geographical

TABLE 2.2

Concerns of Seychellois

| Category of "concern" | A Frequency of mention of "concern" in response to open-ended question | | B Ranking of "concerns" when compared with others on itemized list | |
	Raw Frequency	Percent of Respondents Mentioning Concern	Average Score	Comparative Ranking
Inflation	42	14.4	2.24	14
Tourism development	34	11.6	1.64	4
Political dissension	31	10.6		
Housing	28	9.6	1.28	1
Educational development	18	6.2	1.36	2
Political independence	16	5.5	1.54	3
Unemployment	12	4.1		
Conservation	8	2.7	2.18	12
Road safety and development	8	2.7		
Agricultural development	8	2.7		
Decay of moral values	8	2.7		
Economic development	6	2.1		
Poverty	5	1.7	1.75	6
Foreign interference	5	1.7		
Inequality	4	1.4		
Church-state relations	4	1.4		
Overpopulation	3	1.0	1.90	10
Crime prevention	3	1.0	1.83	7.5
Drugs	2	0.7		
Drunkenness	2	0.7		
Pollution	1	0.3	2.34	16
Development of trade	1	0.3	1.89	
Communist countries' interest in area	1	0.3	2.00	11
Problems of elderly	1	0.3		
Foreign ownership	1	0.3		
No response	38	13.0		

("Concerns" not mentioned in response to open-ended question)

Political apathy			2.55	17
Taxes			1.83	7.5
Western countries overreacting to communist countries' moves in area			2.65	18
Recreational development			2.23	13
Lack of funds from U.K.			2.32	15
Disease			1.68	5

Source: Compiled by the author.

18

entity. This does not exclude loyalty to a larger entity (including a mainland territory, or to a group of islands—e.g.,
the Philippines), but it is apt to generate feelings ranging
from local pride to zenophobia.[5]

How does this differ from the feelings that separate, for instance,
the Basque and Breton from France?

These feelings are not necessarily different from the in-
group loyalties of tribal, religious, linquistic or other
communal groups in mainland societies; but by virtue
of being expressed within confines of a visibly separate
geographical area they may appear a "legitimate" and
even to the spectator, an attractive manifestation of
particularism. Hence, the wide-spread sympathy with
the Anguillans in their revolt against the authority of
St. Kitts.[6]

De Smith's inference that island separation enhances the legitimacy
of ethnic differences, both for the contesting groups internally and
for outside acceptance of its independence, is hard to prove. The
variety of reactions to Nigeria's ethnic rupture of 1966-70 was based
more on the political theories of the evaluators: There is little to
indicate that Julius Nyerere's support for Biafra or Leonid Brezhnev's
for the federal side was conditioned by the continental (rather than
islandic) nature of Nigeria's tribal strife.

Unfortunately, no survey results were collected that would shed
measurable light on the degree to which Western Indian Ocean islanders substantiate de Smith's statement. The author had planned to
give the Bogardus Social Distance Scale, adapted for local conditions.
Through comparing results from different societies on this popular
scale, some conclusions on the vigor of Comorian or Seychellois
self-perception, and on their specific emotional relationship with
other ethnic and racial groups, would have emerged. Research on
how much island separateness stimulates cultural identity is still
needed.

It is also not difficult to see that cultural identity—a sense of
distinctness that may be increased by isolation—does not mean that
cultural differences and rivalries will be absent. Conversely, it is
understandable that in the pressure-cooker politics of a small island
undiluted by national and international considerations, the fixation
with what is, in a comparative perspective, local politics, exacerbates
divisions. To use an Indian Ocean case: Maldivians are conscious of
themselves as one group, when the alternative is the Indians, the
Japanese, or the Americans. Among themselves, however, the inhabitants of one Maldive island lose no love over the neighboring

islanders. To the extent island remoteness causes the Maldivians to spend a greater percentage of their political energy "among themselves" than do mainland peoples, cultural differences may well be increased.

What are we to learn from this analysis? The most troublesome conclusions from the intensifying effects of isolation on the social division within islands are these: Small island cultures, whose ability to operate as autonomous states in the modern world is objectively in grave doubt and who would stand to gain by cooperative federal constitutional solutions, may be the hardest of all to conjoin effectively.[7] Indeed, the ability of islands to stay together in an already established unit may be jeopardized by the maritime nature of their separation. Such well-known cases of fissiparous tendencies as the Caribbean and Malaysian federations attest to this.[8] However, in the light of similar continental examples (Nigeria, Central and East Africa), any conclusion that only island settings produce such strains must be stated with extreme care.

One can easily observe this phenomenon in the Western Indian Ocean. The Mauritian racial balance of two-thirds Indians to one-third Creoles is reversed on Rodrigues, its small possession to the east, and the relationship between the two islands tends "toward fragmentation."[9] The Maldives, with 220 inhabited islands, offer similar potential for centrifugal tendencies, though racial diversity has not been to blame for political stress there.[10] And, in the Comoros, historical traditions and perhaps ethnic, religious, and linguistic differences have produced an intense challenge to Comorian unity from Mayotte Island.

Outside forces may exacerbate the trend toward demands of independence from distant colonial masters. Along with several other very small countries, the Maldive Islands "are accepted by the outside world as independent or internationally autonomous areas, for a variety of reasons," while larger, distinct subcultures within established states "would in normal circumstances not now be considered by the outside world as entitled to any form of international recognition."[11] The United Nations has at times served an important catalyzing role for nationalism,[12] though, once again, one cannot be sure how powerful island status is in explaining why Maldives and Mauritius were accepted as separate entities. Recalling the international acceptance of Gambia and Equitorial Guinea is enough to breed caution here.

In searching for other factors, we return again to the historical context rather than to differences between islands and mainland cultures. The colonial powers helped to divide cultures that might otherwise have developed a natural and binding experience of communications. The divisions of the Mascarenes into French Réunion and British Mauritius is an example of how colonial powers inhibited communications: For example, colonial empires and economic approaches led the British to import Indians. Today the islands are culturally very different, but colonial intrusion sometimes had the opposite result.

> The intrusion of colonial powers into an oceanic area tended
> to harden divisions among the islands by inhibiting freedom
> of movement and informal cooperation, and by introducing
> religious sectarianism and promoting uneven levels of eco-
> nomic development. At the same time those powers im-
> posed an often artificial cohesion on island groups under
> their own administration. [13]

To conclude, the impact on relationships among islands, and between islands and other areas, may not be as powerful in explaining the cultural development of Indian Ocean societies as are certain other factors. We have discussed the varying impact of colonial forces. In addition, some of the islands of the Western Indian Ocean have quite dense populations, a condition that worsens communal cleavages within the island. Mauritius has shown severe problems along these lines, but the country's survival proves "that lack of homogeneity is not sufficient to undo a small territory." [14]

THE PROBLEMS OF SMALL SCALE

Although there is no fool-proof test of when a politico-economic system must be considered "small" in scale, most measures that do exist are in agreement (with the exception of Madagascar) that the Western Indian Ocean islands qualify as "small." This is a significant issue for the study of politics generally, for there are more countries near the small end of the size scale than at the other. [15]

Perhaps the most deeply studied of the problems that attend small scale are the economic consequences. Simon Kuznets (who includes all states under 10 million population in his category of "small") pointed out that size affects "diversity of resources, range of possible industries, dependence upon foreign trade, and other problems of economic efficiency," and that these difficulties apply "with greater force to nations whose population is below five million." [16] These problems of small scale are not necessarily crippling to economic development. Cultural unity can act as a balancing force. In fact, Kuznets argued that smaller-scale societies may have an advantage in developing their economies because greater social cohesion will breed quicker acceptance of change: "The small states are likely to have an easier task because of the closer ties among the members of their smaller populations; because of a possibly greater community of feeling among these smaller populations." Kuznets based this hope on the possibility that smaller size will often be accompanied by "long background of common historical experience and . . . lines of communication and connection . . . that are closer than in a large country with its diversity of regions and multiplicity of local interests." Kuznets probably had the Netherlands in mind here, rather than most small new countries. He explained that small countries "driven by the existence of sizable and hostile minorities or split almost in two by religious, linguistic, and other differences" may face a less optimistic prospect for economic planning. [17]

Most of the Indian Ocean societies are heterogeneous, and their attempts at economic planning may face a situation Kuznets described as more applicable to large countries, especially if their island nature worsens existing social divisions. "Among the larger nations this task is far more difficult, since the ties among the various sectors of their populations are looser and regional and other cleavages can more readily develop."[18] In other words, size per se may be less important to the social contributions (or hindrances) to economic development than are historical and social factors.

Problems of scale reduce the small territorial government's ability to provide either the necessary organizational structure or the services that people expect during this modern age. Holding constant the problems that have more to do with economic underdevelopment than with small size, the UNITAR study perceived two specific limits of size: (1) the diseconomics of small scale for resource base and product variety, and the resulting proportionately greater vulnerability to disaster, crop disease, and market fluctuations and (2) limits in human resources that strain the small system's capacity to provide what people consider "essential" services in today's world. [19]

A final economic consideration is the possibility that small size will leave a state at the mercy of the larger markets and countries. According to Robert Triffin, "Everything else being equal . . . the smaller nation will be more vulnerable than the larger nation to the action of its neighbors, since its ability to concentrate on—and exploit to the full—the lines of production for which it is best fitted by natural advantages will be more dependent on its freedom of access to foreign markets for its exports and imports."[20]

It is difficult to pin down the role of size and island isolation as forces contributing to these economic problems. A majority of the new African countries are so small, so isolated by the artificial boundary-making of the 19th century, and so "single crop" as a result of colonial era "dual economics" that they face the same problems as Seychelles or Comoros. An important difference would emerge if it were possible to prove that small islands as economic systems will find it harder to break away from these economic patterns because they are islands.

A second variety of effects that smallness may have on island societies, particularly operating in conjunction with isolation that reinforces parochialism, is impact on the personality of islanders. Burton Benedict notes that islanders guide their relationships with others in their society on a very personal level. Everybody of consequence is likely to know everyone else who matters. In larger societies, more objective standards must be established to regulate interpersonal contact. People who do not know each other personally need to know the categories of identified offices and specific functional roles as guidelines for their interactions. The "universalism" of an office, to use Talcott Parsons's term, helps us to know what to expect from the person who holds it. People in small societies are in the odd situation of seeming to need many of the governmental and political structures of large countries in order to administer modern programs effectively (and even to classify as "governments") but of needing these structures less than they realize in terms of the sociological aspects of organization. Large percentages of the populace already know so much about the person who occupies a post that they will be likely to feel: "I know what he will say!" Also, there is less reason to accept the administrator's position as one that indicates proven achievement. Since "he's a friend of the prime minister," that must explain how he got his job.

I am certainly not arguing (the Watergate events so fresh in our memories) that political position in larger complex societies is always "achieved" rather than "ascribed" through nonpolitical status (family, church, and so on). Ascription is still an important recruitment characteristic in the most large-scale impersonal societies. It is a question of degree: The key to very small societies is that people are so aware of the ascriptive features that they guide their expectations by them. Benedict has described a typical situation arising in a highly personal, relatively small, society:

> It becomes difficult to remove an inefficient employee on grounds of inefficiency alone because he is attached to the employer by kinship and political ties. Impersonal standards of efficiency, performance, and integrity are modified by the myriad relationships connecting the individuals concerned.[21]

Thus, according to this line of reasoning, small island political systems would serve as good examples of the effects of Weber's traditional society struggling to employ Gesellschaft structures. When everyone knows everyone else, it is harder to judge "what a person does, rather than who he is."[22] Survey data could be collected to study this by asking how people obtained their jobs or promotions. While the responses would be only impressionistic, it is, after all, the impressions that count. Hypothetically, islanders would have accounted for more of these occupation data with ascription-related answers than would British or American respondents. No such data have as yet been collected.

Benedict predicts that when small, isolated territories attempt to accomplish what the large societies are doing, the more particularistic effects of their small social fields will restrict their achievement: "industrialization would appear to be most dependent on universalistic role-relationships; cottage industries, commerce and agriculture perhaps less so."[23]

De Smith adds a second factor, besides the inefficiency of ascriptive society:

> In the first place, considerations of social status, kinship, friendship and personal background tend to matter more than individual merit when questions of leadership and promotion arise. This is perhaps a very broad generalization, because even in communally divided or socially stratified societies like Mauritius and St. Kitts, men of humble origins (Ramgoolam and Bradshaw, for example) can rise to the top. But rigidity of social structure usually makes for inefficiency.

Similarly, regardless of the type of economic activity going on, an important decision in a factory or plantation will affect larger percentages of people in the small-scale society of an island.

> . . . if deep political cleavages and animosities based on community, ideology or personal faction, arise on a small island, the lot of those opposing the group in power is apt to be miserable. There may be no effective refuge, no place to hide, no alternative source of remunerative or prestigious solace. And it follows from this that the incentives to achieve political power and to cling to it are all the greater. Third, particularly where the economy is narrowly based and the island poor, the activities of government are pervasive: government is the main employer; competition for good jobs in the public service is intense; accusations of nepotism and corruption abound. Fourth, it may be extremely difficult to find able persons with the requisite degree of impartiality, or at least persons who are generally accepted as being impartial, to fill posts in which impartiality is of paramount importance. Politicians will often demand that senior and middle-grade civil servants and police officers be their active champions.[24]

De Smith's view is weakened somewhat by the rather awful plight of political oppositions in new and larger continental countries, as well as in some established democracies. His point is difficult to prove, but worth looking for in the six island studies that follow. The Seychelles respondents, for example, are quite aware of the fascination they have for politics: "Political dissension" in Table 2.2 stands for a response that was variously termed "political fighting," "we are committing political suicide," and "too much politics."

The bureaucracy and structures of government may also be affected by the emphasis on personal relationships that is fostered by isolation and small scale. Budgetary restrictions and other valid reasons for constructing a "mini-cabinet" system with four to six ministers, as in Seychelles, result in fierce competition for the available positions and sharp focus on the question of who does staff the government posts. There may be fewer qualified competitors, to be sure, but the narrow list of "target jobs" compensates for that.[25] The personal rivalries that result have caused some observers to suggest that very small island systems consider hiring outsiders, professional bureaucrats, to govern in a more nonpartisan manner than any "resident" can do.[26] Of course, such proposals come up against the very political pressures they are designed to alleviate, and this reduces their chance to succeed.[27]

CONCLUSION

Obviously, the state of theorizing on island societies is not far advanced. The literature is largely impressionistic, for which there are at least two reasons. First, the statistical basis for testing hypotheses related to the potential uniqueness of islands is absent. Islands that would classify as "small" but still significant political entities in their own right are not very numerous. Perhaps for this reason, smaller island societies escaped the scrutiny received by virtually all phenomena that could serve as targets of the "behavioral revolution." Second, and perhaps more important, interest in islanders per se has not been nearly as keen as studies that dealt with definable areas or regions. Empirical study of Latin America or African political systems, for example, is itself a young field, but it has at least begun. There are no "islandists" (save in the sense that some of us enjoy visiting such places), and the field, if it exists, is a new one.

NOTES

1. Stanley de Smith, Microstates and Micronesia (New York: New York University Press, 1970), p. 60.

2. Ibid.

3. Philip M. Allen, "Self-determination in the Western Indian Ocean," International Conciliation 560 (1966): 14.

4. Jacques Rapoport, Ernest Muteba, and Joseph Therattil, eds., Small States and Territories: Status and Problems (New York: Arno Press, 1971), p. 202.

5. De Smith, op. cit., p. 57, emphasis mine. For a Pacific corollary, see W. T. Roy, "Independent Fiji's External Relations," Round Table 243 (July 1971).

6. De Smith, op. cit., p. 57.

7. Roy, op. cit., p. 404.

8. Rapoport et al., op. cit., p. 49. The study cites the Caribbean Federation and U.S. Pacific Trust Territories. One could add Malaysia and Indonesia.

9. De Smith, op. cit., p. 63. See also p. 70.

10. On the Maldives, see de Smith, op. cit., p. 63, and Rapoport et al., op. cit., p. 49.

11. Rapoport et al., op. cit., p. 51.

12. See de Smith's strong criticism of the UN role regarding Mauritius, in Proceedings of the American Society of International Law, 62d Annual Meeting (1968), p. 182. See also his Microstates and Micronesia, op. cit., pp. 45, 51-2, 69.

13. De Smith, Microstates, op. cit., p. 72.

14. Rapoport et al., op. cit., p. 51.

15. For a statistical approach to a taxonomy based on the size of states, see Charles L. Taylor, "Statistical Typology of Microstates and Territories: Toward a Definition of a Micro-state," in Rapoport et al., op. cit., pp. 183-202.

16. S. Kuznets, "Economic Growth of Small Nations," in E. A. G. Robinson, ed., Economic Consequences of the Size of Nations (London: Macmillan, 1963), p. 14.

17. Ibid., p. 29. See also C. D. Edwards, "Size of Markets Scale of Firms, and the Character of Competition," in Robinson, op. cit., p. 128.

18. Kuznets, op. cit.

19. Rapoport et al., pp. 149-50. See also de Smith, Microstates, op. cit., Ch. 6, especially pp. 93-94.

20. R. Tiffin, "The Size of the Nation and Its Vulnerability to Economic Nationalism," in Robinson, op. cit., p. 248. See also Douglas Hague, "Report of the Proceedings, Summary Record of the Debate" (September 11, 1957), in Robinson, op. cit., p. 349.

21. Burton Benedict, ed., Problems of Smaller Territories (London: Athlone Press, 1967), pp. 47-48.

22. Ibid., p. 49.

23. Ibid., p. 50.

24. De Smith, Microstates, op. cit., p. 94. See also Rapoport, op. cit., pp. 150-53.

25. Rapoport, op. cit., pp. 154-56.

26. Benedict, op. cit., p. 8.

27. De Smith, Microstates, op. cit., p. 95.

3

**MADAGASCAR:
THE AUTHENTICITY
OF RECOVERY**
Philip M. Allen

THE TSIRANANA REPUBLIC, 1958-72:
A POSTCOLONIAL PROTECTORATE

In 1972, as though undergoing a "timed release" from imperialism, the 14-year-old Malagasy Republic began to declare itself a
nation. Under some painfully odd rules of self-determination, the
aspirations of Malagasy nationalists had to pass through an ordeal
of adolescence even after the formal end of colonial rule. From the
moment the young "autonomous" republic received its articles of
independence from France in 1960, Madagascar's energies had been
engaged in an irrevocable downward spiral of economic and political
stultification. (See Table 3.1.)

By 1895, France had finally become exasperated with what
historians termed a "phantom protectorate" over the Merina monarchy. [1] Reversing the transition, in 1972, the Malagasy turned
against what they regarded as a phantom republic, constituting in
effect a French protectorate. A varied but geographically disinte-
grated rural economy continued through the first republic, wallowing
in shallow productivity. Only its foreign exporters, civil servants,
millers, middlemen, and non-Malagasy plantation concessionaries
found the era rewarding. French interests owned almost 75 percent
of property other than real estate and conducted some 70 percent of
Malagasy foreign trade. Subsistence agricultural standards had changed
changed from colonial times only in respect to the numbers of un-
productive persons clamoring from city sidewalks to be fed—on
diminishing resources of land and technology.

More fortunate Malagasy joined a new urban consumer class
addicted to empty formulas of "development" without cultural dynamics,
making "deals" for foreign capital that invariably followed the

TABLE 3.1

Political and Constitutional History of Madagascar

To ca. 1787: Political/economic dispersion of migrating ethnic groups with developing hegemonies (for example, Sakalava kingdom in the north) and relative cultural homogeneity

1787 to 1810: Consolidation of centralized Merina* hegemony under Kings Andrianampoinimerina and Radama I, radiating out from central plateau to cover two-thirds of the land surface (three-fourths of the population)

1810-1885: Independent monarchy with fluctuating European (primarily British) influence at court

1885 to 1896: Gradual subjugation by France, culminating in conquest of 1895, abolition of the monarchy, and declaration of colonial status in 1896

1896 to 1958: Formal French colonial period

1958 to 1960: Quasi-autonomous republic within Fifth French Republican Community

1960 to 1972: Independent republic under informal French protection governed by bilateral articles of interdependence

1972 to present: Referendary interim period supervised by plenipotentiary military regime

---

*The Merina compose the largest ethnic group of the island (about 2 million of 7.6 million), inaccurately called hova by early British writers. Relatively pure Asian lineage and culture, they occupy the central plateau area around Tananarive and hold the major civil service and professional occupations in modern Madagascar.

Source: Compiled by the author.

MAP 3.1

Madagascar

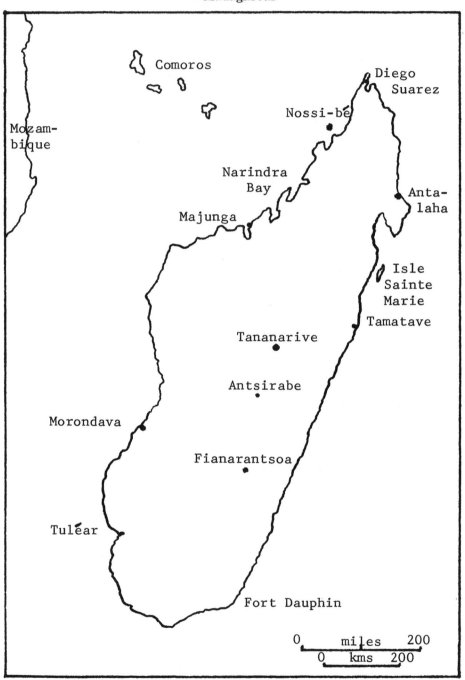

Comoros

Mozam-
bique

Diego
Suarez

Nossi-bé

Narindra
Bay

Anta-
laha

Majunga

Isle
Sainte
Marie

Tamatave

Tananarive

Antsirabe

Morondava

Fianarantsoa

Tuléar

Fort Dauphin

0   miles   200

0   kms   200

prejudicial short-circuits of an excessively gracious investment code. The less fortunate simply clung to family farm or pasture land, doing their best to meet the demands of taxation without mobilization. Some accumulated in the towns, burdening lifelines to the traditional family but scorning the hopeless countryside. These "transitional Malagasy" grasped at opportunity's occasional straws and seethed in frustration against a conspicuously privileged elite. Political participation became equated with political power, held and exercised by an aging, self-serving, functionally incestuous oligarchy that had received the deeds of the republic in Paris and defended their own titles in her name. Eventually, inevitably perhaps, massive popular apathy "liquefied" into protest against the noisy futility of postcolonial politics.

Engaged in a vast, self-contradictory program of national reconciliation within international dependence, patriarchal President Philibert Tsiranana governed by exhortation, ceremonial adulation, and scapegoating. Restricting political access and socioeconomic rewards to loyal elements of his Social Democratic Party (PSD) in a multipartisan state, Tsiranana's strategies consisted essentially of an alternation between manic international dependence both for friends and enemies of the state and depressive domestic control. His statecraft rested on four main pillars. (1) Imported solutions prevailed (usually made in France), which had low price tags and little impact on Madagascar's deepening poverty. (2) Conversely, he expected unflinching respect for the structure of protection maintained by France over its residual interests in the island. This he justified in official rhetoric by the presumed affinities between the two nations so that France was understood to be protecting Madagascar as well. (3) He assumed nearly universal allegiance to his own person as the republican apothesis and comrade of Charles de Gaulle, whatever the vicissitudes of party, policy, or performance. (4) Finally, he tolerated an official opposition party and press as security valves for whatever dissent his own personality might fail to embody.

During his 14 years as president, Tsiranana vacillated between rigorous party patriot and superpartisan "father-of-his-country," "assimilated" friend of the French and self-made, folksy ex-cowherd. Endowed with great vitality, oratorical skills (in virtually all dialects of Malagasy), comprehensive powers of recollection, and selective skepticism (particularly acute in regard to the ambitions of his chief mandarins), he never yielded or shared power. He held the titles of both chief of state and chief of government and consistently refused to designate a prime minister. In late 1970, under the advice of his French counselors, and by then weak and convalescent, Tsiranana designated four vice presidents to head superministries and conceded heir-apparent status to the first of the four, the dynamic Interior minister and PSD secretary general, André Resampa. But within four months, he had begun the demotion of this directorate and the contrived humiliation of Resampa. Interethnic unity could never be achieved except in Tsiranana's person, and reliance on France could never be guaranteed without him. [2]

In its brief prime, from 1960 until 1968, Tsiranana's strategy maintained stability on the Great Island* and ensured modest export preferences for Malagasy coffee, sugar, and other tropical products within various global systems responsive to French influence. French aid, estimated at an average of $30 million per year (not counting military support expenditures or multilateral assistance) bolstered the illusion that protection with dependence would somehow generate prosperity.

When the real advantages of dependence policy—security and statistical economic growth—crumbled, the illusions of development went with them. Poverty threatened survival in the countryside; international economic participation was weakened, and great-power strategies began to cast long shadows over the island; statistical growth could no longer be claimed (let alone criticized). As Gaullist France revealed diminishing ability to sustain its protecting presence, the security of the dependent relation disappeared and, with it, the pillars of Tsiranana's political strategy.

This process became evident during the revolutionary European movements of May 1968 and their international sequel. [3] The Fifth French Republic was beleaguered by overriding commitments in Europe and the contradictions of its Atlantic strategy yet jealous of its privileges in the third world. French diplomacy has relied increasingly (if cunningly) on cultural mystique, personal intimacy among heads of state, and on skillful manipulations of multinational associations—the European Economy Community (EEC) European Development Fund, the United Nations Educational, Scientific, and Cultural Organization (UNESCO), and the new Francophone Agency, for instance—to lighten French responsibilities without weakening the essential position of patron toward its dependencies. [4] Once de Gaulle's mystical nationalism had been shaken by the challenges of 1968, exposing the umbilical cords of protection and dependence, a radical change on Madagascar became almost inevitable. De Gaulle's successors after 1969 have been realistically attentive only to irreducible French interests in their overseas spheres of influence.

---

*Stability under the First Republic was constantly rallied, as explained below, by sudden alarms and threats to security.

Where those interests still appear consistent with local power preferences and strategies of political and economic growth—as in the Ivory
Coast, Gabon, Tunisia, and, for a time, Senegal—France encounters
little serious opposition in the client state or among greater powers.
But wherever lines must be drawn between French strategy and apparent interests of the dependent society—as in Mauritania, Dahomey,
Upper Volta, Niger, the Comoro Islands, and Madagascar—the results
involve some jolt toward national self-determination.

The "jolt" in Madagascar ejected Tsiranana, reduced France to
an unprecedentedly low position of "foreign interest," and precipitated
the Great Island into a search for nationhood, emerging both out of
the precolonial past and the uncertain present.

THE PAST: FROM DOMESTIC IMPERIALISM
TO CONTROLLED INDEPENDENCE

Ruled by a proud, well-organized, indigenous monarchy throughout most of the 19th century, Madagascar (or at least its ruling elites)
developed a sense of international prestige comparable to that of
contemporaneous Siam or Morocco. Consequently, privileged Malagasy
resented the French conquest of 1895 with particularly intense humiliation—more so than most of the subjugated West and Central African
territories whose own impressive political organizations had fallen
into disarray by the time European imperialism was prepared to
swallow the continent. Acting in competition with Britain and Germany,
ensuring her property concessions on the Great Island (and on Réunion
and Comoros as well), befriending rival coastal tributary kingdoms
of the Merina, France required from Madagascar not the complicity
of a "civilized" monarchy, as in Morocco, but the conquest and
colonization of an entire dominion thousands of miles from home. For
comparison, on the sub-Saharan continent, the shock of 19th-century
imperialism came with comparable force to Ashanti, but with a very
different sequel. Colonial British rule certainly affected the "Gold
Coast Colony" far less profoundly than the total imperialism of the
French, sometimes rationalized under the euphemism of "assimilation." The contrast is manifest in the relatively rapid, almost inevitable triumph of Gold Coast nationalism in the 1950s, [5] as opposed
to the complex, compromised, dialectical, and still continuing "recovery" of autonomy in Madagascar.

Late-19th-century Madagascar was largely a Merina oligarchy
governing three-quarters of the population for a monarchy that had
achieved its unification. In earlier centuries, successive waves of
artful East Asian maritime people had brought new technology, a
rich oral culture, and a pastoral economy from Java, Southern India,

and the Swahili littoral. The immigrants conquered and absorbed the indigenous Malagasy,* carried African slaves across the Mozambique Channel, and accepted other African, Asian, and Arab newcomers until a moderately consistent cultural pattern emerged throughout the immensities of the (still underpopulated) island.

Madagascar covers a surface of 228,000 square miles, measuring approximately 980 miles from north to south and 360 miles at the widest east-west diameter; peaks reach from 6,500 to 9,200 feet. The population of 7.6 million (recent official estimate) is dispersed among pockets along the spine of the high central plateau (the Merina, Betsileo, and Tsimihety), and along a half-dozen major river valleys and deltas. 6 There are seminomadic peoples in the southern interior, but the majority are farmers of rice and other staple foods, as well as cash-crop farmers in the more accessible areas. Population as reported in the Introduction to the 1974-77 Development Plan is gravitating toward the cities—which represented 13 percent of the population in 1962 and 17 percent in 1970—especially on the relatively prosperous high plateau. Of the population, 56 percent is under 20 years of age.

Political unification had been attempted previously, in the 17th and 18th centuries, by the Sakalava kings of the northwest coast (who were subsequently befriended by the French against the dominating Merina). It was achieved, however, under the Merina ruler Andrian-ampoinimerina of the high central plateau near Antananarivo (Tananarive) and his son and daughter-in-law, King Radama I (1810-24) and Queen Ranavalona I (1824-53).

Using administrative genius and a system of forced labor and acquiring technology when needed from competing Europeans, the Merina consolidated an essentially imperial control over most of the island. Ethnic and cultural affinities between the Merina and their subjects failed to counteract the prejudices of a class structure in which only Merina nobility (andriana) and freemen (hova) possessed slave-holding rights and cosmopolitan cultural privileges. Yet today, all Malagasy speak variations of the Merina language—basically

----

*"Vazimba" is the generic name given to autochthonous Malagasy prior to the arrival of sea-borne Asians. Their nature is little known, so complete has been their amalgamation. Scholars differ on whether they resemble southern African Bushmen or Asian stock dating from periods when the island was linked terrestrially with one or another neighboring continent. (See Nigel Heseltine, Madagascar [New York: Praeger Publishers, 1971], pp. 13, 54-56.)

Malayo-Polynesian with important Arabic, Bantu, and English accretions. They worship according to similar religious principles—a strong animism sanctioned by elaborate codes of behavior subsisting despite the all-or-nothing encroachments of Catholicism and Protestantism, which claim about half the island's population today—and exhibit common aesthetics in their literature, theater, and music (strongest of the Malagasy arts). But, from the period of Merina rule, the plateau people and the côtiers* (coastal peoples) contemplate each other through a geographically based class consciousness often mistaken for "tribalism."

Before fashion or necessity declared Afro-Asian societies fair game for European power, the Merina monarchy was admitted to a kind of junior partnership in 19th-century international concourse. Although large agricultural and trade concessions were awarded throughout the island to almost any Europeans who promised tax royalties to the Crown (except for a period of xenophobic reaction against Europeans under Queen Ranavalona I in the mid-19th century), the Merina pursued fairly consistent policies of favoritism toward British commercial and missionary interests—sometimes as a lesser evil to the colonizing French and the persistent slaving powers. They allowed their elite and their army to be schooled by Englishmen and used basically English phonetics in their written language. A wave of the monarchical hand converted the entire court of Tananarive to Anglicanism in 1869, and Merina queens subsequently wrote letters to their "sister" Victoria. The United States, Italy, and Germany also exchanged diplomatic relations with Antananarivo, and a modest court constellation developed there among diplomats, tradesmen, churchmen, and technical experts invited to work in Madagascar.[7]

These relations held true until revived imperial ambitions in France, frustrated since the Napoleonic Wars by Britain and then Germany, retreated southward from Zanzibari East Africa. The sugar-growing French colony of Réunion, 250 miles east of Madagascar, clamored for accessible sources of labor, food provisions, and other raw materials. The Comoro Islands to the northwest were successively occupied as Islamic hostages to overseas French business, in a clean-up of leftovers from Rule Brittania.

---

*Côtier is French for "coastal resident," used polemically in Madagascar to distinguish the more African-influenced ethnic groups from the interior plateau Merina and Betsileo.

To preserve its valuable East African, Egyptian, and northern Indian Ocean interests from revived French competition, Britain withdrew its historic benevolence over Merina sovereignty in the early 1880s, ceding Madagascar to the French sphere of influence. Britain thus countenanced the imposition of the short-lived French protectorate in 1885 and the conquest-colonization of 1895-96. The Act of Annexation of 1896 inserted this proud Afro-Asian people into an imperial system of political, economic, and cultural exploitation common to the new French territories of West and Equatorial Africa. Queen Ranavalona III and her consort, Prime Minister Rainilaiarivony (who had married three queens successively and held office since 1864), were sent separately into exile, and France became ruler of all the Malagasy.

Beginning with the tenure of the illustrious General Joseph Gallieni (1896-1905), French policy in Madagascar aimed at immediate political control (requiring relegation of the administrative Merina elite), settlement by French planters and overflow French-Réunionnais, and a favored position for French overseas trading companies. A dual legal system (the indigénat) supported this classical colonial favoritism, and a campaign of cultural evangelism operated through state schools, missionaries, and lay institutions. Although a new, ethnically undifferentiated elite was supposed to be created, only 18,000 Malagasy had received French citizenship by 1939, and the vast majority of these were Merina. While installing a European economy and administration on the island, France succeeded in siphoning off talent, especially medical practitioners, whenever Malagasy expertise could be enticed to the metropole.

The European economy in colonial Madagascar was based on large plantations of coffee, bananas, vanilla, sisal, raphia, and other export crops on the east coast, which often were installed without regard for ancestral crop land, pastures, and reserves. It also included subsidized monopolies of foreign trade and a tax and employment structure that forced peasants into surplus production. An obligatory labor program (the corvée) replaced the Merina slave system to ensure execution of public works and the prosperity of European enterprises. With the outbreak of World War II, the corvée developed into large-scale conscription for overseas military and domestic wartime work.

France lacked the investment funds and the quantity of willing settlers to conduct a full policy of colonization. By 1959, the year before Independence, some 50,000 French passport holders, two-fifths of them Réunionnais Creoles, lived on the island. About 6,000 of these French were members of concessionary farm families. Typical of French colonial systems, the remaining 44,000 were dispersed over a broad gamut of positions as government officials, teachers, clerks, military personnel, technicians, and businessmen.

The total overseas community on the Great Island declined by about 7,000 after Independence in 1960, and an equal number left the island after the nationalist upheaval of 1972. Whereas in the days of colonial exploitation, the French were distributed throughout the island in agriculture, mining, and trade, contemporary foreign communities are increasingly concentrated in administrative, technical, and professional roles in the major towns.

French colonial policy succeeded in sustaining the resentment that had developed among subjugated côtiers against the Merina without seriously prejudicing the social and economic advantages of the great precolonial Merina families. In deliberately creating a pattern of economic pockets opened toward external markets, France also developed an enduring case of territorial dependence on the metropole. These two achievements have more than anything else inhibited the emergence of Malagasy nationalism, self-reliance, and economic development in the postcolonial period.

French policy after World War II represented an evolution of, not a break with, imperial principles. Pay-your-way imperialism was somewhat modified for the fourth and fifth French republics by a more subtle mercantilism of national "profit" through the private prosperity of settlers, concessions, and trading companies, as well as the intangible benefits of cultural diffusion and international prestige. Frenchmen began to question the value of such advantages during the 1960s in the attitude dubbed "Cartierisme."[8] But for Malagasy, as for others in the colonial world, the questions had turned, long before that decade, into a bitter wish for decolonization.

Experiences of the war had humiliated France—through abject defeat in 1940 witnessed by 10,000 Malagasy soldiers as well as by students and intellectuals stranded in the metropole; through slavish conformism to Vichy by the island administration; and through invasion and occupation of the Great Island by British, South African, and East African forces in 1942. "Liberation" in 1945 redeemed the French, but not the glory of France. And despite the cheers for General de Gaulle at Brazzaville in 1944, Madagascar was not to be among the liberated. Its troops were repatriated after long delays; the economy remained in wartime doldrums as France sought to organize her own republic; de Gaulle abandoned power in 1946, carrying the promise of Brazzaville into retirement with him; his successors clung to the mercantilist logic of empire—protection for metropolitan interests and favoritism for indigenous leaders who collaborated in such protection.

But the promise of the 1944 Brazzaville conference and of a "new dawn" in world politics had been interpreted in nationalist terms by many Malagasy. Their sense of nationhood, repressed through a half-century of colonialism, reemerged in the Mouvement Démocratique de la Rénovation Malgache (Democratic Movement for Malagasy

Revival—MDRM) political party, dominated although not monopolized
by the Merina sons of the old monarchy. The parliamentary deputies
of that party, elected to sit in Paris with French and French Union
representatives, sought a qualified form of independence for Madagascar within the union. They were rebuffed by the French and ignored
by the rest of the world. Oddly, the supervised autonomy they coveted
(often falsely likened to the British Commonwealth) was soon to prove
unsatisfactory to Vietnamese nationalism. Indeed, it proved viable
for only two years when it was applied in 1958 to Africa under de
Gaulle's Fifth Republic.

Frustration over the "dishonored promise" reached combustion
level in early 1947. On the night of March 29, rebellion swept the
island, and, although hopeless as a step toward political self-assertion, it was not fully repressed for 15 months. Even if the full story
has yet to be told, the 1947 revolt's message was clear: Madagascar
wished to be ruled no longer by a senescent France. But France
understood that message as a threat to the restoration of her international position. The repression was uncompromising, resulting in
the death of 80,000 people throughout the island; the MDRM was
charged with responsibility for rebellion,* its leaders were prosecuted,
its organization was proscribed, and the island was immobilized
politically for almost a decade. France turned to European preoccupa-
tions with security and trade, and to its struggles in Indochina and
North Africa. The events of 1947 were soon forgotten, leaving the
French with their old assumption that the Malagasy were tempera-
mentally addicted to nonviolence.

During the 1950s and 1960s, Malagasy nationalism dwelt where
it had been before World War II, concealed by a combination of Asian
serenity and African dissemblance, which convinced Frenchmen of
Malagasy quiescence. Colonial policy was never able to eliminate
Merina elitism, but its hostility to the Merina ensured an identity
between them (however "bourgeois" as individuals) and revolutionary
nationalism (however Marxist its expression). For want of alternative
resources, French policy was obliged to keep the literate, bilingual
Merina to administer the huge territory, even under precepts of

----

*The three MDRM deputies were arrested and convicted for
plotting the rebellion, although they were not on the island at the time
and denied any such culpability. The evidence seems to point today to
efforts by the MDRM leadership to hold back forces of revolt. (See
excerpts from a doctoral thesis by Jacques Tronchon published in
Lumière [Fianarantsoa weekly newspaper] no. 1985 [June 23, 1974],
and earlier commentary on that thesis by Pierre Sorlin, Lumière,
no. 1956 [December 2, 1973].)

"direct rule." The Merina were indeed accustomed to Europeans and
sometimes accepted by them, although their acceptability to the French
on French standards is usually overstated. [9]

The arrogance of the "assimilation" policy aggravated the resentment of the Malagasy, for, while conveying bonuses of social position and
prosperity, the policy required assent to the presumed superiority
of a physically dominant foreign culture. While condescending to
"make Frenchmen" of suitably qualified Merina, France inevitably
stressed their inherent inequality. When "lending our language for
the expression of your thoughts," as a conscientious French professor
told an audience of elite Malagasy émigrés in Paris in 1962, France
questioned neither the appropriateness of the transaction nor the
degree of voluntary consent allowed the "borrowers."

Whenever assimilation, dissemblance, and the emigration of
intellectuals failed to contain Merina resentment, the myth of Malagasy
nonviolence tended to explode into violence. In 1915, five hundred
young Merina were arrested for conspiracy; in 1939 efforts to awaken
national consciousness through quasireligious appeals were suppressed
by police; in 1947 at Paris, MDRM leaders sought to join Asian movements of self-determination against French policy, with ghastly
results. Even when political activity was permitted to stir again—under
the brief regime of Pierre Mendes-France and the successor socialist
(SFIO) government—the specter of Malagasy nationalism was kept
out of legitimate politics. (Nationalism remained an ingredient of the
Communist Study Groups, labor unions, and youth organizations—most
of them promoted by French-based parent organizations—which replaced overt political activity during the 1950s, and, in some circles,
"nationalism" thus had communist connotations.)

Madagascar remained caught in a plotted trajectory for African
development that would keep French privileges intact, controlled by
"franc zone" credit systems and French institutional standards, associated with the African territories in the "Loi Cadre" of 1956, but
kept symbolically apart from Africa in overseas French nomenclature.
While refusing to permit the island to follow more sophisticated Asian
examples of political development, as the MDRM had sought, France
nonetheless humored Malagasy separatism from Africa in such titles
as Union Africaine et Malgache [UAM], Coopération Technique en
Afrique et à Madagascar, Secrétariat aux Affaires Africaines et
Malgaches—and indeed in issuing a separate CFA franc for Madagascar,
subsequently redesignated Franc Malgache [FMG].

Responding to de Gaulle in 1958, Madagascar earned the status
of a self-governing republic within the French community. This step
amounted to a virtual realization of the MDRM platform of 1946/47,
but the party now in power, Philibert Tsiranana's PSD, had no time
for Merina-tainted nationalism. Composed primarily of côtiers, the
PSD traced its origin to the MDRM's conservative opponents, the

Parti des Désherités Malgaches (Party of the Malagasy Disinherited, PADESM) an also-ran to the MDRM in the elections of 1946 and 1947, created overtly by the colonial administration to separate coastal people from the nationalist cause traditionally identified with anti-French Merina revanchism.

From the beginning of the French Fifth Republic in 1958, it was clear that French tutelage would survive over subordinate Africa and that the Tsiranana program for cooperation with Paris would represent the sole realistic alternative for Malagasy self-government. His PSD was truly national in scope, having incorporated a conservative Merina element led by lawyer Alfred Ramangasoavina, suburban Catholic leader Abdon Andriamirado, and dentist Alfred Rajaonarivelo. Its platform was mildly welfare-socialist (Christian socialist might apply more aptly, except that Protestants and a few northern Muslims entered the hierarchy), guided in its incipient years by the Société Francaise de l'Internationale Ouvrière (SFIO) and its able governor-general, André Soucadoux. Later the party adapted readily to de Gaulle's style of cultural internationalism and obtained in 1958 a 77 percent referendum majority in favor of the Fifth Republic's constitution. Tsiranana then became a member of the French president's fraternity of African directors, holding a junior ministerial position in his short-lived Community government.

In 1960 the PSD began sopping up small-party and independent political factions, readily persuaded that the future belonged to the party of the father of Malagasy independence. Among the new acquisitions was the renowned but aged Merina nationalist, Dr. Joseph Ravoahangy, martyr of the 1915 VVS youth movement* and one of three MDRM deputies convicted of responsibility for the 1947 rebellion. Ravoahangy joined Tsiranana's cabinet and remained there until his death but never exerted significant political influence.

In other respects, the PSD kept its distance from the MDRM spirit—most notably at the congress for independence held in Tamatave in 1958. Although most of the participants at Tamatave were gradually incorporated into the PSD, or neutralized after 1960, the congress did focus a strong and durable urban opposition, which accounted for most of the 23 percent resistance in the de Gaulle referendum of September 1958. The strength of this opposition remained embedded in Tananarive, stronghold of the Independence Congress Party (AKFM), as well as in the island's two major ports, Tamatave and Diego Suarez,

----

*VVS were the Malagasy initials for the "Iron-Rock-Greenstem" movement, a rather mystical fraternity of young nationalists outlawed after being charged with subversive plotting during World War I.

with their organized labor force and relatively cosmopolitan population. In the remote and impoverished south, the PSD could claim overwhelming support only by harassing the populist nay-sayers of the MONIMA (National Movement for the Independence of Madagascar). While Protestant clergy (both missionary and Malagasy) conveyed the perpetually dissident mood of the southern peasantry, the MONIMA almost disappeared in the manipulated electoral exercises of the Tsiranana republic—only to emerge again in astonishing force when the patience of the peasantry ran out in 1971.

Using combinations of French patronage and government porkbarreling, the PSD was able to sweep elections from 1958 on. It delivered virtually 100 percent majorities to Tsiranana in the presidential elections of 1958, 1965, and January 1972 and captured the bulk of provincial, local, and National Assembly delegations (104 out of 107 deputies in 1965 and 1970). Only the Tananarive AKFM managed to occupy the opposition benches during the last seven years of the republic. The Senate, chosen by indirect suffrage and presidential appointment, was entirely PSD.

In 1958 and 1959, Tsiranana's principal aim was to retain French benevolence for the island, keeping the specter of "leftist" Merina nationalism from the political scene. He was reconciled to participation with western African nations in schemes of nominal or metaphorical "regionalism," provided the regional lines passed through Paris. [10] He had no wish to see the Great Island emerge as champion of a ragged litter of Indian Ocean territories, all smaller, weaker, and more alienated than Madagascar from realities of power. Nor did he accept any obvious affinities with the emerging states of former British East Africa, correctly suspecting that such leaders as Julius Nyerere, Jomo Kenyatta, and Milton Obote would have little appreciation for the privileged relations prevailing between Madagascar and France.

Yet once the Gaullist community of republics proved manifestly inequitable for the African "partners," Tsiranana astutely decided to seek a form of independence regulated by reciprocal treaties. The "accords de coopération," signed on April 2, 1960, preserved French privileges in military security and base rights, economics, finance and trade, and cultural (institutional) tutelage, in exchange for a transfer of sovereignty and broad commitments by France to promote Malagasy development interest.

Through the 14 years of the First Republic, resistance to Tsiranana and the triumphant PSD simply did not show in electoral processes— just as the nationalist sentiment of the Malagasy remained swathed in acquiescence. Popular disillusionment emerged in other forms— lagging tax returns (especially in the underprivileged south), civil disobedience of various kinds (cattle rustling, brush fires, and other illegal, sometimes suicidal rituals), satirical minstrelsy, and

intermittent bombings. Each show of dissent was greeted by the
Tsiranana regime as evidence of sinister plots against Malagasy
security, all remotely controlled (téléguidé) from abroad. But the
regime didn't really require evidence for the plots it denounced: in
its waning years it exposed conspiracies with wearying regularity
and spotted powerful enemies behind every wave that washed ashore.
The object was to sustain a state of insecurity that asserted the indispensability of Tsiranana, the man who could distinguish an alien
enemy from a foreign friend. When charges against the Russians
and Chinese began to wear thin, they were replaced by charges against
the United States (in 1964 and 1971). Some Malagasy leaders continued
to suspect U.S. involvement in the 1947 rebellion. [11]

On June 1, 1971, in a magnificent, hallucinatory solo performance,
Tsiranana denounced the U.S. Embassy (by clear implication) and
André Resampa for collaborating in conspiracy. They were subsequently linked with MONIMA and the communist Chinese in the Tulear
Province peasant revolt of March-April. The accusation, apparently
spurious in its entirety, served to remove the ambitious Resampa
from the president's path to reelection, to purge the party of Resampa
loyalists, to blame all party and government failures on the Resampists, to clean the south of MONIMA dissenters, and to expel the U.S.
ambassador and five of his embassy officers. These events demonstrated to the bewildered French that, however reticent they might
be toward Indian Ocean commitments, the Malagasy Government still
considered France unassailable. [12] The whole affair was carried on
for a year, without trials for the imprisoned Resampa or for the
MONIMA leaders, without presentation of the "evidence" that Tsiranana
claimed he held against the Americans, and devoid of any other
explanation. After the May 1972 revolt, Tsiranana conceded that he
had been at least partially mistaken.

To this penchant for witch-hunting, Madagascar's president
added an insular skepticism of the third world and particularly of
"radical militant" states like Guinea, Tanzania, Somalia, Algeria,
and Sri Lanka. As expressed in his celebrated (on Madagascar) speech
at the second OAU chiefs of state meeting in 1964 in Cairo, in his
delegates' votes on Arab-Israeli matters, in doing business with
South Africa and Portugal, and in his admiration for Moise Tshombe
of Katanga, Tsiranana consistently preferred a European-guaranteed
status quo to the vicissitudes of self-determination. At all events,
he was opposed to the kind of experimentation he believed had caused
Guinea, Somalia, and Algeria to trade their secure old masters for
less congenial new ones.

Dependence on European security was even masked on occasion
in a mystical, rhetorical Afro-Asiatism exemplified in Tsiranana's
remarks to visiting statesmen like presidents H. Kamuzu Banda of
Malawi and D. P. Macapagal of the Philippines: "We have until now

pursued an African policy, but must not forget that we are Afro-Asiatics. We have in fact both African and Asian blood. Madagascar represents a natural hyphenation between those two continents inhabited by our brothers who must become our friends."[13] This formula, rhetorically presented as a "both/and," really represented in practice a kind of "neither" for Tsiranana's Madagascar. Claiming status as a bridge or transitional culture, the insular, insecure Malagasy were able to keep their distance from southern African confrontations, East African social experimentation, and intimidations of power in Asia. For Tsiranana, France was the omnipresent "19th tribe," the civilization that had decided Madagascar's own emergence as a civilization. France was the matrix of alliances, the touchstone of decisions, the point of reference.[14]

A dual economy has remained in Madagascar as a result of its deliberate "Westernization." Investment and import privileges are generous to those who send their funds, and reap their standards, outside the country, while Malagasy suffer under highly restrictive credit opportunities. The $95 average annual per capita income quoted for Madagascar meant that for every foreigner who earned $9,500, a hundred Malagasy earned next to nothing. To this day, Europeans, French creoles from Réunion, naturalized Chinese, and French-passport-holding Pakistanis dominate import trade and most exports. In one form or another, French nationals control production of sisal, raphia, cane sugar, and long-grain (export) rice, as well as the mining of mica, graphite, chromite, nickel, fissionable materials, and semiprecious stones. Europeans predominate in major construction projects, textile manufacturing, milling of rice, sugar and vegetable oils, shipping and long-distance trucking, tourist facilities, oil-prospecting, and food-processing.[15] The list of economic activity remains impressive, but costs are high, and the operational dimensions are modest (often so designed in order to maximize returns and keep costs down). The percolation of benefits into the Malagasy economy is remarkably shallow. Any Malagasy government concerned with development faces a legacy of French economic policy that initiated export production in Madagascar primarily as a means of employing French nationals and maintaining equilibrium in Franco-Malagasy trade.

European and Asian prerogatives have left for Malagasy the operation of a huge, French-styled civil service, state-owned railways, and small-scale food markets, handicraft, and subsistence farming. The present interim government has expanded this participation to include a two-thirds' share of the national airlines (Air Madagascar, which had been owned 49 percent by Air France until recently), the commercial banks, and the electricity and water utility. Malagasy farmers produce most of the country's domestic rice (for non-Malagasy mills) and other food staples—maize corn in the south, cassava and taro yams in the west, plantain bananas in the east. Malagasy cultivate

the vanilla orchid in the sultry northeast for sale to Chinese and
European middlemen, coffee in the east for sale to French brokers,
beef cattle in the south and west for slaughter in French-owned
abattoirs, and cloves for export by Asians.

Vitally important agricultural credit is still dominated by rural
brokers, very few of them Malagasy, despite constant official efforts
to promote cooperative and government-guaranteed rural finance
schemes. In addition to banks and utilities, the new regime has formed
public import-export corporations to replace (on a gradual scale) the
ancient, inefficient French conglomerates with their habitually pegged
prices, low volume, inflexible marketing apparatus, and monopoly
control over trade commodities.

Thanks to the political energies of André Resampa, then interior
minister and mayor of Morondava on the west coast, the pois du cap
(cape pea, known in England as the Malagasy butter bean) represented
during the 1960s the sole important export crop produced and marketed
entirely by the Malagasy.[16] The Morondava area also developed a
promising citrus fruit industry, installed under Resampa's aegis with
Israeli assistance. Both Resampa and the Israelis are gone from the
Malagasy development scene, as a new government imbued with self-
reliance principles seeks to assume the momentum.

Technology has also been a costly import for Madagascar, reflecting the sense of inferiority imposed on Malagasy civilization by
the presumed European masters of modernity. All industry, mining,
construction, and transportation techniques are determined by French
companies, French-trained civil servants, efficient Asians, and overseas technical assistance personnel, in consistently European terms.
Educational criteria, mechanical crafts, corporate management, and
civil service norms have all been imported. Agricultural productivity
has been subjected for 70 years to whatever program the French
Government or sociétés d'état might propose to overcome atavistic
peasant conservatism. These schemes included a rural commune
structure that served centralized political control and tax-collecting
purposes but hardly promoted enthusiasm for farming; the BDPA
(Agricultural Production Development Office), which primarily assisted
transplanted Réunionnais; European-styled cooperatives and agricultural
extension programs; animation rurale, patterned after mildly successful
diffusion programs in Morocco and Senegal; the GOPR (SATEC),
Groupement pour l'Opération de Productivité Rizicole (Société d'Aide
Technique et de Coopération) [Association for Rice-Growing Productivity Program], (Company for Technical Aid and Cooperation), rice
production experiments; and high-level research institutes, development planning agencies, and investment codifiers—all engaged on the
thesis that, as the Mauritian historian Auguste Toussaint put it,
"Madagascar must westernize or suffer anarchy."[17]

This vast rural artifice, so attractive in government pamphlets and in project reports of the "implementing agencies," failed to raise agricultural production in step with population increases, to stem the exodus of unemployable Malagasy to the towns, or to channel the fruits of investment into rural areas. Some of its action contributed in fact to the widening gulf between the privileged class (foreigners and their Malagasy dependents) and the unfortunate Malagasy who were constantly being congratulated on the joy of their hard-earned independence. In January 1969, as the entire structure was clearly tottering from its own weight, the French technician Edouard Chapuis was sentenced to 10 months in prison for a pamphlet charging that Malagasy development existed solely on paper, in official speeches, and folk songs. [18]

The revolution of 1972 affected this system of dependency mortgages in several sensitive ways: by curbing imports, undertaking public participation in major industry and finance, restoring a national educational process, and, in its most controversial phase, relocating the nucleus of national development administration in local-option village communities, called fokonolona. But in order to initiate such radically nationalist changes, a new regime required the advantage of an almost total and simultaneous collapse of all the props supporting Philibert Tsiranana's statecraft.

Simultaneity in politics requires process. The collapse of the Tsiranana strategy began on the streets of Paris in May 1968 and ended on the streets of Tananarive exactly four years later. During that period, General de Gaulle resigned, and the presidency of Georges Pompidou revealed French reluctance to pursue the protecting role indefinitely. The vines of Malagasy development policy refused to yield fruit. The incompetence of his administration tarnished the image of Tsiranana's legendary sagacity.

A paralytic stroke hospitalized Tsiranana in France for the first five months of 1970, emphasizing his mortality if not the vulnerability of his leadership. Throughout 1970 and 1971, he sought to patch up a feeble administration, preparing for his succession but refusing to deny his indispensability. As his weakness became manifest, the chronic indiscipline of PSD mandarins degenerated into defiance; old rivalries burst open; new partners and pretexts were located abroad. The economy sagged further, plagued by drought and flood as well as mismanagement, deteriorating terms of trade, galloping population growth, and rural-urban disequilibrium. Dry-season brush fires, cattle rustling, tax evasion, isolated bombings, and intermittent strikes multiplied the signs of popular discontent.

Characteristically, the regime sought scapegoats. Tragicomic arrests, searches and seizures, imprecise denunciations abounded. Without rational official explication, the labyrinthine rumor mills of Tananarive inevitably magnified and distorted the general sense of chaos. The government reacted by seizing newspapers, denouncing unnamed trouble-makers, purging the party structure, and squelching debate. The energetic political press and the island's Christian leadership (both Protestant and Catholic) warned of the consequences of ignoring the fundamental misery underlying the mood of crisis. But Tsiranana himself remained above criticism, clinging to his strategy of concentric dependence, and fanning the crisis with elliptical references to enemies of the state. [19]

On April 1, 1971, the desperate farmers and herdsmen of the drought-stricken, overtaxed, southernmost province of Tulear rose up with knives and pitchforks in a phantasmagoric Jacquerie that left at least 400 dead and 800 in prolonged detention. Several hundred men attacked a dozen government posts on that night, killing one policeman and wounding 11; in reprisal, the police and administrators settled volumes of old scores, especially against the MINIMA party, which had been declared officially extinct for some time. [20]

One year later, in May 1972, the cities filled with rioters, and, on May 18, the Tsiranana republic toppled. Ironically, Tsiranana had been reinaugurated for a third term on May 1, subsequently naming a 45-man government with few new faces and little promise of change.

FACTIONS OF REVOLT: THE URBAN SPEARHEAD

The foregoing account of the first Malagasy Republic is hardly unique in the annals of formerly French Africa. But the process of conversion from stagnation to self-determination, beginning in 1971, revealed a rare synthesis of national impulses. It associated peasantry, organized labor, military patriots, city misérables and student conscience in a sudden alliance of les damnés de la terre et du trottoir outside the two regular institutions of Malagasy nationalism. While Tsiranana's "united front" politics prevailed, the PSD left wing had persisted since 1962 in demanding a more disciplined socialist   - approach to domestic problems and a confrontation with France over the 1960 "accords." This relatively nationalist line was identified with André Resampa, and, although skillfully restrained by Tsiranana for more than a decade, Resampa and his followers were encouraged to speak out at party congresses and allowed to operate in certain well-defined areas (like the Morondava communal syndicates) removed from the heart of power. Resampa was valuable as a nationalist spearhead within the party primarily because, apart from his loyalty and efficiency, he was not a Merina.

The residue of Merina nationalism, which could never become formally reconciled with a French protectionist strategy, was embodied in the AKFM party, technically a parliamentary opposition and urban socialist force, but in effect very much part of the Tsiranana

"containment" system. What the system could not contain, either in
the non-Merina PSD left wing or in the traditional Merina AKFM, was
the revolutionary force of a new generation that did not thank the
French for granting independence and did not need French standards
to define Malagasy aspirations. This new force did not accept the
long-standing myth of Malagasy quiescence—interpreted by foreigners
as supine fatalism, by missionaries as piety, and by employers as
gutless passivity. Acts of violent protest have indeed been frequent
in Malagasy history, and yet they come invariably as a surprise to
authorities. The movement of 1971-72 is no exception.

Equating national security with the longevity of his regime,
Tsiranana misconstrued the moods of his own people. Any challenge
to his strategies of protective dependence was regarded as subversive,
and any subversion was inevitably motivated from abroad. External
enemies were remarkably abundant for so obscure a republic: criticism of French privileges on the island emerged from envy of Madagascar; critics of the regime's outspoken military alignment with
France were assumed to be anti-West. Hence, any Malagasy, French-
man, Westerner, or militant socialist could be regarded as a seditious enemy of the state. If all good and evil came from a foreign
relation, it was probably inevitable that domestic stagnation would
be blamed by the Malagasy on the ubiquity of privileged foreigners
and their fortunate clients in government.

Thus, the Tsiranana regime's insistence on the overseas origin
of crises and solutions boomeranged. It facilitated a convergence of
interest among discontented rural and urban factions that had hitherto kept their distance from one another. In the towns, four different
viewpoints ultimately agreed that the first republican government
sacrificed Malagasy interests excessively to preserve a protective
but humiliating nexus with France.

1. Labor unions, organized in the 1950s along the French
ideological spectrum from communist left through Catholic, had long
been cut off from metropolitan patronage and treated as instruments
of political control (the price they paid, like the AKFM opposition,
for existence). Wages were barely keeping pace with the official
cost of rice (up 15 percent from 1964 to 1970 despite subsidies), and
taxes were biting deeply into earnings, mainly, it seemed, to support
a large, wasteful civil service.

2. A burgeoning Lumpenproletariat, patronized by official remonstrances to return to the land, to trust in Tsiranana, and to seek
favors from the party in exchange for undeviating allegiance, resented
the prevalence of French standards of employability and educability
in the towns.

3. A relatively professional army of 3,500, commanded by St.
Cyr graduates some of whom had fought with the French in Indochina,
was systematically relegated to parading for Tsiranana and to annual

maneuvers in subordination to the French Indian Ocean forces. Junior army officers, many of them Merina, were politically unknown quantities, hence kept in ceremonial functions, often "doubled" by French advisers and hemmed in by the more reliable gendarmerie and the paramilitary FRS (Republican Security Force).

4. University students and graduates contemplated the mediocrity of careers at the bottom of French social and cultural hierarchies in a closed society where politics determined advancement and gerontocracies made decisions. Relentlessly snubbed by their elders in authority as "spoiled wards of the state," their demonstrations, however peaceful, were repressed as politically inspired and their patriotism was constantly deprecated as a version of international radicalism.

Whereas the rural majority was assumed (until Tulear in 1971) to be implacably devoted to its plain-talking president, these urban classes were habitually regarded as uncooperative but manageable. The general population had only to remain wary of Mao, Moscow, and the Merina (and sometimes, when convenient, the Americans). Indeed, the 1972 revolt, like the great rebellion of 1947, has been stigmatized by conservative Malagasy as a Merina tribal putsch, a communist plot, and a CIA shenanigan.[21] But it is hard to overlook the divergent ethnic and ideological loyalties of the four urban groups that merged in 1972—or indeed, the convergence of their interests with those of the Tandroy, Tanosy, and Vezo countrymen in the remote south a year earlier.

The scenario of the 1971-72 revolution proceeds in phases: (1) intense displays of sympathy by urban groups for the overwhelmed insurrectionaries of Tulear; (2) loyalty purges throughout the PSD striking at some comrades for allegedly plotting the Tulear revolt (for example, Resampa) and at others for abusing authority against the peasantry, hence provoking it (for example, again, Resampa); (3) a reinvigorated campaign of adoration for the convalescent president, culminating in his third-term landslide election on January 30, 1972;* (4) prolonged drought, uncontrollable inflation, food shortages, and payments deficits aggravating both rural and urban grievances; (5) a series of largely nonviolent student manifestations

---

*While Tsiranana officially received 99.72 percent of the votes cast, rumors in Tananarive allege that the actual total of votes tabulated from the returns submitted by local party zealots equaled 120 percent of voter registration.

in early 1972 protesting against persistent French dictation of Malagasy education and the retention of political prisoners from the Tulear episode; (6) heavy-handed police repression of the student demonstrations on May 12, 13, and 15, 1972: in three days, 374 students and teachers were peremptorily deported to the Nosy Lava prison camp, some 40 of them dying in detention. Hysterical radio denunciations from Tsiranana and his ministers helped solidify the movement and bring it into the streets.[22] The Tananarive city hall, radio station, and major French-language newspaper were damaged by mobs. Between May 13 and 15, the uprising spread to other cities, involving secondary school pupils, labor unions, and the hordes of unemployed (grouped under the banner of the ZOAM).* The army, which, as usual, had remained out of the activity, intervened on the 15th to stop intensifying repression by the police and FRS.[23]

Probably, Tsiranana had expected help from Paris, either in the form of counterinsurgency action by the 4,000 French troops stationed on the island or in some publicized gesture, as, for instance, an expression of willingness to renegotiate the 1960 bilateral accords. But France did not move to preserve Tsiranana. Direct intervention of the kind that had saved Gabon's president, Léon M'Ba, in 1964 ceased shortly thereafter to be instrumental. (Since then, French forces have allowed such close friends as Presidents Hubert Maga of Dahomey, Maurice Yameogo of Upper Volta, and Hamani Diori of Niger to fall from power.) As for a concession to nationalist grievances, President Georges Pompidou had already proved willing to renegotiate the bilaterals—albeit not eager to flaunt the prospects of liberalization. It was Tsiranana who feared the weakening of the protective aegis once France was induced to yield some of its residual privileges.

On May 18, faced with pandemonium in the streets, a general strike under virtual safe conduct by his own army, and silence in Paris, Tsiranana gave up. He dissolved his government, endowed Army Chief of Staff Gabriel Ramanantsoa with full powers, and subsided into a figurehead chief of state until new elections could restore legitimacy.

---

*"ZOAM" is an untranslatable Malagasy term meaning, roughly, the "down and out." Politically, ZOAM has been linked with the radical Malagasy Association for Class Equality (MFM), in a union of Lumpenproletariat and intellectuals typical of the May 1972 revolt.

That electoral restoration was not to come so soon, however, for General Ramanantsoa discovered the depths of distortion in Malagasy society as a result of Tsiranana's 14 years. Although able to restore order quickly, the general found the urban factions disinclined to disband or to countenance a return to the old regime. They demanded relief from the "reign of politicians" and a fundamental review of Malagasy institutions, especially those that subsisted through conventions with France. The rural population welcomed a reduction in political-administrative tyranny over the countryside, and they quickly won elimination of the ruthless minimum head tax and cattle tax that since General Gallieni's regime had sent so many into rebellion and despair.

So, in the sequel, Tsiranana's major surviving sources of support were isolated in provincial capitals of the north where community leaders were as suspicious of a "return of the Merina" as they had been of the supremacy of the French.* In those towns, continued partnership with France had a reality underscored by French business and military establishments, which accounted for most of the paying jobs. At this writing, fall 1974, Tsiranana and the remnants of his PSD had regrouped in these places—Majunga, Diego Suarez, Tamatave, Antsirabe, and with Resampa's abject return, Morondava—using the specter of the Merina and the shadowy fear of international communism to keep alive the prospects of a revived, protected dependency.

THE MILITARY INTER-REPUBLICUM

From the summer of 1972, the Western Indian Ocean's great island traveled a delicate transitional course toward some form of "second republic." Its military custodians were seeking to read the signs of national self-interest and to mobilize the revolutionary élan that deposed Philibert Tsiranana and his policies of systematic dependence on France. The transition was secured by a five-year mandate given General Ramanantsoa by referendum on October 8, 1972—

---

*Ramanantsoa is a Merina, as were half his ministers and principal aides. He had been careful to compose a government and high bureaucracy consisting largely of military and technical experts chosen from all parts of the island. Tsiranana, a Tsimihety who once governed with four côtier vice-presidents, has bitterly attacked the new regime for tribalism.

technically, therefore, the date of Tsiranana's retirement.* The general's objectives were manifestly national, his temper was cool, his discipline austere, and his strategy at once familiar in postcolonial Africa and unique to Madagascar. The national sensibility, very much alive among the Merina and other groups bereft of their sovereignty by France, had been revived again. But now it was in power, and indeed respectable, for the first time since 1895. What remained was to make nationalism an acceptable credo to the nation as a whole.

Progress under the new government proved paradoxical. The regime suffered under the inherited cleavages and the ethnic aggravation engendered, but largely ignored, by its predecessors. Unencumbered by legislative and other constitutional impediments, the new leaders paid scrupulous attention to expressions of popular sentiment. They encouraged congresses, political seminars, and grass-roots organization. The chief of state and his ministers, although fewer in number than Tsiranana's and better equipped for technical than for political work, traveled regularly into the provinces in search of consensus. Although moving rapidly to sweep away the props of overweening foreign interest, Ramanantsoa maintained a deliberate (and to the more revolutionary factions, exasperating) pace in domestic reform, at least until well into 1974. In spite of its impressive technocratic makeup, the interim government authenticated important aspects of traditional, or at least precolonial, political culture, based on ancestral precedent and the lore of the land.

With a mandate to prepare a second republic worthy of its independence, the Ramanantsoa situation could be compared to some extent with previous transitional African regimes led by Generals Sese Seko Mobutu in Zaire, Sangoulé Lamizana in Upper Volta, Christophe Soglo in Dahomey, and Gnassingbe Eyadema in Togo. Parliamentary and electoral sanctions were suspended for the interim, and the military character, regarded as the antithesis to self-serving, undisciplined politicians, became the agency of an orderly search for "authentic" national institutions. The initial acts of the new Malagasy government did indeed exemplify the austere, "no-nonsense"

----

*The referendum of October 8, 1972, first of its kind in Madagascar since 1958, produced a 96.4 percent acceptance of Ramanantsoa's caretaker mandate; the abstention rate was 16 percent. André Ravatomanga, Lumière's authoritative columnist, concluded (October 15, 1972) that this was "the first really free vote in Madagascar's electoral history" (author's translation).

style of a typical military command, particularly in regard to bureau-
cratic flabbiness, the domestic budget, and currency exchange controls.

Yet there were contrasts between Malagasy experience under
Ramanantsoa and the standard African process. In the first place,
no "revolutionary council" emerged to replace the erstwhile dominant
political party; all previous parties remain legal. Second, elections
did take place, albeit not along party lines; a representative National
People's Council for Development (CNPD) met periodically at Tananarive, if not to enact legislation (Tsiranana's PSD-dominated assem-
blies seldom did more than help clarify executive policy), at least
to issue a series of cogent "recommendations" for government action.
(The CNPD and its energetic chairman, Michel Fety, seem to have
been closely consulted on genuinely "public" issues like taxation,
land-holding, employment policy, and education, but far less so on
such matters as foreign policy and finance.) Third, the military
regime tolerated considerable dissent, particularly among factions
and personalities (like Tsiranana himself) preserved from the dis-
credited First Republic. Labor unions, economic interest lobbies,
a polemical press, and a spectrum of political parties were encouraged
to speak out as participants in a fundamental, painstaking (and not
always successful) constitutional "referendum."

This degree of tolerance provoked criticism among the more
militant urban factions responsible for the May 1972 upheaval. They
distrusted the revolutionary authenticity of a regime that retained so
many props from the repudiated establishment. Their impatience
was exacerbated by the very openness of this complex political
orchestration: Few interests received undue favor, and none was
declared an enemy. All foreign residents were to be treated alike,
even the French (Tsiranana's "19th tribe"). All economic sectors
were convertible to Malagasy control but with appropriate indemnity
and limited participation by former owners.

Insistence that modern Madagascar must somehow draw its
strength from "folk" tradition recalled the "authenticity" campaigns
launched in other states, with Mobutu's Zaire as touchstone. But it
was expressed in Ramanantsoa's Madagascar without the verbal mys-
tifications that have provoked charges of atavism in Central Africa.
The streets of Tananarive have been renamed away from their former
French historical orientations (some of them insulting to Malagasy
pride), and the Malagasy language was being used for important
official, technical, and educational purposes. These were hardly
xenophobic acts, however: The Tananarive City Council had been
trying to change street names since 1963, and Malagasy is a rich,
flexible, nationally understood language that had shared official status
(with French) since Independence. In execution, the recovery of
Malagasy authenticity was remarkably unauthoritarian and took the

form of an exhaustive popular consultation. Official appearances in the provinces seemed to serve not to exhort obedience and impose policy but to ask for "the truth."

THE NATION AMONG NATIONS

In contrast to the comparable military regimes of continental African states, most of which nurtured their inherited international ties with great caution, Ramanantsoa promptly assaulted the sacred umbilical cord attaching Madagascar to France. From the outset, the goal of Foreign Minister Didier Ratsiraka was to redefine France as a foreign power, rather than a protector, and to classify French citizens and business interests as external parties, not members of the economic family. While negotiations on the multifarious accords de coopération stuttered along into June 1973, it was clear to all observers that Paris, not Tananarive, was responsible for the delay. France stood in the midst of an election season and only former President Pompidou's personal intervention could dissolve the most serious of the deadlocks—the status of the Diego Suarez naval base and the privileges of French citizens to transfer currency out of Madagascar. Only at the presidential level could France accept the dissolution of a dual protectorate— (1) the right to defend special interests of Frenchmen and their businesses in Madagascar and (2) the privilege of setting limits on Malagasy options in military, economic, and cultural affairs.

In effect, the new agreements, signed on June 4, 1973, simply canceled the old dependency relationship between metropole and former island colony. Although the exchange value of the new Malagasy currency* remained pegged to the French franc at the old rate of 50 to 1, Madagascar left the franc zone and would no longer depend on credit accounts at the Bank of France for its external financial position. Exchange controls and a new, far more rigorous investment code restricted the export of capital and earnings. For the first time, French nationals must apply for residence visas and other authorizations to settle and operate in Madagascar. The elimination of French citizens' special privileges intensified the emigration of French and

---

*The ariary, ancient nomenclature for Merina currency, which like the fokonolona, never fully expired in rural Madagascar. Ar 1.00 = FMG 5; AR 10 = FF 1.00.

other foreigners from the island after 1972. (According to official estimates, foreign residents, including French, totaled 106,800 in 1959, dropping to 99,000 in 1963—three years after Independence— and to 85,000 at the end of 1973; the current foreign community includes 50,000 Comoreans, 16,000 European French, 13,000 Réunionnais French [Creoles]. About 7,000 European French [including military personnel] and 1,000 Réunionnais left the island between May 1972 and December 1973.)

Once the new financial accords were signed in Paris, the break with protectorate policy became clear, but at the time of this writing, the island still struggled in the backwash of its declared independence. France promptly began withdrawing its troops from the air base at Ivato (near Tananarive) and honored the phased removal of 1,900 naval and 550 Foreign Legion personnel from the Diego Suarez base. The French Government remained joint administrator of the shipyards in that port—ironically one of the traditional centers of opposition to both the pro-French Tsiranana regime and to Ramanantsoa's nationalist reforms.

Tying convertibility of the Malagasy currency to the French franc was highly inflationary from the Malagasy viewpoint, but the interstate bank agreement retained the exchange relationship. Removing French credit and other central banking services without as yet solving Madagascar's serious balance of payments deficits endangered the country's scanty foreign exchange reserves. Rapid enforced national participation in banks, public utilities, manufacturing, external trade, and other activity effectively undermined foreign dictation of crucial economic sectors, but at the cost of a serious reduction of investment capital. Only 10 percent of the new 1974-77 development plan was to be financed by external sources, as compared with over 45 percent in Tsiranana's 1964-68 plan.[24]

In addition to losing the currency spent by France in military support costs and benefits to French civilians, the Malagasy also acted to reduce the overall French presence in cultural institutions. The French scientific and technical research institutes in Madagascar— whose work has been elegant if not dramatically applicable to developmental needs—were put under contract to the Malagasy Government. French technical assistance remained intact, although FAC (bilateral Aid and Cooperation Fund—Fonds d'Aide et de Coopération) loans and financial guarantees began to decline. But Madagascar would now have to recruit and train teachers to replace many of the French technical assistants previously assigned to secondary and higher education throughout the island. Enrollment in secondary schools reached 57,000 in January 1974—22,000 higher than the previous total; France was supplying only 176 of the 1,478 teachers needed at that level, as compared with 893 of 1,165 employed in 1972.

France undertook to maintain French-language schools for 4,000 primary and 2,600 secondary pupils, most of them French nationals or other non-Malagasy. Nevertheless, during the vicissitudes of the difficult changeover to the Malagasy language as the vehicle of instruction and the surrender of protection for Malagasy diplomas in the market where French "equivalencies" are prized, many of the wealthier Malagasy families were sending their own children to France, Réunion, or other Francophone areas to complete their education. (Ironically, these cosmopolitan Malagasy were often found among the most vigorous "nationalists" in other matters, and their Frenchified children returned from Paris to man the barricades against Tsiranana in May 1972.)

In conducting foreign relations under the First Republic, Tsiranana's government maintained freedom of action only where important French interests and direct Franco-Malagasy ties were not involved. The former president enjoyed calling attention to instances where he had chosen policy lines at variance from those of the French. For example, he maintained formal relations with Taiwan after de Gaulle recognized Peking in 1963, continued close ties with Israel after 1967, and authorized British planes to operate out of Majunga for surveillance of Mozambique Channel shipping after the imposition of UN trade sanctions against Rhodesia in 1966. These examples of relative freedom hardly amounted to an offense against French interest. In Taipei, the Malagasy Embassy was probably regarded as a useful listening post for Paris, just as British and Canadian representation in Peking served during the same period to keep Washington informed of developments.

Wherever France was directly engaged (colonial policy regarding the Comoros and Djibouti, nuclear testing and the maintenance of military bases in the third world, EEC association, investment and trade preferences, and cooperation with African and Indian Ocean neighbors outside the French orbit), Tsiranana's Madagascar seldom chose to affront the French. Important relations not specifically endorsed by France (the OAU—Organization of African Unity, southern African liberation movements, UN operations in the Congo, U.S. Peace Corps, and other major power agencies) found Tsiranana ambivalent or hostile.

Shortly after May 1972, Foreign Minister Ratsiraka, a 37-year-old, blunt-speaking naval officer, raised cheers from the nationalist press by flinging some of these windows open for Madagascar. Promptly, the new government exchanged instruments of recognition with China, North Korea, the Sihanouk Cambodian government-in-exile, and the Vietnamese Provisional Revolutionary Government (PRG—Vietcong)—all Asian anathemas to Tsiranana, partly because of exaggerated anxieties related to the subversive potential of a wealthy but sedate Chinese trader community on the Great Island. An entirely new Middle East policy emerged after the October 1973 war. Madagascar broke relations with Israel, one of the First Republic's most vigorous sources of technical assistance, and undertook gestures of solidarity with Algeria, Libya, and other militant Arab states. Libyan financial aid promises announced in mid-1974 amounted to about $100 million. (Unlike the purely technical assistance obtained from Israel during the First Republic, Libyan aid pledges are largely oriented toward financing capital projects: approximately FMG 17,000 million of the FMG 25,000 million total has been earmarked for road improvement, FMG 6,500 million for a new sugar refinery, and the remainder to resume bauxite production at the Manantenina mine fields abandoned in 1973 by the French Pechiney company for lack of adequate Malagasy Government guarantees.)

A clear preference for participation in African affairs replaced Tsiranana's mystical ambiguities on Madagascar's Afro-Asian calling.[25] Madagascar withdrew from OCAM in August 1973 on the grounds that it was more French than African, and it canceled Tsiranana's growing intimacy with South Africa on the premise that no African can ignore the insulting realities of apartheid when dealing with that country.* Renunciation of official ties with Pretoria, announced as

---

*South Africa had participated increasingly in Tsiranana's development program for Madagascar from 1968 on. Pretoria government and Johannesburg banking resources were particularly active in loans, and building contracts, and transportation services for Malagasy tourist sites (in Tananarive, Majunga, and Nossi-Bé island), in minerals-prospecting, educational exchange, and, at least tentatively, the ambitious scheme for a new deepwater drydock at Narindra Bay on the northwest coast. South Africans accounted for almost 75 percent of the 8,000 tourists recorded in Madagascar during 1971; after the 1972 break, total tourist figures dropped to 6,500 (1973), probably still including a significant number of South Africans. Throughout the evolution of relations, both governments expressed concern over growing Chinese and Soviet shipping in their "common zone of security." Tsiranana and his foreign minister, Jacques Rabemananjara, referred with persistent ambiguity to prospects of formal relations with South Africa. They exchanged official visits, permitted the opening of a South African information office in Tananarive, and insisted on the self-evident need to maintain good relations with all neighbors regardless of ideology but expressed disapproval of South African apartheid policy. In 1971-72, it appeared that Tsiranana was counting on Ivory Coast President Felix Houphouet-Boigny's leadership in opening diplomatic relations with South Africa, at least for OCAM members, through the announced Ivoirian strategy of "dialogue."

early as June 1972, imposed an obligation to repay $8 million in bank loans extended at 4 to 6 percent interest for the development of a tourist eldorado on Nossi Bé island off the northern tip of Madagascar. In January 1973, after refusals from France and the United States (which had encouraged Tsiranana toward "dialogue" with South Africa), Ratsiraka obtained the funds on a 15-year no-interest loan from China. Completing its departure from Tsiranana's policy of strict alignment with "the West" (revolving, of course, around Paris, not around Washington), the new regime declared nonalignment to be its principle, participated in the September 1973 Algiers conference of nonaligned states (a forum habitually shunned by Tsiranana) and opened relations with the Soviet Union and other East European states (only Yugoslavia had been diplomatically represented in Tsiranana's Tananarive). A 1964 trade agreement with the USSR, which Tsiranana had refused to implement, came into effect. Both Moscow and Peking opened resident embassies in Tananarive, to the manifest horror of the pro-Tsiranana press.* However, at least until late 1974, Ramanantsoa had denied port rights to both U.S. and Soviet naval vessels and denounced all great-power military activity in the Indian Ocean.

Madagascar's geographical position seems to demand an essential cordiality with East Africa, despite divergent ethnic, cultural, and colonial heritages. Even the Merina monarchy played power interests off with greater avidity than the first Malagasy Republic, obsessed with its delusions of insecurity and of French protection as the solution. Certainly, after the Paris trauma of May 1968 and especially since de Gaulle's abdication, Tsiranana had sought to diffuse his republic's dependence on France. But the effect of diversification during his tenure consisted in the development of limited, often rhetorical cordialities with powers congenial to France. Rather than interpret Malagasy geopolitics in the context of an emerging third world, Tsiranana chose to consider the Western Indian Ocean as a persistently European imperial sea where Madagascar helped France keep a balance against the "Anglo-Saxons."

(See Agence France Presse [September 3, 1970]; Nouvelles Quotidiennes Malgaches [January 10 and 13, 1971]; Rabemananjara interview in Rand Daily Mail [Johannesburg, November 30, 1970].)

*On August 6, 1971, Foreign Minister Rabemananjara used the following delightful non sequitur in an article commenting on China's imperialistic ambitions: "If we recall the name Yalta, it is because we don't want a Munich in Asia." (La République, PSD weekly [Tananarive, August 6, 1971], author's translation.)

Thus, post-1968 Tsiranana policy adapted to French reticence
by offering investment concessions to Japan, West Germany, Italy,
and South Africa, as opposed to strengthening ties with East Africa,
Southern Asia, socialist nations, or even the United States and Great
Britain. The dramatic "opening" toward South Africa was justified
on "strictly business" grounds with occasional overtones of enhanced
Indian Ocean Western security. Similar grounds permitted Malagasy
tolerance of NATO-member Portugal across the channel in Mozambique.
Tsiranana even promised that South African sponsorship of a major
deep-water port at Narindra Bay on the northwest coast would trans-
form Madagascar from a subsistence into a "consumer" economy.
These advances received broad ballyhoo on the Great Island but
proved of negligible national interest. (The most effective foreign aid
programs through the Tsiranana period appear to have been those
[by French FAC, European Development Fund, World Bank, United
Nations Development Program] that established communications
and other infrastructural links; even these major projects served
essentially to restore otherwise heavily deficitary balance of payments
accounts, to keep foreign contractors and suppliers busy, and to
maintain a large expatriate technician population in the country. Very
little job creation, rural participation, or local initiative was engendered in the process.)[26]

After 1972, acute domestic discontent could in part be focused
on the self-evident mistake of dependent alignment with a second-rate
European power losing its initiative in the third world. Ramanantsoa's
conversion of Malagasy foreign policy in the direction of dynamic
neutralism and broadly based diplomatic relations could therefore be
achieved rapidly, effectively, dramatically, and uncontroversially
(except among the Tsiranana rear guard). Nonalignment proved
readily acceptable as the international expression of revived Malagasy
nationalism. Besides, the foreign policies of newly independent
Mauritius offered an example of what might be done by an insular
government with the courage of its nationalist convictions.[27]

Beyond the usual fustian of foreign affairs, these new options seem
to have brought Madagascar some substantial benefits. Not only did
China agree to cover the loans drawn on South African institutions
for Nossi Bé, but also the Chinese have contracted for additional
assistance in food relief, industrial development, and trade.[28] Even
if Peking's aid proves as disappointing as the conventional Western
varieties, Malagasy indebtedness will be far lower. The import
ledger, astronomical without being productive in the Tsiranana period,
has been brought under control, and the national balance of payments
is improving, despite the rise in energy and transport costs.[29]

By 1974, Madagascar was in touch with dynamic forces in Africa
for the first time and seemed to have mastered its insular-ethnic
ambivalence on the subject. Exchanges of visits and diplomatic

relations with Tanzania enabled the Malagasy to clarify parts of their most ambitious "new" program—a return to local village initiative (the fokonolona system) as the basis for rural development. General Ramanantsoa attended the OAU summit meeting at Mogadiscio in June 1974, correcting Tsiranana's trend away from the organization (and Tsiranana's horror at Somalia's "pro-communist" proclivities). The new government contributed to the OAU's African liberation funds and espoused full independence for Portuguese territories.

Responding to similar trends—including symptoms of withdrawal in their respective British and French patrons—Madagascar's smaller Indian Ocean neighbors began following their own paths toward national identity. Once the Comoros, the Seychelles, and Mozambique realized independence, the Malagasy Republic might accede to a position of central influence in the perilous self-realization of a Western Indian Ocean region. For the first time in history, Madagascar was strong enough to accept leadership in what the author called (in 1971) a "new round" for the Western Indian Ocean.[30] Assertion of that role will require an ability to overcome inconsistencies in ethnic composition, culture, colonial heritage, and imperial economics—for the dominant modes of production were established in each island to serve competing metropolitan needs.[31] Madagascar's reported interest in the status of the islets called Europa, Glorieuses, and Juan de Nova, like the recent Mauritian and Seychellois concern for the alienated flecks of the British Indian Ocean Territory, has already agitated French security and brought military reinforcements from the remaining bastion of France in these waters, Réunion.[32] This development, insignificant in itself, bears witness to a new Malagasy sense of responsibility in regard to Europe's residual claims on the Indian Ocean.

AUTHENTICITY AT HOME

For a full year after the revolution of May 1972, in an elaborate series of political seminars and public meetings, the Ramanantsoa regime sought to discover an underlying popular will. The results were more confusing than anything else—but hopeful all the same. The students and town youth who had confronted Tsiranana's police in the streets demanded the enactment of genuinely Malagasy educational and civil service systems, putting an end to the cultural tribute paid by an allegedly "inferior" people to French civilization.* They

---

*Malagasy intellectuals were especially irritated by the persistence of French as the vehicle of instruction and research, simulated French

also demanded the eviction of foreign profiteers licensed to drain Madagascar by the least responsible and least efficient methods.

In the pronouncements of seminarists, one heard the demand for a conversion of leadership roles from high-paid consuming foreigners to high-paid consuming Malagasy, but the seminars were not purely self-service marketplaces. Organized labor joined the campaign for Malagasy performance standards, adding its own welfare demands, which had been consistently frustrated by a government indefinitely under mortgage to franc zone bankers. The city poor insisted on higher minimum wages and labor-intensive investment—far from the customary practice of the old regime. Rural poor to the extent that they were consulted, requested relief from pointless taxation, negligent investment policy, deteriorating prices, arrogant officials, and fair-weather politicians in league with rapacious middlemen.

Ramanantsoa's experts began smartly, with the removal of minimum head taxes that had enraged a penniless peasantry. The overall tax structure was further rationalized in 1973 and 1974, after signature of the new bilaterals between France and Madagascar, permitting more progressive impositions on those able to pay.[33] Under the Constitutional Law enacted on November 7, 1972 following the successful referendum of the month before, Ramanantsoa would have governed by executive ordinance until November 7, 1977 (or earlier) but would have had to remain open to pluralistic dialogue. The law contains a brief bill of individual rights and requires the ultimate Second Republic constitution to be endorsed by a new referendum.[34]

In addition to its strictly utilitarian investment code and its other foreign trade measures, the Ramanantsoa government quickly

—————————

curricula at all levels, examinations prepared in (or reproduced from) France, all leading to French diplomas (the sole freely convertible professional currency in Madagascar, despite increasing numbers of returning graduates from other countries, including the United States and USSR). French training often rendered Malagasy professionals more readily qualified in overseas job markets than at home. Outside the educational system, civil service qualifying examinations and promotional standards for most managerial jobs were also established according to French norms long after the departure of French incumbents, and often in situations inapplicable to Madagascar. The inescapable inference was that French (and especially Réunionnais Creole) personnel would always enjoy cultural advantages over local competitors for jobs.

decreed price benefits for growers of rice, coffee, and pepper, as
well as increased minimum wages. With a cost-of-living curve mount-
ing by 15 percent annually, the Malagasy economy found itself tugged
into disequilibrium at every step on the way to austere solvency. But
the new government sought, unlike its predecessor, to correct chronic
problems by adjustments in domestic relations, rather than through
foreign ventures. The immense twin specters of declining agricultural
production and wasting national resources have been attacked by an
ambitious land reform program calling for the redistribution of un-
cultivated tracts—many owned by French, Réunionnais Creoles,
Pakistanis (most carrying French passports), and Chinese. Following
an elaborate survey of available land, the authorities began in mid-
1974 the arduous project of inducement for unemployed and under-
productive farmers (including ex-military and pioneer youth) to mi-
grate into designated resettlement areas. [35]

Following the first wave of adjustments, major reforms came
slowly, provoking irritation among the impatient heirs of the 1972
revolution. Open protests broke out intermittently in cities, where
rising crime and juvenile delinquency rates, educational miasma,
and a still depressed employment market seemed to mock the hopes
of 1972. In the countryside—still plagued with waves of public despair—
cattle rustling, brush fires, and civil disobedience defied the authorities to demonstrate that anything had changed. [36] To the urban factions,
Ramanantsoa could make such demonstrations. In the great rural
landscape, with 83 percent of the population, his success presupposed
a new spirit, a sense of self-interest in socioeconomic development
among people whose exclusive concern had always concentrated on
primary practicalities of survival, and a new confidence in the rhetoric
of authority after generations of apathy and disillusionment.

Rural immobilism, that misconstrued nemesis of every development policy, may well frustrate Madagascar's reborn nationalism
more seriously in the long run than any other obstacle, domestic,
French, or foreign. So often confounded with quietism, fatalism, or
plain moramora (sweet apathy), the unresponsiveness of the Malagasy
peasant greeted what inevitably seemed to him to be senseless, uncertain, and, above all, other-imposed demands for action. Inertia
seemed perversely justified by the manifest ability of the peasantry
to survive well beyond the longevity of the brave programs recommended by authority for their benefit. [37] By bestowing rights of
initiative and operational control on communities at grass-roots
levels, the Ramanantsoa regime hoped to correct the crippling fault
in previous development strategy. And yet, it at once encountered
the very same problem: is self-determination genuine if it has to
be granted from above?

The unavoidable reply is affirmative, for what was being imposed
had only to do with institutions and process; what would emerge out of

that establishment must be a quality of self-reliance and self-determination. In late 1973, after a year of apparent torpor,* the regime
began dismantling the highly politicized, psuedo-socialistic structure
of rural communes installed in the early years of the Tsiranana republic. Under that system, a replica of centralized French administration, popularly elected communal councils designated mayors
who acted under authority (and revenue grants) from préfets and sous-
préfets appointed by the national minister of the interior. Not only
did the local electoral processes prove thoroughly vulnerable to PSD
patronage, intimidation, and election-rigging, but the very source
of authority at the head of the ministry was, until his fall in 1971,
PSD Secretary-General Resampa.

A number of other strands ran parallel to the party and prefectoral
lines from the central government to local administration—in police
and public order, agricultural policy, rural commerce, education,
public health, and public works. Operating what observers termed
la République de Papa,[38] Tsiranana and his surrogates indefatigably
toured the vast Malagasy landscapes listening to petitions and deciding
whether or not to grant them. Despite constant reference to grass-
roots development throughout the Tsiranana period—usually phrased
as exhortations to "do what we say"—the system operated largely to
drain finances, technology, manpower, and, most crucially, initiative
and responsibility, toward the central authority in the towns. Thus,
the First Republic never received the necessary quantum of confidence
on the part of a skeptical and practical peasantry and never ceased to
deplore the absence of reciprocity by the rural population to its own
energetic démarches.[39] Because it simulated the structural patterns
of industrial France, however, the process was readily characterized
as "modernization."

The post-Tsiranana alternative for rural administration was
conceived and conveyed with comparable energy by the interior
minister, Colonel Richard Ratsimandrava (former commandant of the
gendarmerie who had occupied a choice position for observing the
conduct of the previous system). Viewed as benign destruction,
Ratsimandrava's approach had three facets: decolonization of the

---

*The overall strategy was promptly announced, in General
Ramanantsoa's radio speech of July 27, 1972. On March 27, 1973,
the strategy was defined in an ordinance, but the fokonolona was not
given its articulation of powers until August 4, 1973. The firaisam-
pokonolona was characterized by an ordinance on June 21, 1974.
JORM (June, 29, 1974).

concepts governing rural development policy, disentanglement of local administration from partisan politics, and decentralization of decisions affecting agricultural production, marketing, and public services. Expressed more positively, these steps involved an empirical approach to specific rural needs, conversion of civil authority into a nonexecutive technical advisory role, and an entire reorganization of the rural territory to permit inductive flow of projects and decision upward from semi-autonomous village units (<u>fokontany</u>) and their respective village councils (fokonolona).

Under the new system, rural Madagascar was divided into 10,498 village communities averaging about 500 inhabitants. Each of these fokontany was to form its own fokonolona as it saw fit, provided, however, that all residents shared membership in the council and that decisions reflected universal consensus. The actual content given these concepts took root in soils that underlie Tanzanian and other communitarian socialisms,[40] rather than Western political theory, returning in nomenclature and spirit to the principle of total communal participation in the determination of survival. In a sense, the fokonolona extended the principle of family solidarity and mutual aid into the larger village economy. By requiring consultation of the entire economic community prior to individual or family decisions affecting the community, the traditional structure diffused responsibility for consequences, neutralized the inherent (and abhorred) egoism of competitive motives, permitted private property as a secondary privilege after the priority of social survival, and assured reciprocity of obligation among community members.[41]

Conceived metaphysically, the communal council continues on a lateral level (earth) the current of vitality transmitted vertically from ancestral spirit through the generations of living individuals into the land out of which life springs, and for which the living community is responsible. In practical terms, the individual survives through the efficacy of the community in production, distribution, communal defense, and self-regulation. Communal officers are obliged to consult the membership on all decisions not directly authorized in previous decisions (<u>dina</u>) and are subject to strict review by ombudsmanlike agencies (comparable in some ways to the "secret societies" of West African civilization). Unanimity is achieved despite egalitarian voting rights through a belief in the inspiration of the most persuasive orator. This process of "right rhetoric" is enshrined in the elaborate traditions of the <u>kabary</u> (peroration), which defend the community against the temptations of demagoguery while protecting its privilege to be entertained by eloquence.

Obviously, technological innovation, the generation of economic surpluses, and other opportunities unprecedented in the survival orientation of original fokonolona culture require flexibility and enlightenment in the community. Historically, the fokonolona has indeed adapted to new conditions, producing new forms of association and new agencies to cope with change.[42] It foundered against the machinations of tyranny under the late 19th-century monarchy and in the assertion of French military superiority at the end of the century. From the perspective of 1974, neither circumstance could be predicted to recur under the present Tananarive regime.

To ensure that the contemporary fokonolona would make appropriate adaptations from survival communalism to the developmental world, each council was to have an executive economic commission (vatoeka) of 5 to 15 members, maintaining consultative relations with government technicians. Technical liaison agencies were to connect with district groupings (firaisam-pokonolona) of five or more fokonolona, and report to regional headquarters for rural services at the level of the fivondronam-pokonolona, roughly corresponding to the prefecture. Eventually, the faritany (province) organizations are to include these smaller groupings as well as urban communities. The upward process of consensus is to focus at the national level in the National People's Council for Development, newly defined[43] as the two-directional consultative link between central executive and the population.

At the outset, in 1974, the fokonolona were entrusted with the distribution of unexploited land (on the principle that all Malagasy families are entitled to own their plots). They were to encourage production, warehousing, and marketing of agricultural products, with group procurement, to initiate self-help projects, and solicit state loans for larger-scale projects within the terms of the 1974-77 development plan. Villages (fokontany) that have failed to form operational fokonolona are to lose out on these advantages. Further powers of legislation and administration of justice are to accrue to the councils as the system matures.

At least two previous efforts to apply fokonolona principles to 20th-century Madagascar were evidently frustrated by central authority. During the abortive 1945-47 revival of Malagasy nationalism, a conflict developed within the MDRM between "Europeanized" party notables and certain rural leaders who had envisioned an egalitarian state for Madagascar based on fokonolona principles of consensus. Some observers interpreted the tragic March 1947 rebellion as a protest movement by the rural traditionalists against the party leadership, although both sides ultimately suffered in the drama.[44]

In the early years of the Tsiranana regime, Ministry of Agriculture officials developed a project to encourage peasant cooperatives (fokotantsaha) along fokonolona lines. The idea was suppressed out of concern for its potential conflict with the new, quasi-French system of rural communes.[45] However, in its decree of July 24, 1962 (during a period of attempted national mobilization through special executive powers granted the president by the National Assembly), the

First Republic recognized the utility of fokonolona as an administrative arm of the central government in villages too small or too remote to function properly through rural communes. The councils were given limited jurisdiction over public order but never received initiatory powers or the resources needed to become an executive agency. Yet, informally, and behind the administrative scene, fokonolona operated continually throughout Madagascar to regulate civil disputes, issues of ritual and custom, and the external relations of villages.

Revival of the fokonolona system in 1973 met general, albeit not unanimous, approval in Malagasy political and journalistic circles. The new structure resembled ancestral tradition sufficiently well to be acceptable in rural regions where the fokonolona had never expired, and it was certainly a departure from slavish imitation of France. Mobilization of technical expertise along nonpolitical lines leading into a popular, communal executive matrix captured the imagination of many nationalists. Ramanantsoa's disciplined military services appeared competent to assure orderly transition, public peace, and the "depoliticization" of the rural environment. An impressive array of technical cadres began to emerge from the limbo reserved for them by a party oligarchy that had been manifestly jealous of their competence and suspicious of their political tendencies.

Primary resistance to the new institution came from two sources. (1) PSD vigilants, including Tsiranana himself, after regrouping and allying with the most forgiving André Resampa in the new Malagasy Socialist Party (PSM), pursued a fervent crusade against any inclination toward Merina "tribalism." They denounced the fokonolona strategy as an imposed Merina institution dating from an indigenous 19th-century "colonialism" (over the côtier population) more pernicious than the 20th-century French variety.[46] PSM sources also warned against the government effort to induce fokonolona to deal with Malagasy middlemen instead of French companies, a step that would tend, in their view, to enrich the middle-class Merina. (2) An assortment of Marxist and Maoist commentators, many of them Merina, decried the atavism of an archaic communalist system incorporating undue reverence for age and precedent.[47] Skeptics from all positions of the ideological spectrum questioned the practicality of traditional communitarian techniques in a competitive world. A noncoercive, self-operating institution appeared unlikely to enlighten peasants very effectively regarding the realities of their interests. The coordination of particular decisions on a national budgetary level suggested chaos. Cities and towns and indeed any culturally heterogenous society would seem excluded from the fokonolona process—thus aggravating the cleavage between urban and rural life. Rural credit mechanisms remained in the hands of usurers, petty monopolists, and other exploiters, even after the departure of the great French companies: how could local councils effectively liberate farmers from their financial burdens, stimulate incentives, and promote local circuits of liquidity? How can the system defend itself against a return to political mandarinism and domination by village bosses, especially if parties are eventually permitted to campaign for council offices, as demanded by the nationalist wing (the Resampists) of the PSM?[48]

Indeed, the revived system requires not only that villagers deliberate astutely over their interests and prospects but that eminently middle-class civil servants convert psychologically to the role of disinterested advisers to the village communities. The difficulty of such a conversion within the authoritarian "Frenchified" bureaucracy has been deemed sufficiently formidable to cripple the experiment, even without legitimizing partisan politics.[49]

Midsummer 1974 developments continued to warrant such skepticism over the success of the fokonolona strategy. Villages were reported either to have failed to launch their councils into operation, to have made a start without obtaining the resources or services needed for efficacy, or to have resented the urgency of the government's remonstrances. Others reported fokonolona officals behaving with the incompetence and corruptibility characteristic of civil servants in the old days. There were fears that the reforms were being applied too hastily and anxieties over the laggard pace of change. Perennial seasonal shortages of such staples as soap, cooking oils, matches, and foodstuffs were now blamed on the fokonolona, as some areas were inevitably favored (for example, rice-growers, coffee and pepper planters) over others (for example, forest economics, banana-growers).

To cope with these difficulties, the Ramanantsoa government appeared to be adopting some of the futile reactive tactics of its predecessor—issuing empty appeals to "work," without providing tools or jobs; insisting on the value of education without undertaking the promised revitalization of a sagging school system; celebrating processions of foreign emissaries to Tananarive and of Malagasy officials abroad without evidence of results; using the national radio and press for dithyrambic pronouncements all too reminiscent of the "adoration-of-Tsiranana" propaganda programs. Austerity as a strategy has always affected populations unevenly and invidiously. This time, however, it seemed to be hurting the very elements that created the 1972 revolution.[50]

"And yet," as a Malagasy journalist recently declared, "we are actually breathing in an air of freedom. The theoretical [military] dictatorship coexists with a factual state of liberty. So, go understand it all!"[51] The bewilderment and tolerance implicit in this ejaculation typify Malagasy attitudes toward the complicated process of nationalizing the nation under Ramanantsoa's interim authority. The official answers were often slow to emerge, and the performance of new ventures like the fokonolona system has hardly had sufficient time to be measured. Yet agricultural production, a primary target of policy, has begun to move upward (favored in 1974, for the first time in over a decade, by the absence of hurricanes) and "may have reached a level 30 percent higher than 1973," according to Economics Minister Albert-Marie Ramaroson.[52] Most of the serious strikes, including those of university students and teachers, were more or less settled in mid-1974. The firaisam-pokonolona were getting organized. Even the cost of living seemed to be leveling off in June 1974!

Finally, in response to honest critics who question the applicability of an ancient instrumentality like the fokonolona to a changed economic and technological situation, the Malagasy have at least a provisional reply. They can argue with Frantz Fanon that peasant misery has remained a constant throughout the phases of third world history, that the rural world has failed to participate in the transformations glibly designated as "modernization," and that subjugation and humiliation can only be corrected by the self-assertion of the subjugated. Even if "fokonolona nationalism" fails—or is substantially modified through experience—it will have represented an effort to extend to the "wretched of the earth" an irreducible responsibility for their own fortunes. And, in the last analysis, that effort has to be made from inside, not from the position of the dominant, as in Madagascar's colonial period under France and its extension, the First Republic under Tsiranana.

General Ramanantsoa's regime became the victim of its own dynamism, rather than its torpor. In January 1975, Ramanantsoa was forced to yield power, under pressure from the Tsiranana PSM and allied military factions, not from the impatient revolutionary forces of May 1972. After an unsuccessful attempt at an "officers' coup" on New Year's Eve, Colonel Brechard Rajaonarison and other côtiers joined forces with dissidents in the Mobile Police Force, representing in effect the remnants of the FRS, which had sought to crush the 1972 movement. Charging favoritism for the Merina, these pro-Tsiranana elements held Tananarive in suspense for several weeks, forcing dissolution of Ramanantsoa's government on January 26, followed by the general's resignation on February 5.

Interior Minister Richard Ratsimandrava, the former commandant of the gendarmerie, who under Ramanantsoa had been charged with implementing the fokonolona program, succeeded to the presidency but was assassinated on the 12th, after only a week in office. The Rajaonarison units moved into Tananarive, engaging the regular army forces under the command of General Gilles Andriamahazo, Ramanantsoa's minister of Public Works. After skirmishes in which 15 rebels and 6 regular military were killed, the loyalists overcame Rajaonarison's insurrectionaries, and Andriamahazo took charge of the country. He arrested Resampa and sent manhunt parties to round up the remaining rebels and the prisoners freed by Rajaonarison from the Tananarive jails during the putsch. After several days of martial law, some tranquility seemed to have been restored. However Andriamahazo and his military junta may handle the troubled political situation, the PSM-Rajaonarison putsch has demonstrated the residual strength of côtier resentment, pro-French and pro-Tsiranana sentiment, and suspicion of government programs throughout Madagascar.[53]

NOTES

1. See Hubert Deschamps, Histoire de Madagascar (Paris: Berger-Levrault, 1961), Ch. 7; Nigel Heseltine, Madagascar (New York: Praeger Publishers, 1971), pp. 131ff.

2. For Tsiranana's "indispensability complex," see Philibert Tsiranana, Le Cahier Bleu (Tananarive: Imprimerie Nationale, 1972); Virginia Thompson and Richard Adloff, The Malagasy Republic (Stanford, Calif.: Stanford University Press, 1965), Ch. 9; the author's "Rites of Passage in Madagascar," Africa Report 16, 1 (February 1971): 24-27.

3. For accounts of the insurrections of May 1968 in France, see Jean-Jacques Servan-Schreiber, Le Reveil de la France (Paris: Denoel, 1968); Edgar Morin, Claude Lefort, and Jean-Marc Coudray, Mai 1968: la Brèche (Paris: Fayard, 1968); J. Sauvageot, A. Geismar, D. Cohn-Bendit, and J.-P. Duteuil, La Révolte Etudiante (Paris: Editions du Seuil, 1968).

4. For analyses of French overseas policies under the Fifth Republic, see Edward M. Corbett, The French Presence in Black Africa (Washington, D.C.: Black Orpheus Press, 1972); Waldemar A. Nielsen, The Great Powers and Africa (New York: Praeger Publishers, 1970); the author's "Francophonie Reconsidered," Africa Report 13, 6 (June 1968): 6-15.

5. See Kwame Nkrumah, The Autobiography of Kwame Nkrumah (London: Nelson, 1957); W. E. F. Ward, A History of Ghana (London: Allen and Unwin, 1966); Alan Lloyd, The Drums of Kumasi (London: Longmans, 1964).

6. See Heseltine, op. cit., pp. 23-50.

7. See Jean Valette, Malagasy Foreign Relations in the Nineteenth Century, trans. Shelby Williams (Tananarive: Impremerie Nationale, 1964).

8. After Raymond Cartier, author of a series of critical editorials in Paris Match in the early 1960s, regarding French overseas commitments at the dawn of a new Europe.

9. See Heseltine, op. cit., p. 156.

10. See the author's "Madagascar and OCAM: The Insular Approach to Regionalism," Africa Report 11, 1 (January 1966): 13-18.

11. See Thompson and Adloff, op. cit., p. 178.

12. For reportage on these episodes, see Africa Report 17, 7 (July-August 1972): 4; Jeune Afrique, no. 564 (October 30, 1972); Latimer Rangers in Jeune Afrique, no. 543 (June 1, 1971); André Ravatomanga in Lumière (June 6, 18, and July 25, and August 1, 1971). For an account of French beweilderment, see C. L. Sulzberger in New York Times (June 25, 1971). The link between Resampa and the MONIMA was as improbable to those who knew Malagasy politics as a 1971 joint conspiracy between Washington and Peking: Resampa had been responsible for vigorous harrassment of MONIMA during election campaigns in the early 1960s; he also seldom had contact with the U.S. Embassy at Tananarive (whose major preoccupation at the time seems to have been the pursuit of investment opportunities for U.S. businessmen in Madagascar).

13. Nouvelles Malgaches Quotidiennes (Tananarive: Imprimerie Nationale, November 7, 1965), author's translation.

14. See the author's "New Round for the Western Islands," in Alvin J. Cottrell and R. M. Burrell, eds., The Indian Ocean: Its Political, Economic and Military Importance (New York: Praeger Publishers, 1972), pp. 309-11. See also the author's Self-Determination in the Western Indian Ocean (New York: Carnegie Endowment International Conciliation series No. 560, 1966), pp. 17-18, 27-28, 50-51; also Heseltine, op. cit., pp. 6-7, 191-96.

15. For criticism of the European economy in Madagascar as a kind of "slave trade, "see Rene Gendarme, Economie de Madagascar (Paris: Cujas, 1961) and René Dumont, L'Afrique Noire est Mal Partie (Paris: Seuil, 1962), Ch. 2, Annex 2, and elsewhere.

16. See Heseltine, op. cit., pp. 256-62.

17. Auguste Toussaint, History of the Indian Ocean (London: Routledge and Kegan Paul, 1966), p. 244. For background on problems of agricultural technology, see M. J. Dez, "Un des Problèmes du Développement Rural: la Diffusion de la Vulgarisation Agricole," in Terre Malgache, Tany Malagasy (Tananarive: Ecole Normale Supérieure Agricole), no. 1, n.d., pp. 41-70; also Heseltine, op. cit., Chs. 1, 7, 8; also Annual Reports of the Institut d'Emission Malgache (Tananarive: Imprimerie Nationale).

18. Edouard Chapius, Dix Ans de la République (Tananarive: privately printed, 1969). Declining agricultural production through 1972 was confirmed in L'Annuaire 1972 of the Service de la Statistique Agricole du Ministère du Développement Rural (Tananarive: Imprimerie Nationale, 1973); see also Marchés Tropicaux (June 14, 1974).

19. See L. Rangers in Jeune Afrique, no. 543 (June 1, 1971); no. 564 (October 30, 1971); Africa Report 16, 5 (May 1971): 10-11.

20. For accounts of the 1971 Tulear revolt, see Lumière (April 11, May 2 and 9, 1971); Africa Report, 16, 5 (May 1971), pp. 10-11. Curiously, American Lutheran missionaries in the south, repeatedly suspected since before 1947 of seditious behavior on behalf of aggrieved parishioners, were denounced by MONIMA leader Monja Joana in a Paris speech in June 1974 for collaborating with the government in suppressing the 1971 revolt; see Lumière, no. 1988 (July 14, 1974).

21. See Colin Legum, ed., Africa Contemporary Record, 1972-73 (London: Rex Collings, 1973), pp. B-168-76; see also interview with Philibert Tsiranana in Jeune Afrique, no. 564 (October 30, 1972).

22. A shocking statement, broadcast on the radio on May 13, 1972, threatening to mow down the demonstrators, with Tsiranana's voice imitating machine-gun fire, "lost [Tsiranana] in a few minutes all the esteem he had acquired over 14 years' rule." Africa Contemporary Record, 1972-73, op. cit., p. B-171.

23. For comment on the army's role, see Bechir Ben Yahmed's editorial in Jeune Afrique, no. 595 (June 3, 1972). At the time of the revolt, Malagasy army strength was 3,700, the navy was 250, the air force 150. Tsiranana's loyal FRS had about 4,000, as did the gendarmerie and the French forces stationed on Madagascar.

24. The new 1974-77 Development Plan has been critically analyzed in Lumière, nos. 1987 and 1988 (July 7 and 14, 1974); it is summarized in Marchés Tropicaux (March 1, 1974). The plan calls for a modest 3.2 percent average annual increase in GNP (which grew by only 1.4 percent in 1973), with a total investment of FMG 169,200 million; 64 percent of revenues are to be acquired through public domestic financing. Principal developmental priorities concern expanded agricultural production (especially foodstuffs) and equitable distribution of revenues and services (including education).

25. Compare Tsiranana's constant references to Madagascar as a "bridge" between continents to Foreign Minister Ratsiraka's blunt statement that "We are completely African." Interview with Jeune Afrique, no. 698 (May 25, 1974).

26. See Heseltine, op. cit., pp. 294-95; Africa Contemporary Record, 1972-73, pp. B-179-88; the author's essay in Cottrell and Burrell, op. cit., pp. 318-20.

27. For an account of Mauritius's experiments in nationalist foreign policy, see the author's essay in Cottrell and Burrell, op. cit., pp. 321-23.

28. See Marchés Tropicaux (February 8, 1974); also Paul Bernetel in Jeune Afrique, no. 687 (March 9, 1974); also the Economist Intelligence Unit's Quarterly Economic Review, no. 1 (London, 1974), pp. 14-16.

29. Ibid., no. 4 (1973), p. 17. Nevertheless, as 1974 proceeded, the Malagasy Government estimated a necessary subsidy of FMG 22,000 million for the importation of 200,000 tons of rice, with self-sufficiency in food staples calculated as still three years away.

30. See Chapters 4 and 7 in this volume; see also the author's essay in Cottrell and Burrell, op. cit., pp. 307ff. Previous regional associations had almost exclusively occurred under French sponsorship—for example, the creation of the Indian Ocean Tourist Association (ATOI) with a growing network of air links from April 1969, the use of Malagasy beef markets for Réunionnais and Comorean meat purchases, free Comorean immigration into Madagascar despite political and social dislocations, cultural exchanges with Mauritius under the symbolic aegis of "Francophonie."

31. See the author's Self-Determination, op. cit., pp. 55-65.

32. The incident, unconfirmed by official sources, was reported in Jeune Afrique, no. 704 (July 6, 1974).

33. For tax reform legislation, see Journal Officiel de la République Malagasy—JORM (December 31, 1973); see also Marchés Tropicaux (January 11 and 18, 1974).

34. See the astute constitutional analysis by Charles Cadoux in Lumière, no. 1984 (June 16, 1974).

35. JORM (June 22, 1974).

36. See Lumière editorial, no. 1985 (June 23, 1974); also no. 1984 (June 16, 1974).

37. For discussion of the complex relation between Malagasy peasant temperament and development, see Heseltine, op. cit., p. 251 and the author's review of Heseltine's work in Africa Report 17, 3 (March 1972): 39, 40. About three-fourths of Madagascar's 3.2 million actively employed workers are agricultural laborers (the total is less than half of the working-age population) but that majority produces only one-fourth the annual GNP; approximately 100,000 young people enter the labor force each year, only a tenth of them capable of being absorbed in the nonagricultural job market.

38. Paul Bernetel in Jeune Afrique, no. 687 (March 9, 1974).

39. See B. Chandon-Moët, in Lumière, no. 1923 (April 8, 1973).

40. It is nonetheless erroneous to draw too close a comparison between the fokonolona process and the "ujamaa" system as operated through the TANU party and other peculiarly Tanzanian institutions. (See Lumière, no. 1989, July 21, 1974.)

41. For theoretical and historical descriptions of the fokonolona, see Paul Ramasindraibe, Le Fokonolona (Tananarive: Imprimerie de la Mission Catholique, 1962); Richard Andriamanjato, Le Tsiny et le Tody dans la Pensée Malgache (Paris: Présence Africaine, 1960), pp. 38, 73-74; Jacques Dez in Terre Malgache, no. 1; Guy Hanicotte in Terre Malgache, special issue no. 15 (June 1974).

42. See Dez, in Terre Malgache, op. cit., p. 50.

43. JORM (July 20, 1974).

44. See Jacques Tronchon thesis, excerpted in Lumière, no. 1985 (June 23, 1974).

45. See René Teissonière in Terre Malgache, no. 1, p. 40.

46. Actually, as Tronchon points out in Lumière, no. 1985 (June 23, 1974), the fokonolona is far older than the period of Merina hegemony: British and French missionaries campaigned against it in the mid-18th century. Even the PSM weekly La République tacitly recognizes the seniority of the institution in calling Ramanantsoa's decision to revive the fokonolona "a 300-year leap . . . backwards." La République (April 13, 1973).

47. See André Ravatomanga, in Lumière, no. 1925 (April 22, 1973); see also Espérat Rakotazafy, in the same issue.

48. Basy Vava, pro-Resampa daily, Tananarive (April 13, 1973). Political parties operating (albeit not electorally) in Madagascar during 1974 included the MFM, whose slogan is "Power to the Little People"; the traditionally Merina-socialist AKFM (Independence Congress Party), which has clung to strands of loyalty to the Ramanantsoa government, although by tactical mistakes, it failed to participate in the May 1972 revolution; the rural-populist MONIMA, revered by the southern peasantry and respected by authorities although it has broken with the "bourgeois dictatorship" of Ramanantsoa; the small Christian Democratic Party (PDCM), revived in Tamatave; and the PSM (Malagasy Socialist Party), a reassemblage of the remnants of Tsiranana's PSD and Resampa's short-lived Malagasy Socialist Union (USM). Following the Tsiranana-Resampa reconciliation in March 1974, the PSM has attacked the government for dictatorial usurpation, narrow (anti-French) nationalism, Merina tribalism, and procommunist folly, while seeking early elections to be able to form a parliamentary government under what it assumes will be a Ramanantsoa presidency. A rapid return to party politics is opposed by all other parties and press organs and seems excluded by the constitutional ordinance of November 22, 1973 (JORM, July 20, 1974), which makes the CNPD "the sole legal and institutional forum for dialogue between the people and the government."

49. See André Ravatomanga, in Lumière, no. 1925 (April 22, 1973).

50. For accounts of the 1974 malaise, see Lumière, nos. 1987 and 1991 (July 7 and August 14, 1974), and Philippe Decraene in Le Monde (July 1 and 7, 1974).

51. Nivo Rakoto, in Lumière, no. 1987 (July 7, 1974).

52. Lumière, no. 1992 (August 11, 1974).

53. In June 1975, Andriamahazo's military directorate designated Captain Didier Ratsiraka as the new Chief of State; Ramanantsoa's ex-foreign minister, Ratsiraka has pledged to restore momentum to the 1972-74 program.

4

THE POLITICS OF
COMORIAN INDEPENDENCE
John M. Ostheimer

In the late 18th century, the southwesternmost islands of the
Indian Ocean were interlocked in the economic embrace of the slave
trade. Malagasy slavers carried away Comorians for sale in the
French islands to the east, Ile de France (Mauritius) and Ile de
Bourbon (Réunion). Once again, two centuries later, Madagascar
plays a pivotal role in the region. The 1970s finds these islands
affecting each other's politics in significant ways as the recent movement of the Western Indian Ocean's "Great Island" toward more complete independence from France reverberates throughout the region.
Relationships between France and the two remaining French Indian
Ocean possessions—Comoros, an Overseas Territory, and Réunion,
a Department, or integral part of France—have undergone new strains.
In the former, a break with France has brought a constitutional time
table that promises to lead to complete independence. In Réunion,
to be described in the following chapter, the strain has thus far been
absorbed without weakening the structures of departmental status to
the breaking point. Nevertheless, problems exist.

Midway between Madagascar's northern tip and the African mainland lie the four main islands of the Comoros Archipelago.[1] The
nearly 300,000 people of these four islands are to some degree homo-
geneous in racial, linguistic, historical, and especially religious
terms, although at least the southernmost one, Mayotte, provides a
contrast that has contributed to recent political turmoil.

This chapter is a substantial revision of "Political Development
in Comoros," African Review 3, 3 (1973):491-506.

MAP 4.1

Comoro Islands

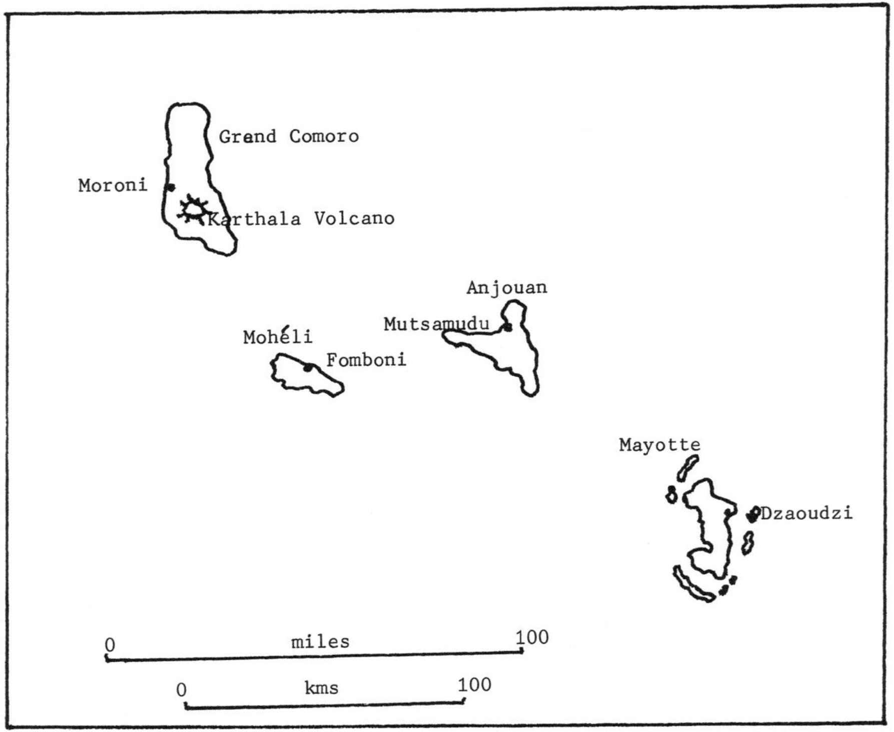

Grend Comoro

Moroni

Karthala Volcano

Mohéli

Fomboni

Anjouan

Mutsamudu

Mayotte

Dzaoudzi

miles   0   100

kms   0   100

BETWEEN AFRICA AND ASIA

Three of the six political units included in this volume were
settled prior to European exploration: Comoros, Madagascar, and
Maldives. Unfortunately, the anthropological records for Comoros
are very thin, since no extensive anthropological field work has yet
been carried out there. Even the most basic generalizations about
the racial and geographic origins of the Comorians have been the
subject of extremely divergent views.[2] The people appear to be
African, but with significant contribution of "Arab" features (via the
East African Coast) in the three northernmost islands, and of Malagasy
blood on Mayotte.

African origins, perhaps first from the Mozambique coast as
early as the 5th century A.D., were followed by intrusions of Malagasy,
Shirazi, and Zanzibari. The order of these immigrations is debatable.
During the late 18th and early 19th centuries, Malagasy contributions
increased, particularly toward the southern end of the island chain,
as a result of a series of invasions in search of cattle and slaves.[3]

The islanders think of themselves as Comorians, but there is a
measure of pride in contributions from abroad, for example among
those who stress their Arabness, or increasingly in recent years
among the "Mahoris" (Mayotte was previously known as Mahore), who
emphasize their Frenchness partly in order to elicit French support
for their separatist cause.

Historically, the Comoros have served as a stepping stone for
human and technological interchange between Madagascar and Africa.[4]
But though their isolation has produced a degree of ethnic, linguistic,
and cultural unity, the four islands also have differing cultural and
historical experiences and traditions that have contributed to strong,
and at times destructive, interisland rivalries. Culturally, Arab
and Islamic influence is probably a stronger unifying force than language, for each island has developed enough uniqueness in its use of
Swahili so that travelers can be identified off their home island.

Interisland rivalries played key roles in the 19th-century sequence
of events that led to French domination, and they are still supremely
important in the politics of Comoros today.[5] In fact, the manner of
French acquisition of the four islands may have added to the differences
among them. France had claimed control of Mayotte in 1841, under
circumstances that are not completely clear. One historian has argued that Mayotte was so troubled by incursions from Northwestern
Madagascar's pirates that the island "deliberately gave herself to
France on April 25, 1841."[6] A more recent interpretation is that the
era of Malagasy piracy was finished by then and that the Mahoris were
simply attempting to play the French off against potential enemies
within the island chain.[7] In any case, France ruled Mayotte until

1878 through an administrative union with the Malagasy island of
Nossi-Bé. Particularly after that time, Nossi-Bé and other settlements of northern Madagascar have served as receiving centers for
Comorian emigration. Although French rule was also declared over
the three islands during the mid-19th century, the French presence
was far more extensive on Mayotte than to the north. First, the
French developed Mayotte as a possible naval base, but it proved
disappointing. Sugar plantations were the next French thrust. The
relative tardiness of French control in the other three islands is
demonstrated by the fact that the negotiations leading to the final act
of abdication by the Sultan of Anjouan did not take place until 1909.[8]
Also, during the 1880s Grand Comoro witnessed confrontations between the Germans and French that illustrated the tenuous nature
of French control.[9]

The scramble for colonial territories, such a dominant event in
the 19th-century history of the African continent, did not pass the
Comoros by. It is at least partly true with French control of the less
valuable islands (Grand Comoro and Mohéli particularly) that international rivalries precipitated colonialism as a system of real control,
as opposed to mere claims of sovereignty. The French saw little
value in Grand Comoro, except when their influence throughout the
area was threatened by other European empires. In the British case,
the flag may have followed the establishment of trade, and then only
with great reluctance, but, for post-Waterloo France, "reluctance"
was a more relative thing. Beginning with the adventure in Algeria,
the French flag followed any excuse to salve the wounded national ego.
In the Comoros, interisland rivalries and political maneuvers within
each island elite found a willing "victim" in the French, who extended
their rule through treaties of "protection." The Comorians soon
learned to play the Europeans against each other. For example, a
chiefdom on Grand Comoro flew the German flag briefly in 1886 (the
Germans may not have been aware of this officially) in order to stress
its autonomy from other chiefs of their island. As a result, the
French moved in more permanently.

It was in 1909 that all four Comoro islands were added to France's
colonial administration in Madagascar. French administration brought
some of the more immediately transferable benefits of 20th-century
life. Health standards soon began to improve, as the population
increase of 50 percent between 1900 and 1960 manifested. As one
French historian has written, not all of the changes brought by French
rule were so "healthy." According to André Bourde, "the effects of
French rule were by no means entirely beneficial. The Comoros appear
to have attracted fortune seekers rather than statesmen. France originally wanted [the Comoros] to compensate for the loss of Mauritius
in 1815, but on the whole she took very little interest in them."[10] The
economy, which had been rather self-sufficient, given the emigration

of Comorians over the years either by free will or the slave trade, was steered away from crops that could be consumed or sold within the region, in favor of the standard colonial "dual economy" relationship. Vanilla, the perfume musk tree (ylang-ylang), coffee, sisal, citronella, cloves, pepper, and cocoa were planted. Land ownership came increasingly under the French agricultural sociétés (corporations) or under the control of the traditional elite. The old society was not fundamentally disturbed; members of its elite were merely "employed" in the colonial administration's subordinate roles. They retained their dominant social position.

World War II finally brought the beginnings of change. With Madagascar in the camp of Pétain, the Comoros had to be invaded by England, whose ships used the island chain as a base. After the war, the Comoros were severed from the Madagascar connection, becoming an Overseas Territory, more self-governing than a colony but without the proportional access to the French power center that Overseas Departments enjoyed. The national referendum of 1958 in all French possessions found Comorians voting to remain a territory. In spite of this vote, more complete self-government soon followed in 1961, when the territorial legislature's size and powers were expanded. Under President of the Council of Ministers Said Mohamed Cheikh, the more powerful Chamber of Deputies made policy for the great majority of internal problems. Foreign relations and defense were still under the control of the French High Commissioner. The prevailing view of Cheikh's government was that continued territorial status was an absolute essential for the economic and political stability of the Comoros. Cutting off the support of France, a disaster that could result from the affront suffered by the metropole when a colonial people choose complete independence (Guinea), would represent a blow that the poor Comoros could not afford. The Zanzibar revolution of January 1964 served as an even better warning of certain other consequences of "political radicalism." The leaders of the Comoros feel related to the Arab elite of Zanzibar, and the brutality that attended Zanzibar's Independence cast independence itself in a very unhealthy light.

These political advances toward self-government were accompanied by the opening up of the islands to the outside through an air travel route in 1947 to Madagascar and through French investment aid, though the pace of these postwar changes must be categorized as painfully slow. A look at the world map helps to remind one who would blame French neglect alone for the turtlelike pace of Comorian colonial development that geography is somewhat responsible. Particularly after the opening of the Suez Canal in 1869, the Comoros lay in a uniquely bad location for increasing contact with the outside world and for maximizing the potentials for development.

Thus, although the Comoro Islands share some aspects conducive to a unity of outlook, access to modernity has been limited, and, as shall be obvious in the review of Comoros politics to follow, features of diversity are of primary importance.

Added to the recent historical difference between the islands is a visible age difference, in a geologic sense. Like the other three, Mayotte is the top of a volcano, but the island has "decayed" to the point where its soils are comparatively rich and deep, its mountains not significant as communication barriers, and its waters protected by an extensive coral outer reef. This final difference is added to the others to defend Mahori claims to the right to select their own destiny. Marcel Henri, the leader of the Mahori Movement (MM), puts this very strongly; he points out that Mahoris speak Swahili differently from other Comorians and are discriminated against when they travel to the other islands. Their greater amount of Malagasy blood helps to ensure that they will not escape recognition. [11] Politicians from the other three islands constantly fight this threat of separation by Mayotte with statements stressing the unity of the Comorian experience and asking for subsequent unity of actions. As Ahmed Abdallah, president of the Governing Council, put it:

> Comorians, [unity] is not only the reunion among the
> political parties. Also it is foremost for all of you a
> new way of thinking and living together. It is searching,
> without passions, for solutions that preserve the tradi-
> tions of religion and custom to which we are powerfully
> attached, which treat with respect the particularisms
> of each of the islands, which place in harmony the
> heritages of the past with the necessities of the modern
> world, with the needs of a new society . . . [12]

Today, the Comoros could certainly never be used to bolser an argument for the "benefits of empire." They are pitifully poor and backward; there is virtually no press and only a single secondary school. Per capita income is surely among the lowest in the world. [13] The economy is based on plantation agriculture, and thus dependent on crops that need price supports in order to keep the effects of changing world demand off the farmers themselves. Until recently, this economic dependence was used as a major argument favoring continued attachment. According to a former Comorian president of the Governing Council, the Comoros must remain "at the bosom of the French Republic." [14]

Some of the Comoros's problems are, to be sure, preordained by geographical factors. No significant mineral resources have been discovered. There is not even a surface water supply on porous Grand Comoro, only man-made catchments and wells, so that the potential

of the volcanic soil is hard to tap. Fishing has little developmental
potential because continental shelves and banks are virtually nonexistent. To add to this, there are periodically disastrous cyclones.

Although all the islands are poor by world standards, the poverty
is unevenly distributed. Table 4.1 indicates the relative poverty of
Anjouan and Grand Comoro. One result of this uneven distribution
is varying nutritional standards. Mahoris and Mohélians are better
fed, with caloric intakes of over 3,000 units per day, as compared
to an average of 2,250 on Grand Comoro and 1,900 on Anjouan. [15]
Politically, differentials such as these explain much of the interisland
dissension over the Comoros' future. The richer islands, especially
Mayotte, fear the pressures of the two more populous, but less rich
ones. These jealousies cause the major internal political issue of
the islands: unity with independence, or separation?

Each island government is severely limited in its attempt to deal
with developmental problems because of the lack of revenues. For
example, the district government for Anjouan was forced to cut the
budget for 1973 to roughly 90 percent of the 1972 level. [16] French
Government aid has not been sufficient to overcome even the most
basic problems stemming from underdevelopment. As the Comorian
deputy to the French National Assembly pointed out to that body, the
number of doctors on some of the islands has actually fallen. [17] The
economic and social repercussions of this underdevelopment will be
more fully explored below.

The political results of underdevelopment have been quite pre-
dictable, although the timing of events has not. For many years, the
Comoros slept, politically somnolent while the more educationally
advanced populations of Africa and Asia were each reaching their
respective national "years of awakening." Only small, very unrepresentative groups of Comorians who had reached the outside world
had drawn the obvious lesson of comparison and dared to think the
situation of their islands could also change. Then, finally, from the
1971-72 period on, the political leaders still in the Comoros have
decided, in a complete turnaround, that their islands would be more
likely to develop with greater independence from France. After a
brief survey of the current governmental structure, this study will
concentrate on the development of independence politics in Comoros—
a place that one expert in French politics stated in 1962 was "unlikely
to seek independence in any immediate foreseeable future." [18]

THE STRUCTURE OF COMOROS GOVERNMENT

Currently, the Comoro Islands are formally governed by a High
Commissioner who reports to the minister of Overseas Territories
and Departments (TOM and DOM) in the French Government. [19]
Several legislative changes since the Fifth Republic's beginning

TABLE 4.1

Comoros: Selected Economic Data

	Grand Comoro	Anjouan	Mayotte	Mohéli	Average Totals
1) Forest (percent)	11	25	19	21	16
2) Pasture (percent)	10	0	6	7	7
3) Cultivatable Ground (percent)	35	64	64	59	48
4) Useless (percent)	45	12	11	14	29
5) 1958 Pop. Density per Sq. Km. Total	79	146	62	25	82
6) 1970 Pop. Density per Sq. Km. Total	114	220	97	35	121
7) 1958 Pop. Density per Sq. Km. Cultivatible Ground Only	227	229	97	42	170
8) 1970 Pop. Density per Sq. Km. Cultivatible Ground Only	327	346	151	60	251
9) Growth Index (1958 = 100)	144	151	156	142	148

Note: Column 9 applies to both columns 6 and 7.

Sources: Columns 1-4: B. Mennesson, "Situation Economique et Sociale des Comores," Promo al Camar (June 1970), p. 16. Columns 5-9: Territoire des Comores, "Annuaire Statistique des Comores," February 1972, p. 9.

FIGURE 4.1

Comoros Government Structure

The French Government: Ministry of Overseas Departments and Territories

The Commissariat at Moroni

French High Commissioner and Staff

Powers: Foreign relations and defense, internal security under "emergency conditions," immigration and emigration, French aid, information and broadcasting, police, judiciary, higher education, commerce, and finance.

"In all other domains, the Territory is sovereign"

The Chamber of Deputies of Comoros

39 members elected for a five-year term. Islands have proportional representation. Chamber of Deputies elects president of Chamber and also president of Governing Council

Powers: Enacts law relative to internal problems of Comoros. May be asked to advise High Commission on foreign relations

May pass "motion of censure" of the Governing Council.

The Governing Council of Comoros

Includes presidency and ministries for Interior, Economic Affairs and Planning, Finance, Public Works and Tourism, Rural Development, Public Health, Employment, Cultural Affairs, Education.

May propose dissolution of the Chamber of Deputies, to be decreed by French Council of Ministers

Subterritorial-Level Governments

Prefectures (one prefect for each island)
Subprefectures on each island

Source: Terr. des Comores, "Organization Politique et Administrative," Rapport Socio-économique sur l'Archipel des Comores, April 1973, pp. 1-5.

81

increased the internal autonomy of the islands,[20] but essentially, it was still correct to say that France held the preponderance of power, especially in the important realms of internal security.* Figure 4.1 indicates the distribution of governmental powers in 1974.[21]

After 1962, the Comoros were allowed a Territorial Legislature (now 39 members) with a Council of Government (cabinet) of from 6 to 9 ministers. This sytem could be called a modified parliamentary structure. Members of the legislature of the territory (Chamber of Deputies of the Comoros) might be asked by the president of the Council of Government to serve as ministers in his government, in which case their seat in the Chamber was filled by their "replacement." The names of these replacements were stipulated prior to the election, and in this way by-elections were avoided while the Chamber was kept at full strength. The life of the Chamber was five years. (See Table 4.2.)

The system differed from the pure parliamentary type in that cabinet ministers did not keep their seats, but it was similar in the important concept of "vote of confidence." An important example of the confidence vote took place on June 25, 1973, when Council President Ahmed Abdallah evoked a strong vote of support for his independence bargaining with France. The Council of Government was "responsible before" the Chamber of Deputies, while, to balance this, the Chamber of Deputies could be dissolved by decree taken in the Council.[22]

It was not necessary for legislators to be replaced if they were also serving in the French Government. One of the two Comorian deputies to the French National Assembly, Mohamed Ahmed, and the senator from Comoros to the French Senate, Said Mohamed Jaffar (the current president of the Comoros Chamber of Deputies), occupied such dual roles.[23]

---

*It is significant that according to Article 72, Section 3, the High Commissioner "shall be responsible for the national French interests, for administrative supervision, and for seeing that the laws are respected." The degree of French control over the Comoros during the last decade is, of course, a matter of interpretation. According to André Bourde, from the perspective of 1964, the Comoros had "complete internal autonomy" after December 1961. "The role of the French High Commissioner is only advisory in certain matters, such as defence and foreign policy." As Bourde saw it, the Comoros were "virtually independent." ("The Comoro Islands," Journal of Modern African Studies 3, 1 [May 1965] : 95.

TABLE 4.2

Party Composition of Chamber of Deputies, Comoros, 1974

Island	Party	Number of Seats
Grand Comoro	RDPC (Democratic Assembly of Comorian People)	10
	UDC (Democratic Union of the Comoros)	8
Anjouan	PSDC (Social Democratic Party of Comoros)	3
	UDC	10
Mohéli	RDPC	3
Mayotte	MM (Mahorais Movement)	5
Total		39

Source: Compiled by the author.

It is ironic that the Comoros possessed such an elaborate system of local government and representation on a political base that was extremely shallow. The systems of organized political groups* and written political communications were virtually nonexistent,[24] indicating a population that was basically without experience in or inclination toward participatory politics. Yet, below the territorial level, each island possessed a district-level government (circonscription) complete with a legislative Chamber, and these island governments were subdivided into legislative districts for leadership purposes and into subprefectures for administration.

One can perhaps explain some of this void in political development by the long-term effects of emigration. The French encouraged emigration, which seemed a wise thing to do given the lack of resources and development, making it easy by a concept of citizenship that entitles Comorians to all the rights of Frenchmen; for example—French consular protection. But an important effect of this on the islands

---

*Although 100 dock-workers did recently strike in Moroni (Info-Comores [March 17, 1973], p. 8), there are no trade unions at all, and no other "political associations" of any type other than the political parties and the business organizations such as the Chamber of Commerce, the planters, Air Comores, and so on.

was that many of the more active minds left, defusing the islands'
politics and delaying the independence attitude. However, it could
be also that the same demoralizing effects of underdevelopment that
long caused Comorians to emigrate did finally serve to stimulate
interest in independence. The mood in 1971, which seems to have
been the year that changed many minds on the independence issue,
was called by an editorial in the islands' only journal "pessimistic,
morose, and undeceived."[25]

POLITICAL DEVELOPMENT

The major Comorian political parties of the early 1970s are
difficult to keep straight because of the importance of personal relationships in determining membership. An example of this was the
Turqui family, which had three brothers; all three served different
political parties, as there was not "enough room" in one party.
  In spite of the relative importance of personality at the expense
of policy and ideology differences, it is possible to generalize about
the major parties of the immediate pre-Independence era. There
were essentially two varieties of Comorian political party: traditional
parties based on the established elite, and ideological-reformist
parties. The analysis becomes easier when it reaches the smaller
parties, of the ideological-reformist type, which were not represented
in the Chamber of Deputies but were crucially important in the
overall process of political development.
  The majority party in the 1972 popular vote, the RDPC (Democratic Assembly of the Comorian People), was created in August
1968. It had central committee membership in each island (four
members from each, plus five founders), and these planners met
formally once a year in party conference. (The most forceful RDPC
leader in 1972 was Mouzaoir Abdallah, the secretary general.)
During the year, four regional RDPC committees handled party business and directed the activities of the local committees on each
island.
  While the RDPC was certainly one of the "traditional" parties
in the sense that its leadership was derived directly from the leading
stratum in the population, and although it did not advocate basic
reform of the society, its program included a certain measure of
reform. RDPC leaders began after 1972 to make statements concerning land reform and at times to come out against monopoly, whether
in the hands of indigenous or French investors. Its views were
strongly Francophile, but in the liberal tradition, stressing reorganization of administration where necessary. Furthermore, the party
was officially in favor of the liberation and emancipation of Comorian
women, not a small reformist step to take in such a traditionalist

Muslim society. Among the traditional parties, the RDPC made the clearest statements of position (although as was usually the case in the Comoros, it was nearly impossible to find such statements in written form) and had the best organizational structure. It was basically "middle class"—which in the Comoros meant civil servants, teachers, and shopkeepers—and had had some success in establishing ties to the youth.

Perhaps some of the strength of the RDPC comes from the fact that it was long an opposition party, with less organizational structure, as a group that had for years been called the "whites" (parti blanc). (The terms "greens" and "whites" refer to the color of the ballots used by the largely illiterate electorate. They can be best understood in historical perspective. The followers of Dr. Cheikh on Anjouan used the green ballots. The traditional elite of Grand Comoro [the Cheikh group's counterpart] used white ballots, as did their allies on Anjouan, the PSDC.)[26]

Until 1970, during the UDC presidency of Dr. Said Mohamed Cheikh, the RDPC was the voice of reform against a government that represented the most traditional of options. After Cheikh's death in 1970, the RDPC took advantage of the competitions of personalities within UDC, accepted some ministerial posts, and became part of a coalition by fall of 1972. The RDPC leader, Prince Said Ibrahim, was president of the Council of Government for a time, but his position typified why one must be cautious of generalizing about the traditional parties. The policy positions ascribed to the RDPC above did not apply to Said Ibrahim, and he resigned because of conflict with these developing positions, and eventually founded a new party. Said Mohammed Jaffar, who made the call for independence, and Mouzaoir Abdallah, chief architect of the new multiparty coalition, were more typical of RDPC views.

The election of December 3, 1972 gave the RDPC (in conjunction with its allies from Anjouan, the PSDC) the relative majority of the popular vote, although the Democratic Union of the Comoros (UDC) still controlled the majority of Chamber seats by a margin of 18 to 16 and has control of the Governing Council.

The UDC derived from the traditionally powerful group, which had been identified since elections began as the "greens" (parti vert). The latest form of this group was created in December 1968, like the RDPC, for the purposes of competing in the 1970 elections. Its structure resembled that of the RDPC, with a central committee of 24 (6 from each island) that met three times each year. (The UDC leadership is more or less synonomous with the current Governing Council. After Ahmed Abdallah, president of the Governing Council, the second most important UDC politician is probably Said Attoumane, minister of Interior, who has been taking charge of the presidency when Ahmed Abdallah travels.) Formally, the UDC possessed structure down to party sections on each island and subsections that coordinated the activities of the village cells. But, in reality, the UDC's organization was perhaps the weakest of all parties, in relation to its size.

UDC policy attitudes are usually characterized as more conservative and traditional, more concerned with the maintenance of the status quo, which had served the "greens" well. They were the "big families" of Anjouan, and although by 1974 they had become leaders of UDC, until 1970 they were only the supporters of Dr. Cheikh, who was from Grand Comoro. The new UDC leader, Ahmed Abdallah of Anjouan, was president of the Governing Council. He was strongly pro-French, but by 1972 he saw independence as a political necessity and was determined not to let it get out of hand. His model of an independence relationship with France is along the lines of that established from 1960 to 1972 by Madagascar. He feared any French attempt to cut Comoros off, as she had Guinea. In his speech before the French Senate in 1970, Ahmed Abdallah took the frank position that although Comorians wanted to remain with France, the meagerness of French aid placed Comorian politicians who defended this idea in an "extremely difficult situation." He stated further,

> You well know, Mr. Minister [of TOM and DOM?], that
> several parties have been created in Comoros, one for the
> status quo [UDC?], another for independence [PASOCO
> and RDPC?], the third for departmentalization [MM?].
> Which will have the majority some day? No one can know,
> but you have put us [UDC] in an impossible situation.[27]
> (Brackets added.)

The party system reflected interisland rivalry as well. That part of the Grand Comoro elite that was <u>not</u> in control, the "whites," tried to resist UDC preponderance of power in territorial affairs by gaining support in the other three islands. They eventually controlled Moheli, had formed a working alliance with the Mahori Movement, and had identified allies on Anjouan among those who were for some reason (usually personal) alienated by the "greens" there. Their basis of success was certainly not the slight ideological differences between themselves and the "greens," but rather the fear of domination by Grand Comoro.

The third major party of the early 1970s, Umma (an Arabic word meaning "the people") was perhaps the most difficult of all to understand, and the most typical of the basic thesis expressed here, that Comorian traditional political parties were merely personal alliances between individuals tied together by their own shared distrust of other individuals. Its leader, the former president and RDPC head, Prince Said Ibrahim, was one of the most important feudal-style

landlords on Grand Comoro. Along with several followers, he split
with RDPC—probably in order to be in a position to offer either group
a coalition if this was necessary in order to form a government.
Said Ibrahim's splinter party was joined by Ali Sohili, a younger reformist whose policy outlooks were perhaps the most socialist of any
member of the three traditional political parties. Sohili was leader
of a group called Mranda, a collection of reform-oriented younger
politicians. It is impossible to take seriously the prospects of such
a union as Umma lasting for long. There is even one line of thought
that holds that Umma was formed by Said Ibrahim after the influence
of the Gaullist Jacques Foccart, secretary general for the African
and Malgache (Francophone) Community, in an attempt to salvage
influence for France through a "swing" party.

Among the political parties that did not merit the label "traditionalistic," the oldest was MOLINACO (National Liberation Movement of the Comoros), which was formed in 1962 by Comorian intellectuals living in the Tanzanian capital of Dar es Salaam. There were
several locations that could have witnessed such a development, as
Comorians have emigrated for years in search of work, and large
Comorian communities exist in the northern cities of Madagascar
(Majunga, Diego Suarez), on Réunion, in Seychelles, in Mombasa,
and in Dar es Salaam.[28] But the founding of the MOLINACO in Dar
es Salaam proved to be fortuitous, as by 1965 Tanzania was taking
a leading role in the development of a "radical" stance toward liberation of the remaining colonial territories. The permanent office
of the Organization of African Unity's Liberation Committee was
located in Dar, and the Tanzanian Government has been a continual
source of aid to MOLINACO and other liberation movements. The
OAU has also been useful, such as during the internal crisis within
MOLINACO that occurred during 1970-71, when a radical youth wing
tried to gain control of the party to turn it toward active and forceful
(military) tactics to oust the French from the Comoros. The secretary
general, Abdou Bakari Boina, weathered this storm and, with his
handful of fellow organizers, seemed to have embarked on a new
approach by 1973.

Until 1967, little was done by MOLINACO inside the Comoros,
perhaps because of the effectiveness of French control. MOLINACO's
account of the following incident gives an idea of the nationalists'
difficulties:

> The group of militants operating within the country al-
> ways faced the greatest hardship. Several of them were
> arrested in 1968 following a demonstration of students
> of Moroni Secondary School against French domination.
> The Comorians protested against Colonial abuses and
> dehumanization practices of the French administrators.

They were clamoring for "respect," self-determination,
and "human equality" as in the United Nations Charter
which was signed by France among other nations. A
total of over 300 appeared before the court, some were
sent for 50 years in closed prisons while others were
deported from the islands for 10 years. Important
names among the lot were Aberhman Ahmed and
Abdillahi Ali Hassan. The French lawyer (they were
not allowed to make use of the services of lawyers
other than French) Maurice Buttin, of the Appeal
Court in Paris, who appeared in Court for the ac-
cused was tricked by Air Comores—a French company operating air services to the Comores—who
changed the itinerary of their services so that Mr.
Buttin would not catch his flight from Dar es Salaam
to Moroni. He was flying from Paris, and although
he missed the Air Comores flight he did manage to
get to Moroni in time for the trial. MOLINACO had
to charter a plane from TIM AIR in Dar es Salaam to
Moroni. Had Mr. Buttin not gone on the chartered
flight, the case would have been conducted in Moroni
in his absence! [29]

MOLINACO was purely an expatriate party, and efforts were
concentrated on organizing branches in Madagascar and Réunion,
and in recruiting financial aid, mostly from the OAU and the USSR.
After that time MOLINACO became much more active through agents
in the Islands and through two parties that were formed locally to
represent its views. March 1968 saw a demonstration at the secondary
school in Moroni, and MOLINACO successfully lobbied at the United
Nations to have Comoros included on the list of territories under
"colonial domination" (UN Res. 1514 (XV)).

In August 1969 a group of young people, mostly students, formed
PASOCO (Socialist Party of the Comoros) to attempt to spread the
message of independence and socioeconomic reform in the islands.
This party had a hard time with the authorities, who thought of it
primarily as communist-inspired and tactically violent. PASOCO
was also subject to internal dissensions. In 1971 the PASOCO
treasurer, Ali Abdallah Himidi, switched to the conservative UDC,
a remarkably facile intellectual maneuver, given the differences
between the two parties, and served in the Chamber as the elected
UDC member from the ninth arrondissement.

Until June 1971, Boina's group in Dar es Salaam officially considered PASOCO their "arm" in the islands. Several trends then
coincided to convince MOLINACO that a change of tactics was called
for. First of all, PASOCO had failed to gain instant popularity.

Second, Boina had by this time overcome more radical opposition within his party. Third, the shape of post-Cheikh Comorian Government proved more pragmatic and less conservative as politicians dared to voice more openly their dissatisfaction with French rule.

As a result, in 1972, the Party for the Evolution of the Comoros (PEC) was formed, and this group seemed capable of hiding its dislike of the traditional parties while supporting their growing feeling that the Comoros could do better economically as an independent country. The PEC formed a part of the new "union," which must now be described.

Cooperation between the RDPC (and Anjouan allies, the PSDC) and the UDC had become very close by 1973. Since the UDC had moved toward slightly less traditionalistic and antireformist positions during the previous two years, the cooperation between the two parties culminated in the formation in September 1972 of the Union for the Evolution of the Comoros. It was premature at the time of writing to call this Union a political party. Although leaders of both the traditional parties that formed the bulk of the Union insisted that it was in fact a replacement for the older individual parties, and that their central committees had been merged, it was more correct to label the Union an electoral alliance.[30] This is particularly true when one recognizes that the PEC and other more radical reformist elements had joined the Union. The most that could be said for the prospects for continued unity was that the Union's diverse participants shared a desire, whatever their various reasons, for greater independence from France. But it is important not to lose sight of the fact that most participants in the Union had only joined the independence issue recently, that their differences were of much longer standing, and that these would be likely to emerge afresh after Independence, perhaps even exacerbated by the contest over the spoils of power. Although even MOLINACO leaders were working cordially with the "mainstream" politicians, during 1973,[31] their perspectives on the UDC and RDPC cannot have changed greatly. Perhaps the tongue in cheek, MOLINACO's view on the UDC was that "It used to be regarded by nationalists as a puppet party."[32] By 1974, the level of cooperation between MOLINACO and the governing coalition had begun to drop. From a high point of cooperative politics in January 1973, when the parties signed a memorandum of agreement on Independence at an OAU meeting in Accra, relations soured when MOLINACO representatives condemned the coalition's conservatism, in August. As predicted, the alliance with MOLINACO proved quite fragile.

One final political party remains to be described; the Mahoris Movement of Mayotte. Member and foe alike insisted that it was not really a political party at all; but it shared all the definitional features of one. (During the last election, MM used the title Union

for the Defense of the Interests of Mayotte.) For many years Mayotte
was the most advanced of the Comoro Islands economically and was
the center of French administration. Then, as the elites of the larger
populations of Anjouan and Grand Comoro became more active under
French control, power shifted to those islands, leaving Mayotte (and,
as always, Mohéli) in the backwash. Under the regime of Dr. Said
Mohamed Cheikh, the capital was moved from Dzaoudzi, Mayotte,
to Moroni, Grand Comoro, an event that proved of supreme significance
in the political development of Mayotte. The Mahoris felt that their
island had been badly neglected even in the context of comparative
overall neglect of all the Comoros. Mahori leaders talked about the
dismantling of the refineries that processed their sugar and of other
resources they were denied over the decades.[33] As anyone who has
braved the Hotel le Rocher can attest, the tourist industry has by-
passed the island. Even Radio Comoros has been moved to Grand
Comoro.

The removal of the capital was the most important of these blows.
Symptomatic of the political consciousness it created was the relative
overdevelopment of the political role of women that could be observed
in Mayotte. The MM has shown great skill in bringing attention to
the economic impact of the loss of the many domestic work positions
that are no longer available. One of the party's leaders, Madame
Zaina N'dere, was responsible for seeing that every Mayotte village
has one cell leader, frequently a woman, who kept track of the party's
fortunes there.

The tactics of the MM have been to emphasize the differences
between Mayotte and the other islands and to lean on French desires
to keep some position of influence in the Indian Ocean, at a time when
things were not going France's way.[34] Marcel Henri and other MM
leaders supported their claims to continued French protection by
pointing out that they welcomed the French Foreign Legion garrison
that has long been stationed at "the Rock" on one of Mayotte's smaller
islands; that their giant lagoon is capable of serving as an anchorage
for the French area fleet; and that, of the Comorian peoples, the
Mahoris are least dominated by Islam and the most Europeanized
(the Henri family is Franco-Malgache and Catholic) and would be the
most economically viable if only some attention were given to their
problems. On the subject of Mahori tactics, one must also mention
a series of violent events, the worst in October 1969, which at least
twice resulted in fatalities. During the December 1972 elections,
for example, MM "goon squads" apparently entered villages where
immigrants from Anjouan and Grand Comoro were concentrated and
intimidated them, discouraging them from voting.[35]

The Mahoris were clearly banking of the possibility that the
French really do care what happens to their part of the Indian Ocean
and therefore wish to keep some position of influence there. France

has on occasion encouraged them to feel that way. In November 1970,
Minister of TOM and DOM Henry Ray scolded the Mahoris for their
problems of "morale": They had allowed the removal of a few offices
to upset them, but they should recognize the inherent richness of
their island.[36] Then in 1972, Pierre Messmer, Ray's successor,
assured the Mahoris that there would be no independence without
allowing the populations of each island to rule by referendum on their
political futures. During early 1973, Marcel Henri, Abdullah Houmadi,
and perhaps others from Mayotte made plans to attend the Paris deliberations of May to June to remind Messmer, then prime minister,
of his year-old promise. As we shall see below, the French role
vis-a-vis Mayotte was to remain a disrupting influence.

    To emphasize their displeasure with the increasing domination
of territorial affairs by the other islands, although somewhat destructive to their own position perhaps, the Mahoris pursued a policy
of boycott. For months after the 1972 election, the cabinet included
no one from Mayotte. According to the government, a minister from
Mayotte would be "designated in agreement between the parties of
the Union and interested Mahoris."[37] It was not clear whether Ahmed
Abdallah's government intended to wait patiently for the MM leaders
to accept the unity of the islands or whether they would actively seek
other Mahoris who sympathize with that position. (The inclusion of a
Mahori, Youssouf Said, in the cabinet during 1973 indicates some
success with this tactic.) From the president's recent statements
and from past speeches, it would appear that he had little patience
with Marcel Henri's group, and had as well some reservations about
the French intentions. As a senator, Abdallah once indicated his
suspicions in a remarkably candid speech to the French Senate:

> It seems surprising to me, to say the least, that at the
> moment when all the giant powers are sharpening their
> penetration of the Indian Ocean, France seems to wish
> to renounce her well established position in the Comoros,
> the strategic importance of which is evident, and is driving
> us little by little to seek Independence. This French state
> of mind may be mere unconsciousness, but many Comorians
> think France is preparing another contrivance. That would
> consist of setting up one island, Mayotte, as a French De-
> partment and abandoning the other three to their own ends.[38]

Events were clearly not moving in the Mahori Movement's favor, and
they would continue in that direction unless France were to decide
to separate Mayotte off from the other islands. Interisland migration
filled whole villages on Mayotte with people from overcrowded Anjouan
and Grand Comoro. This migration was perfectly legal, but MM
leaders feel that it was being unjustly stimulated by politicians on

TABLE 4.3

Election of December 3, 1972, Comoros Chamber of Deputies

	Registered Voters	Valid Number	Votes Cast Percent of Registered	Pro "Union" (UDC, RDPC, PEC, and Allies) Number	Percent	Umma Number	Percent	Other Number	Percent
Grand Comoro	70,749	54,574	77	39,777 "Union"	72	13,021	23	1,776*	3*
Mohéli	5,562	4,216	75	2,409 576 (PASOCO)	57 13	1,231	29		
Anjouan	36,330	34,178	94	34,178	100				
Mayotte	16,428	11,885	72	2,351 (UJPM)	19	9,534	80		

*Front Patriotique Unie(?).

Source: Territoire de Comores, "Listes Proclamée Elue," December 7, 1972.

the two biggest islands. The election data in Tables 4.3 and 4.4 indicate one impact of these movements. It is significant that Mayotte had the highest nonvoting rate on the four islands. This could be partly explained by unrest around villages that had many more immigrants from other islands. There were more than 19 percent of the people on Mayotte who were unhappy with MM's message, and in future elections the "hand-shakers" (as the MM derisively call those from the other parties who stress Comorian unity) may do successively better.[39] A Mayotte-based party, UJPM (Union of Youth for the Progress of Mayotte) was advocating unity with the other islands and independence.[40] The French model of administration would act, in practice, to further this trend. The prefect of Mayotte, M. Abdouraquib, and the economic adviser, Ahmed Soilih, were examples of "pro-unity and independence" officials who served to undermine the MM position.[41] These efforts were already beginning to bear fruit, as the March 1973 elections for the French National Assembly (Table 4.4) showed 28 percent of Mayotte voters supporting the Unity candidate. In any case, this electoral arithmetic would mean little as long as France were to stay with her decision to observe the dominant international and Comorian pressures to give the four islands independence only as a single unit. Ahmed Abdallah had campaigned for the December 1972 election with a vow to establish a timetable for Comorian independence, but without threatening a future working relationship with France. This was a difficult "middle" course, for there were many who wanted either greater independence or retention of more complete ties with France.

TABLE 4.4

March 4, 1973 Election: French National Assembly

	Registered Voters	Votes Cast (All for Uncontested Unity Slate)	Percent Participated
Grand Comoro	76,383	62,730	82
Mohéli	5,914	5,394	91
Anjouan	36,965	34,937	95
Mayotte	16,272	4,347	28

Source: Info-Comores (March 17, 1973), p. 4.

The agreement signed June 15, 1973, promised that the referendum would not allow a single island to opt for continued dependence relationship with France.[42] France agreed in October 1974 to hold the referendum within six months. It seemed apparent that the Comoros would soon become independent and that the Mahori cause was lost; the referendum was held December 22, 1974, with 95 percent of the votes in favor of independence. Lumping all four island results together obscured the dominant view of Mayotte, where 64 percent of the voters chose departmental status.

Thus, there are a variety of tactics that the UDC-RDPC governing coalition may employ to reduce the troublemaking capacity of Mahori separatists. They can encourage "infiltration" of Mayotte by pro-unity Anjouanais to reduce Mahori voting power, both in the independence referendum and in the Chamber of Deputies. This tactic might make it easier to govern Mayotte; as things were in 1973, government leaders had a difficult time even visiting the island without evoking hostile receptions.[43]

A more conciliatory approach had also been shown at times by Ahmed Abdallah's regime. Though he rejected a French attempt during the negotiations of 1973 to count separately Mayotte's ballots in the forthcoming independence referendum, the accords signed by Abdallah did include preservations of "regional rights and interests," and he has repeatedly insisted that Mahori leadership is welcome to join the government in constructive mutual solutions to problems.

It will be hard to isolate the "Mayotte problem" without a clearer picture than presently exists of the evolving French role in the region. On examining the physical setting, it is hard to perceive of the French actually deciding to replace their lost Ivato and Diego Suarez bases on Madagascar by moving en masse to Mayotte. But the September 1973 speech by the French Minister of DOM and TOM Bernard Stasi surely left the impression that some officials, at least, favor such a policy. Stasi followed his statement on Mayotte with remarks in the French National assembly that indicate strongly the failure within Franco-Comorian communications: Stasi, at least, believed the accord allows Mayotte to decide her own fate.[44]

As of this writing (December 1974), it is by no means clear that the political setting within France is adequately stable to confront the cacophony of adverse international sentiment that would be sure to follow such a French move. Even the Anglo-American scheme for Diego Garcia has occasioned serious international opposition, and in that case of a nearly uninhabited, politically irrelevant island, both immediately concerned governments, Mauritius and Seychelles, gave tacit consent.

Editor's note: In July 1975, the Comorian Chamber of Deputies attempted to precipitate events with a 33-0 vote for immediate independence. Mayotte's deputies were absent.

ECONOMICS

Presumably, all of these political problems will be resolved in due course, but, one way or the other, basic social and economic underdevelopment will remain. The Comoros have relied heavily on France for development capital, and for the trained personnel to administer the modest development that has taken place. After World War II, the islands began to receive at least a small share of French development funds under the first FAC (Fonds d'Aide et de Coopération), and then the expanded FIDES (Fonds d'Investissement et de Développement Economique et Social). These programs have been responsible for the transfer of many millions of francs to Comorian development; aid that was approaching the CFA 1 billion level (c. 225-50 Francs CFA = $1). This is over and above the operating budget deficits that France has annually subsidized. The budget for 1974 was anticipating a 21 percent deficit. (The 1973 budget showed revenues of 1,779 million francs CFA, which included a French subsidy of 419 million francs CFA against expenditures of 1,610 million. For 1974's revenues of 2,311 million francs CFA, the French subsidy was to total 469 million.)[45] In spite of the obvious importance of France's contribution, it must be pointed out that though the Comoros account for more than one-half of the total population of French Overseas Territories,* the Archipelago received only 20 percent of all FIDES aid set aside for those territories.

Agricultural development is badly needed. One might also say that Comoros agriculture needs to be "redeveloped," away from some of the emphasis on raw agricultural goods purchased by France for her own domestic perfume, spice, and then secondary industries, towards rice, coconuts, bananas, and other basic crops that the Comoros themselves need. This process would reduce import value and increase self-sufficiency. Food and other consumer items amount to 70 percent of the imports bill. Land reform may be an essential aspect of producing such a change. One third of Anjouan's land remains for the peasants, after European sociétés and individual plantation owners, and the few Arab elite, are discounted.[46] The

---

*The population figures for 1966 were Comoros, 225,000; French Polynesia, 90,000; St. Pierre and Miquelon (CN atlantic), 5,000; New Caledonia, 93,000; Wallis and Futuna, 8,000.

economic pressures of land hunger, serious on Anjouan and Grand Comoro, may be an even better reason than politics for relocating Comorians onto Mayotte.

Another significant change would be to encourage light industry based on existing agricultural potential. Mayotte had several sugar refining mills before they were dismantled years ago. A good sign is that the Comoros will soon have a new refinery as part of French aid. The Comoros have no mineral resources, but more could be made of the fishing industry, in a geographical region now dominated by Japan, and forestry could be developed for greater export potential.

Yet another direction for development is tourism, and a new jet port on Grand Comoro may stimulate tourism potential after its completion in 1974. Nonetheless, the traditionalistic nature of Comorian Islam does not bode well for smooth tourism developments. It is needless to say that with a 3 percent population growth rate, some basic development is going to be necessary.

SOCIAL DEVELOPMENT AND THE
CULTURE OF NATIONALISM

The continuing social and educational underdevelopment, in islands that are still characterized as "sleepy," may soon erupt into political problems of crisis proportion. December 1973 brought riots on Grand Comoro that had to be suppressed by French forces brought in from Réunion by invitation of the Abdallah government. It is against these unfortunate levels of backwardness that the future strength of PASOCO, MOLINACO, and other militant groups of Comorians, such as ASEC (the Association of Comorian Students and Trainees in France) should be gauged. Only one-quarter of the school-age youth are attending public schools, a figure that would be swelled by defection from current enrollment in Koranic schools. But the question is whether the hard-pressed governmental resources could provide more educational facilities.

Educational problems, the shortage of medical personnel, and other difficulties of provisioning basic social services show the true depths of Comorian poverty. There is little left for the "frills," such as communications media. For years, the only printed "news" source on the islands was the amateurish Promo al Camar, which ceased publishing in 1972. A new PASOCO weekly, Uhuru (Swahili for "freedom") was being picked up by government agents in 1973 before it could spread too widely. During 1973 the French began a new mimeographed paper, Info-Comores, which preferred a rather innocuous reporting diet of official speeches.

In view of the very weak status of interisland communications, the feeble development of the media and of educational and social infrastructure, and the variety of Comorian outlooks ranging between pro-French sentiment to immediate independence, one of the more difficult future Comorian problems may be to establish a true national will and spirit. Whereas Madagascar's problem is to resurrect an authentic traditional base on which to peg present unity, Comoros must forge such a spirit for the first time. It is hard to see how this can happen quickly. The author recalls the efforts during the 1960s to establish a history that might be capable of molding pride among the students in new African countries. Even then, with larger, comparatively wealthier societies, with national universities and corps of historiographers (ironically, largely expatriate) to reinterpret the past, and with better communications systems, progress was slow (and still is) in establishing a sense of being Tanzanian or Nigerian.

The material probably exists for constructing a historical interpretation on which Comorians could base a pride in their identity as a separate and distinct culture,[47] but with such mediocre infrastructure and educational progress, the forces pressing for national unity may derive little support, at least soon, from such cultural sources of assistance.

Meanwhile, the pressures of politics in an isolated context, may well work in the other direction.

NOTES

1. Information on the Comoros is sparse. According to a U.S. bibliographer, "Political development is given little room in the specialized studies which form the bulk of significant literature on the Comoro Islands during the late nineteenth and the present centuries." Barbara Dubins, "The Comoro Islands: A Bibliographical Essay," <u>African Studies Bulletin</u> (September 1969), p. 134. Furthermore, the most complete present statistical study warns readers that, given the quality of the figures, "statistical rigor is debatable." Territoire des Comores, <u>Rapport Socio-economique sur l'Archipel des Comores: 1970-71</u> (Moroni, 1973). In part, the paucity of anthropological and sociological research on Comoros may be because, as Dubins put it, the research has "been conducted by and for agencies of the French Government, and the findings [have been] published in reports which are not widely circulated." Dubins, op. cit., p. 136. Dubins, op. cit., p. 136.

2. Comorian ethnohistory is treated in the following writings by Urbain Faurec: <u>L'Archipel aux Sultans Batailleurs</u> (Moroni, <u>Promo al Camar</u>). "Voyage aux Iles Comores," <u>La Revue de Madagascar</u>

(July 1937; reprinted in Promo al Camar, March 1971), pp. 6-15; L'Histoire de l'Ile de Mayotte (Moroni, Promo al Camar). See also Said Ahmed, "L'Histoire d'Anjouan," Promo Al Camar (May 1971), pp. 36-39. Other writings on the 18th and 19th centuries are suggested by Barbara Dubins, "Nineteenth-Century Travel Literature on the Comoro Islands: A Bibliographical Essay," African Studies Bulletin (September 1969), pp. 138-46.

3. For an example of these pressures, see "Piraterie Sakalawa; Raid sur les Comores," extract from "La Ville des Antalaotra Majunga," Promo al Camar (May 1971), pp. 13-15. See also M. A. Gevrey, "Notes aux sujet des incursions Malgaches aux Comores du XVIe au XIXe Siécle," among the documents in the collection of the Museum of Archaeology, University of Madagascar, Tananarive; excerpts in Lumière (April 28, 1974), p. 5. This work was published by Gevrey as Essai sur les Comores (Pondichery, 1870). At the moment, the most complete general bibliography of Comoros' history is Barbara Dubins, "The Comoro Islands," op. cit.

4. An interesting study of the Comoros' bridging role between Madagascar and Africa has to do with the origins of the Ngalawa, or outrigger canoes, of the region. See James Hornell, "The Outrigger Canoes of Madagascar, East Africa and the Comoro Islands," Mariner's Mirror 31 (1944).

5. An example of an intra-island confrontation is described in what is certainly the best extant study of the precolonial era: Barbara Dubins, "A Political History of the Comoro Islands, 1795-1886" (Ph.D. dissertation, Boston University, 1972).

6. Faurec, "Voyage aux Iles Comores," op. cit., p. 11.

7. Dubins, "A Political History," op. cit., p. 88.

8. Acte d'Abdication de Said Mohamed Sultan d'Anjouan, reprinted in Promo al Camar (August 1971), pp. 27-28.

9. See Dubins on scramble, A Political History, op. cit., pp. 231-33.

10. André Bourde, "The Comoro Islands: Problems of a Microcosm," Journal of Modern African Studies 3, 1 (May 1965): 93.

11. Marcel Henri stressed this and other features of discrimination in a personal interview at Dzaoudzi, April 28, 1973.

12. Speech of January 26, 1973; published in Info-Comores, February 3, 1973, p. 3. For other calls for unity see the speeches of former president, Said Ibrahim, October 2, 1971, in Promo al Camar (October 1971), pp. 12-20. All translations from French used in this chapter are by the author unless indicated otherwise.

13. Estimates are $20 by P. DeCraene, The Guardian, December 23, 1972; and $60 by The People (Seychelles) (December 6, 1972), p. 12.

14. This June 1971 speech by President Said Ibrahim is a good example of the dependence argument at work. Promo al Camar, (July 1971), pp. 4-8.

15. Terr. des Comores, Rapport, op. cit.

16. Info-Comores (January 22, 1973), p. 6.

17. Speech by Mohamed Ahmed, Paris, November 5, 1969. Cited in Promo al Camar (November 1969), p. 2. This state of affairs provides the radical Comorian nationalist movement based in Dar es Salaam with some of its most effective propoganda. See "Comorians Demand Their Independence," The People (Seychelles) (November 22, 1972), p. 11.

18. Dorothy Pickles, The Fifth French Republic: Institutions and Politics (New York: Praeger Publishers, 1962), p. 161.

19. Other Overseas Territories are French Guiana, French Territory of Afars and Issas (Djibouti), St. Pierre and Miquelon, Polynesia, and New Caledonia. Their status is determined by Article 72 of the Constitution of 1958. A report on Overseas Territories appeared in Le Monde (June 19, 1973), p. 8.

20. These are Law No. 61-1412 of December 22, 1962, and the Law of January 3, 1968. Articles 73 and 74 of the 1958 Constitution allow such modification.

21. Judicial structures were not analyzed in this report. They are described in Promo al Camar (December 1970), p. 14.

22. Description of current Comorian Government occurs in Terr. des Comores, Rapport, op. cit. The "replacement system can be seen in action in the cases of five members of the current Governing Council." See Info-Comores (March 17, 1973), pp. 6-7.

23. French law pertaining to the Comorian electoral process for senatorial elections is found in Info-Comores (March 17, 1973), p. 3, and (April 2, 1973), p. 5.

24. Until April 1972, an interesting, informative monthly, Promo al Camar, was printed by BDPA (Bureau pour le Developpement de la Production Agricole) in Moroni. Then in January 1973, a French Chief of Cultural Affairs Services was recruited to put out the new bimonthly, Info-Comores. Outside of this governmental effort, there is no established private press, only a recently appearing underground PASOCO paper, Uhuru.

25. Promo al Camar (March 1971), p. 1.

26. For an account of the development of the political party system, see P. DeCraene's article in Le Monde (April 1971), and Cedric Saint-Alban, "Les Partis Politique Comoriens entre la Modernité et la Tradition," Revue Francaise d'Etudes Politiques Africains 94 (October 1973): 76-91. Saint-Alban's article includes a detailed chronology of Comorian events from 1841 to 1968.

27. Promo al Camar, (December 1970), pp. 2-6.

28. P. DeCraene, Le Monde (December 1 and 2, 1972). More on the Comorian "diaspora" is found in Paul Guy, "Islam Comorien," in Jean Paul Charnay, Normes et Valeurs dans l'Islam Contemporain

(Paris: Payot, 1966), pp. 145-58. It is probable that more Comorians have emigrated and are living in East Africa, Madagascar, and other places than the total who remain in the Comoro Islands. These expatriates cannot help but exert an important influence on the politics of the home islands.

29. The People, (November 15, 1972), p. 11.

30. Conversation with Minister of Interior Said Attoumane, May 2, 1973.

31. See account of Boina's welcome of Ahmed Abdallah in Uhuru (Dar es Salaam)(April 4, 1973). For Boina's views of the PEC coalition, see the interview with Boina in Africa, 21 (May 1973): 38.

32. The People (November 15, 1972), p. 11. See also the enlightening comment by the Tanzanian journalist Musa Kibasi: "Independence for the Comoro people is now a question of time. MOLINACO will then have to press for economic independence. It will have to introduce urgent land reforms." "A Chameleon Called France," Daily News (Dar es Salaam)(December 5, 1972). See also, the official Tanzanian Government statement on the Comorian elections, December 1, 1972.

33. Karrim Essak argues that this condition was general throughout the Comoros, where French policy has been directed toward the positive destruction of Comorian industry. Using data probably provided by MOLINACO, he argues, for example, that between 1844 and 1905 all 14 sugar factories were dismantled. Daily News (Dar es Salaam) (October 16, 1972).

34. For example, during the visit by the French High Commissioner to Mayotte in March 1973. For a statement of the Mahori view, see the speech by the Mahori member of the Comoros Chamber of Deputies, Younoussa Bomana, on the occasion of the visit by the French Minister of DOM and TOM, November 1970, to Mayotte. Promo al Camar (November, 1970), pp. 7-8.

35. Info-Comores (March, 1973), p. 3; also cites "incidents" on February 19 and 20, 1973.

36. Promo al Camar (November 1970), pp. 9-11.

37. Info-Comores (January 22, 1973), p. 3.

38. Speech printed in Promo al Camar (December 1970), pp. 2-6. See also the New Year's speech of former president Said Ibrahim, which was largely concerned with the subject of Mayotte. Promo al Camar (January 1972), pp. 1-4.

39. One must note here that MM has benefited in the past from a favorable French press, notably in the person of Le Monde's P. DeCraene, whose articles have stressed the positives of the Mahori position.

40. An interview with UJPM's leader, Mohamed Mrandjae, appears in C. Hoche, "Comores: A Quel Prix, l'Indépendance?" Le Figaro (January 20 and 21, 1973).

41. See also P. DeCraene's account of activities of Muslim holy men who argue that MM is subverting the correct domestic role of women. Le Monde (December 1 and 2, 1973).

42. On the prospects of international uproar should France decide to "hive off" Mayotte as an Indian Ocean base, see Daily News (Dar es Salaam) (October 16, 1972). For more analysis of this topic, see P. DeCraene, Le Monde (June 9, 17, and 18, 1973). Also Le Monde-Guardian (English Edition, June 16, 1973).

43. Accounts of Franco-Comorian discussions of 1973, leading to the independence accord are found in Marches Tropicaux (July 27, 1973), p. 2360; Le Monde (June 9, 1973); Jeune Afrique (January 13, 1973 and July 7, 1973). The July 1973 visit by Ahmed Abdallah to Mayotte, which resulted in demonstrations and the arrest of the Mahori leader Younoussa Bamana (on charges of instigating unrest) is described in Marchés Tropicaux (August 24, 1973).

44. Stasi's travels and statements are reported in Marchés Tropicaux (October 12, 1973), pp. 2963, 2990-92, 3025.

45. Marchés Tropicaux (June 8, 1973 and November 23, 1973).

46. A good discussion of land tenure and inequality problems is found in Bourde, op. cit., pp. 96-97.

47. For example, Barbara Dubins's reinterpretation of the French takeover of the Comoros during the 19th century contradicts the Eurocentric view that the Comoros had been destroyed by the vicious slave trade and was hopelessly backward, ready for colonial rule. Her reexamination of the 19th-century records leads to the conclusion that Comorians were important, perhaps determining, actors in the events. See, for example, "A Political History," op. cit., p. 234.

5

RÉUNION: FRANCE'S
REMAINING BASTION
John M. Ostheimer

Four hundred and twenty miles from Madagascar lies the imposing island of Réunion, its forbiding shoreline a symbol of French
determination to retain a presence in the Indian Ocean region. The
visitor to this French bastion soon develops a feeling similar to that
experienced while routing mainland France—a sense that history is
everywhere. But Réunion's is a very different sort of history; a story
of multiracial immigration, dominated by the impact of each successive
"wave" upon the developing culture: a curious combination of intrusion
from outside with unique isolation. Probably best known outside French
circles for curious (and in many cases recently extinct) forms of
bird and other animal species that evolved there, a contemporary
Réunion seems to retain the ability to gestate compelling environmental disequilibriums. But today's problems are very human. As
one French writer put it, "The demographic problem is today the
sore point of the island's economy."[1]

An egg-shaped island of roughly 40 by 30 miles, Réunion has a
total land area of 970 square miles. The Réunionnais numbered
466,000 by 1972, concentrated along the coastal area from Saint-
Benoit around the north and west of the island to Saint-Joseph. There
are smaller settlements on the high plateau between the two volcanoes:
extinct Piton des Neiges in the northwest and the active Piton de la
Fournaise on the southest side. For the most part, the southeast
corner of the island is quite barren and useless.

HISTORIC BACKGROUND

The majority of Réunionnais are called Creole, a racial mixture
that derives from the various immigrations that have occurred since
the French settled the uninhabited island in the mid-17th century.

MAP 5.1

Réunion

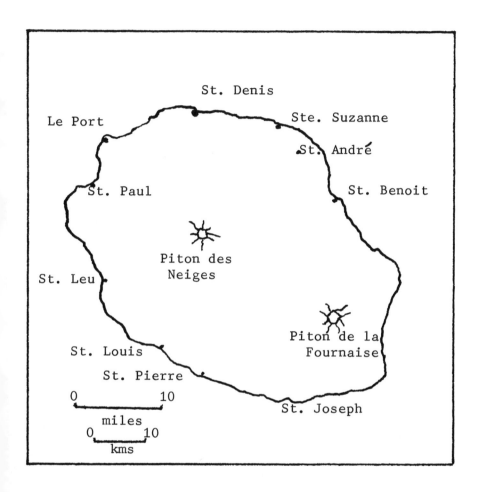

French historians divide the history of Réunion into five major episodes, and this historiography helps one understand the island's present racial composition.[2] The first period, from settlement until 1715, saw slow growth into a community that numbered around 1,200, composed of French and their African slaves. The economy was based on a variety of activities such as hunting and fishing, as well as some early plantation crops (sugar, tobacco, and so on). For the next century, coffee and spices predominated. It was during this period that French designs for empire east of India fell apart, and control of Réunion was no longer justified only because the island was a stop on the way to far more significant French holdings. Finally, French mastery even over Réunion was questioned by the Napoleonic defeats, which caused the island to fall under British rule for five years. The Treaty of Paris in 1815 returned Réunion to France, but at least as significant for the French outlook on Réunion was that Britain kept other Indian Ocean islands taken from Napoléon.

At least economically, these events proved momentous for Réunion. France's previous reliance on Ile de France (Mauritius) was necessarily replaced by a long period of sugar emphasis on Ile de Bourbon (Réunion). The population grew spectacularly under the impetus of immigration for plantation labor. Many thousands, mostly Malagasy, were imported as slaves, swelling the population from 17,000 in 1800 to over 100,000 by 1830. When these laborers proved an unreliable work force (many left the plantations after slavery was abolished in 1848), Indians were brought to replace those who had fled into the mountains to avoid plantation labor. Besides the Indians, there were also Arabs, Indochinese, Polynesians, and more Africans and Malagasy. By 1865, more than 200,000 people swarmed over the island, producing a remarkable population density (for those days) of over 200 per square mile.

During the 1860s Réunion's fortunes began to decline, because of a combination of natural and competitive forces, the worst being an infestation of sugar cane borer and the growth of the Cuban cane and French beet sugar crops. In 1881, England cut off the supply of Indian labor after charges that they were being mistreated on Réunion. Finally, malaria's arrival in the 1860s proved a depressing factor well into the 20th century. Thus, the fourth period of Réunion's past was a somber, neglected span of 80 years, which improved somewhat after World War I as sugar once again became profitable.

Réunion's modern era began in 1946 with departmentalization. Since then, an impressive stream of investments and administrative personnel have come from the metropole to turn a miserably underdeveloped island into what is, in many respects, a demonstration of what the French can do when motivated. Réunion was opened to the outside world: Travel outside the island doubled between 1967 and 1971.[3] By the 1970s Réunion had become as prosperous as Comoros was neglected; in fact, visits paid to Réunion by several Comorian politicians helped convince the latter that in comparison to department-alization in Réunion, their own status of Overseas Territory was the least satisfactory of future options.

Much of France's motivation, certainly the majority of it since 1963, came from the deputy to the National Assembly for the first Réunion constituency, Michel Debré. Réunion's star was tied in large part to the "second ascendance" of Debré, and it is essential to understand his significance. A lawyer and political scientist by training, Debré served the Fourth Republic briefly in the Foreign Affairs Ministry and as a senator for 1948-58. Finally in 1958, he became minister of Justice in de Gaulle's cabinet and took charge of drafting the Fifth Republic's Constitution. He helped during that time to form de Gaulle's new party, Union pour la Nouvelle Republique (UNR). The general made Debré premier from January 1959 until April 1962, when he was replaced by Georges Pompidou. Though not originally from Reunion, Debre chose to reenter politics through a 1963 by-election on the island and won as the UNR candidate. He was subsequently returned via this seat in the 1976, 1968, and 1973 elections.

Prime Minister Pompidou summoned Debre to his cabinet in 1966, and he served continuously until April 1973, holding the portfolios for Economy and Finances, Foreign Affairs, and National Defense. Then, sponsor of the loi Debre, a tremendously unpopular bill ending key types of draft deferments for educational purposes, Debre failed to negotiate a suitable position in Pierre Messmer's cabinet after the March 1973 elections.[4]

The most impressive and visible changes that were observable in the island resulted from funds procured after Debré's return to influence with the Gaullists. Add together the continuing development of the road system (including the spectacular new Saint-Denis-Le-Port road, carved out of the cliffs), with the residential development and museum-university complex around Saint-Denis, and Debré's impact cannot be denied. Nor may one pass off this sudden attention for an island 9,600 kilometers from France as cynical vote-getting by Debré, although votes may have been one result. Debré typified the Gaullist attitude toward France's grandeur and her role in world affairs. Réunion represented more than just his ticket to the National Assembly. It was (and is) a French outpost in a hostile world. Symbolically, hundreds of ancient cannons, all pointing toward the sea, testify to the difficulties post-Napoleonic France had in remaining a world power. Those cannons were once used against Britain, and visitors have a gnawing sensation while in the more francophonic islands of the Indian Ocean that the "enemy" is still England or at least "Anglophonie."

Many Réunionnais feared that Debré's fall from influence in April 1973 would mean a decline in the fortunes of the overseas department. As Debré himself had written, "Réunion is today a very living expression of France."[5] But Debré's fall may be balanced

by new attention given to Reunion in the wake of the French ouster
from Madagascar, and the full independence, in 1975, of the Comoros.
France's sense of mission in the Indian Ocean also has included overtones of defending the area from the rivalry between the United States
and the Soviet Union, a view not unlike the Gaullist perception of the
French role in Europe. The United Nations' report on Diego Garcia
and other developments in the U.S.A.-USSR rivalry (referred to in
Chapter 1) were reported extensively in Reunion's government-supported daily paper. [6]

After a brief account of the governmental structure and political
forces, this chapter will review the French strategies for Réunion's
development as they evolved during the Debré era, considering the
process the options suggested by critics. Development has stimulated
great antagonisms among the Réunionnais, and, ironically, the power
of the autonomist groups has risen along with the scale of French
investments. The chapter will conclude with an evaluation of the
issue of autonomy and of the opposition movement's strength and
prospects.

GOVERNMENTAL STRUCTURES

Article 72 of the 1958 Fifth Republic Constitution, cited in the
Comoros chapter in reference to overseas territories, also provided for overseas departments (DOMs). Under Article 76, Réunion
chose, by decision of the Territorial Assembly, to adopt this form
of relationship with the metropole. Departmental status does not
provide for any constitutional development toward independence, but
Article 73 does appear to give DOMs some recognition that their
unique qualities may require their "administrative organization to be
modified by measures intended to adopt them to local conditions."[7]

France has been a highly centralized and hierarchical country
since the days of the Bourbon monarchs. Fundamental political
arguments have been over whether the centralized system should be
ruled by a monarch, a representative assembly, or a Bonapartist
dictator. Each group has desired control over a strong center, rather
than a peripheralized, federal system. As one of 99 departments,
Réunion is governed by a prefect who is nominated by the minister
of Overseas Departments and Territories (DOM and TOM) and appointed by the president of the Republic. The departmental prefect's
powers to carry out the laws and decrees of France are extensive,
but his ability to reshape the policies to suit local conditions (or
encourage his advisory "General Council" to do so) are minimal.
Beneath the departmental prefect, the administrative cabinet and sub-
cabinet officials are housed in the impressive Hôtel de la Préfecture,
in Saint-Denis. It is interesting that, besides the various administrative departmental officials such as Information and Press, Police,

Education, there is a Reunion office of the intelligence and defense
establishment. Under this departmental administrative structure are
three subprefectures, installed in the towns of Saint-Pierre, Saint-
Benôit, and Saint-Paul.

The principal legislative structures are of two levels: On the
Departmental level, there is a general council consisting of 36 elected
members from Réunion's 23 communes. In 18 communes the mayor
of each commune's main town is represented in that commune's General Council delegation, a fact that lends significance to the council
itself, given the importance of the office of mayor in French government traditions. [8] On the national level Réunion is represented in
Paris by five elected officials to the National Assembly, three members of the Chamber of Deputies, and two senators who are elected
indirectly to nine-year terms (1/3 every three years), and by a
member to the Economic Council.

The departmental system of administering France has traditionally
been the largest unit for tying together the huge network of 38,000
"communes" that has always been the basis of French community
life. But in the competition for resources that has typified modernizing France since World War II, departments have proven too
small and specific for effective coordination. For this reason a
regional system was decreed in 1959-60, blending the 95 metropolitan
departments into 21 regions, and the general evaluation had been
that more efficient social and economic planning and development
have resulted. [9]

The regional system was based on the logical similarities and
infrastructural ties among departments, and the four overseas
departments were therefore ignored. It was increasingly clear that
Réunion's bargaining position in the competition for developmental
funds and priorities would suffer from lack of regional status. Each
regional prefect (a department prefect selected from the appropriate
departmental prefects to preside jointly over the region as well as
his own department) speaks with the authority of several departments.
In 1974, Réunion was still in the position of being a single department,
and without the counterbalancing influence of a Debré in high position,
ways to give Réunion (or perhaps the four DOMs together) regional
status were being considered. An example of how lack of regional
status had hurt Réunion was in the relatively underdeveloped organization and financing of social health facilities. [10]

POLITICAL INPUT STRUCTURES

Réunion differs from Seychelles and Comoros, and is more like
Mauritius, in possessing a very modern-looking, well-developed
system of political organizations, groups, and print media separate
from government. Interest groups are numerous and employ the full

gamut of techniques. An effective public opinion campaign by GEPEBA, an association for the economic expansion and promotion of building and artisanry, informed Réunion's powers-that-be in late 1974 that unless cement supplies (badly depleted by important public road-building projects) were augmented, trucks owned by the group's members would form roadblocks until officials took the necessary remedial steps. Réunion politics frequently reflects such tactics, directly derived from the French continental examples. [11]

Most professional, educational, occupational, and cultural areas appear to be well-represented by organizations. To some degree, these mirror not only the tactics but also the main configurations of French metropolitan politics, particularly for the extreme left. The Communist Party (PCR) masses are completely organized, with a newspaper, Témoignages; a union, CGTR, patterned after the mainland's CGT (General Confederation of Labor); youth groups, JAR (Autonomist Youth of Réunion); women's groups; and so on. Their main strength was the Port city area, and their leader, Paul Vergès, was mayor of Le Port.

Among noncommunists, too, there exists a broad range of interest groups. Indeed, in some fields, the tendency to form groups has worked against unity for the interest itself. For example, agricultural groups, confronted with adverse prices and rising costs, have insisted that Réunion faced economic chaos if the trends continued. But division between the two main farmer's organizations has lessened their collective impact. [12]

The political party system of Réunion is somewhat less complicated than that of France as a whole. The only "complete" party, from the perspective of organization, is the PCR. The Gaullist Union of Democrats for the Republic (UDR) depended heavily on the personal connections maintained by Debré. Even should some new face (Michel Jobert or Jacque Chirac perhaps) revive Gaullist fortunes nationally after their decline of 1973-74, it is unlikely that Réunion's Gaullists will easily regain the dominance they have known. It is possible that no political force, other than the Communists, will be able to organize effectively. The French population is more transient than the Creole, on which the PCR is based. This does not mean that PCR dominance must inevitably increase. The Gaullist majority was based for 16 years in the "metropole" on a mass of Frenchmen who had sickened of party politics generally; in a sense the UDR and its progenitors were replacements for party politics.

There is much fluidity in Réunion's other political party formations. In the early 1970s, there were several tendencies located along the political spectrum between the Gaullists and the Communists-gradients of opinion that were concerned with two dominant issues: (1) internal socioeconomic problems, and (2) autonomy versus departmental status. In the center stood the Mouvement pour le Socialisme par la Participation (MSP, also called the "Gaullist Left"), which shared Debré's zeal for continued departmentalization but was critical of failure to deal with economic and social deficiencies. To the left of MSP were intellectual elements, socialist to varying degrees, eager to remain French but even more reformist in their criticisms of French domestic policy impacts on Réunion. Albert Ramassamy, leader of the Reformateur Party, was perhaps the best known of this brand of local politician.

Then, between these elements and the Communists stood those Socialists who founded the Réunion Socialist Party (PSR) after a series of crucial events; there seemed to be little difference between the harshest critics of Réunion's administration other than their outlook on autonomy. The Paris conference of Socialist and Communist elements in May 1972 and a meeting at Morne Rouge in Martinique the same year had produced a common front among the many groups that signed the final proclamations on the issue of autonomy. Their position was that France had been systematically denying the peoples in the overseas departments and territories their constitutional right to choose self-determination, using electoral fraud, persecution, and other insidious techniques. These meetings were watersheds in the development of Réunion's politics, for many Réunionnais (and also many French living on the island) who were reformist in their assessment of Réunion's problems could not stomach the prospect of separation from France. A great deal of party formation and reshuffling occurred between 1972 and 1974. These conferences on self-determination proved to be a watershed. Ramassamy and others formed departmentalist-reformist parties, such as the Reformateurs, while Wilfrid Bertile, mayor of Saint-Philippe, formed the PSR on an autonomist-reformist program.

POLITICAL COMMUNICATIONS

Réunion's radio and television systems are government-controlled and perform according to guidelines decreed in Paris. Their activities are politically significant in two ways: Unlike the British practice of political neutrality, insured by the nonpolitical nature of the BBC, French radio and television are under more direct political influence. Autonomists have pointed out in the past that, in their opinion, programing makes the most of visits by Debré and leaves unmentioned important events pertaining to the other parties. [13]

A great variety of political viewpoints does emerge in the printed media, but most papers have circulations that are far from impressive. By spring 1973, Journal de l'Ile, the government daily, was printing 25,000 copies, while the only other daily, the PCR's

Témoignages, claimed a circulation of 2,000. None of the others, mostly weeklies, could boast of circulations exceeding 500. They ranged from the left-wing Témoignage Chrétien and PSR's Le Progressiste to papers that were more friendly to Debré: Action Réunionnais and Democrate Réunionnais; Cri du Peuple, which supported Alain Poher over Pompidou for the presidency in 1969; Le Creole; Hebdo-Bourbon (which included articles by Ramassamy) and Gazette de l'Ile (these two papers were MSP-oriented); and finally, on the right, Le Combat National (which acknowledges Debré as its founder). In this researcher's opinion, the island's most impressive paper was Croix-Sud, a weekly of moderate-liberal Catholicism, which covered domestic problems without hysteria but with scathing reformism where it was called for. Croix-Sud seemed to sympathize with the Reformateur Party.

ECONOMIC DEVELOPMENT DURING
THE DEPARTMENT ERA

The official French version of how development is to proceed for Réunion emphasizes three factors: (1) continued exploitation of the primary agricultural products for which Réunion has a natural advantage within the overall French market, (2) industrialization based on these products' processing needs and on infrastructural and social overhead capital projects, and (3) tourism development to take advantage of the Indian Ocean tourism boom. [14] The third of these aspects of development will be dismissed rapidly below; Réunion appears quite unconcerned with tourism, in contrast to Mauritius and Seychelles, which have made obvious efforts to develop this industry.

Developments in the economic and social categories have been important facets of Réunion's politics. This analysis begins with the agriculture and fisheries sectors, then considers the industrial, construction, and infrastructural aspects of the economy, concluding with some general evaluation of the French role in Réunion's development. Emphasis is placed on Réunion's economic system because it is so classically "colonial" in certain very important respects. Réunion's politics is incomprehensible without this solid economic background.

Lacking major mineral deposits or other forms of extractable wealth, volcanic Réunion has always been dependent on agricultural production. The island's agricultural system has particularly relied on sugar cane. Nearly three-quarters of the actively farmed land is devoted to sugar, and much of the industrial system is oriented to sugar products, particularly rum. Other exports are also based on agricultural production. Perfume essence is derived from geraniums, vetiver, ylang-ylang, and patchouli. While export crops dominate the acreage, food must be imported. Similarly, livestock production falls short of satisfying needs.

Complaints heard about the status of Réunion agriculture are not unlike those in other lands where the forces of industrialization are active (even though these pressures still are rather weak in Réunion). During April 1974, a demonstration in Saint-Denis gave insight into the frustrations many farmers felt. It was becoming harder, they argued, for the smaller and medium sized farmers to break even. The trend being toward mechanized farming, smaller farms could not afford to purchase or maintain the equipment. Many were being forced to leave their farms for work elsewhere.

These may have been natural pressures that are, economically speaking, a sign of "development," but they were politically unpopular and brought to light a series of interrelated demands: (1) Sugar cane planters felt that government subsidy was not adequate for their product to be competitive with other sources of cane sugar imported to France, or even with French-grown beet sugar; (2) farmers complained of inadequate assistance in obtaining fertilizer, which had become more a question of buying imported chemical mixtures as opposed to using manure produced by the island's livestock; importers came in for criticism by the farmers for their intervening role with this imported fertilizer was to increase its price; (3) a program of public works was advocated to employ the smaller sugar farmers and farm workers squeezed out of that sector and into the ranks of the unemployed; (4) among the larger growers, the price paid for sugar was deemed too low when compared with other sources of sugar entering the Common Market; and (5) the larger Réunion sugar cane growers complained that they were being charged transportation costs to the factory while French beet-growers were subsidized to compensate for these costs. [15]

Every source agreed that the Réunion sugar industry was troubled, both in the adverse effects its internal changes were having on Réunion's social development, and in its failure to compete within the new, multi-supply-source sugar economy of the Common Market. The solutions for sugar price and fertilizer cost support, and other policies announced by the secretary of State for DOM and TOM in July 1974 were not considered adequate by a variety of observers. Four hundred million francs were to be allocated annually for price support instead of the eight billions recommended in a previous government study. According to Croix-Sud, "the government will provoke chaos and finally the death of the sugar economy in entirety." [16]

Perhaps what was lacking, and badly needed, was an overall development policy within which agriculture fits. In the continued absence of such a policy, the conclusion of many, particularly the

PCR, was that the impoverishment of Réunion's farmers was a purposeful campaign intended the keep the prices for Réunion's products low. Driving "surplus" laborers off the sugar fields through mechanization would create unemployment, which was essential, according to the Communists' analysis, to provide a low-wage, low-cost industrial program. Thus, the Communists saw the decline in farm laborers (from 22,000 in 1961 to 12,000 in 1972) and in sugar cane planters (from 24,000 in 1961 to 13,500 in 1972) as an indication of conspiratorial maneuvering of the Réunionnais by France. [17]

French emphasis on continued production of Réunion's traditional plantation crops had also failed to alleviate the land-poverty suffered by many islanders. The structure of land ownership left French administration open to charges that they were presiding over a feudal system: 2 percent of the landowners occupied 60 percent of the land, while 72 percent had only 7 percent of the land. To a large extent, perhaps, economic efficiencies explained the trend toward fewer, larger estates. But many Réunionnais considered these land ownership trends, and the failure to develop more of the potential of industries that are directly related to sugar and perfume base, as an indication of intentional "neocolonialism." [18]

Meat and fish production were good examples of weak planning for a diversified economy. Meat production based on locally raised stock was actually declining, as Table 5.1 demonstrates. The growth in the total meat industry was accountable to imported animals, which were, at least, slaughtered locally. This was a ridiculous situation when one considered that Réunion had the potential (pasturage and so on) to be a meat-exporting land.

Another way of demonstrating the decline in meat production is through the number of animals, as shown in Table 5.2. The figures obviously do not contribute to the Gaullist argument that Réunion has prospered under UDR policies, even with Debré's impressive and fruitful support. Human population increases were matched with declining domestic production of cattle. Obviously, the autonomist viewpoint was bolstered by these trends. They saw these economic policies as designed to better the lot of the island's notables by impoverishing the bulk of islanders, consciously turning them into a force of low-cost labor. Whether or not these trends represented conscious policy, they were bound to appear that way to the autonomists. Gaullists, backers of Debré, and defenders of the policies of post-1958 administrations in Réunion passed off the adverse economic and social trends that dominated agriculture by pointing out the great natural obstacles that needed to be overcome. Climate, soil conditions, lack of water where it is needed—these were the forces that really explained why Réunion's products have difficulty competing. Certainly, there was some truth in these arguments. [19]

TABLE 5.1

Réunion's Meat Production
(tons)

Year	Total Tons Consumed	Local Production in Tons	Imported Tons
1960	1,538	836	702
1965	2,568	1,010	1,558
1970	3,166	770	2,396
1971	3,369	720	2,649
1972	3,307	808	2,499
1973	3,635	567	3,068

Source: Croix-Sud (June 21-28, 1974), p. 9.

TABLE 5.2

Livestock Trends: Réunion
(numbers of animals)

Animals	1943	1957	1973
Beef cattle	43,313	40,000	19,800
Milk cows	27,964	n.a.	7,100
Pigs	102,000	100,000	79,500
Goats	24,686	n.a.	39,800
Sheep	6,087	5,000	2,300
Human Population	230,000	300,000	470,000

Source: Croix-Sud (June 21-28, 1974), pp. 8-11.

A strong fishing industry has not been easy to establish around Réunion. Geography (lack of continental shelf) is largely responsible for this, but geographic factors are not entirely to blame. Comparisons are frequently made between the success of Mauritian fishing cooperatives, using deep sea equipment, and the lack of similar success in Réunion. To the local Communist Party theorists, this failing fits in well with their stock explanation of Réunion's agricultural underdevelopment: Réunion existed, in their analysis, merely as a market for French goods. Réunionnais must be "encouraged" to remain laborers with their wages absorbed in purchasing French-made goods. An inefficient, high-priced fishing industry provided no competition for the frozen fish from France.[20]

Neither lighter forms of coastal fishing nor the deep sea catch have done well. The former, many fishermen feel, suffered from a form of occupation registration dues (taxe de rôle) that fishermen, represented by the APAR (Association des Pecheurs Artisans de la Réunion), argued were set at unreasonable rates. APAR maintained, in a series of arguments with the Préfecture, that they are forced to sell their boats and join the growing ranks of unemployed or simply break the law by continuing to fish without a license. According to official figures, the total catch, as of 1973, was worth about 340 million francs CFA divided among the 900 fishermen (of which at least 200 were fishing without paying their enrollment fee). Thus, the dues of 14,000 francs CFA equaled nearly half the individual's monthly gross profits. The solutions were, quite simply, either to levy a tax on imported fish that would increase profits for domestic producers, to directly subsidize Réunion's fishermen, or to allow the island's fishing industry to die out. The fishermen put their case simply. Administrative decisions, particularly the unpopular taxes de rôle, were indeed threatening the death of their trade.[21]

With the precarious status of agriculture and fishing, many Réunionnais need employment in some other sector. Industry and construction have not been keeping pace with these pressures. Industrialization, treated in more detail below, has made some progress, with new plants producing cement and prefabricated houses, and some ancillary development from the sugar sector, notably production and distribution of liquors.[22]

This limited progress in industrialization indicates some thorny problems ahead, because it does not compare with developments of a social and educational nature. Tremendous housing projects provided many jobs during the 1960s, and the construction industry has been generally in boom conditions during the past decade. Symbolically, the University Center in Réunion (of the University of Aix-en-Provence) was opened in 1963 and began to occupy its new complex outside Saint-Denis in 1973-74. New secondary schools are now turning out unemployable youth, and Réunion appears to be making

some of the same mistakes many newly independent underdeveloped
countries have made. When the rush of infrastructural developments
slow down, jobs will thin out, and unhappy, unemployable school-
leavers will increasingly become a source of political alienation
during the middle and late 1970s.

It is apparent that, just as the flood of Debré-caused construction
has eased off, the unemployment problem is becoming far more
serious. Several factors are converging to aggravate the situation.
Between 1954 and 1969, a total of 12,000 jobs were lost from agricultural employment. But during the succeeding four years, 10,000
more agricultural jobs were lost, and during that latter period, the
ranks of young, employment-age Réunionnais increased to 10,000
annually.[23] The documented rapid rise of unemployment, from
figures that were quite manageable as recently as 1970, is, according
to the PCR, only the tip of the iceberg. "The real number of unemployed is, as we know, considerably higher, as it proved by surveys
of the INSEE. It remains a fact that growing pressure of unemployment is such that the government services are unable to hide it."[24]

Further, the Communist argument runs, unemployment is 10
times higher in the overseas departments than in the metropole. Unemployment is increasingly recognized as the number one economic
problem facing the island. Meanwhile, development of local transportation and derivative industry has lagged.

Other economic woes add to this argument over whether or not
it is France's intention to retain Réunion as a "colonial" appendage
of the metropole's econonomy. The stimulation of a handcraft industry would be a logical adjunct to tourism, but this has been painfully slow to develop.[25] Also, critics of contemporary development
point out that the changes are mostly "high-visibility projects" in
Saint-Denis particularly, and are designed to benefit the French
sector, though not so obviously so as to cost the regime political
support. An example is the lack of public transportation. Bus companies do exist, but compared to the large investment in roads
(notably between the capital and Saint-Gilles, where many French
have their beach cottages), the public transport facilities are admit-
tedly terrible.

Most damaging of all, this lack of response to the problems of
development and diversification of the agricultural and industrial
sectors cannot be passed off as natural results of emphasis of
tourism, as one could claim of the Seychelles Government between
1971-74. Although French functionaries are fond of talking about
Réunion's beauty, little has really been done to promote tourism.
By early 1975, hotel bed capacity was still under 500, compared to
Mauritius's 5,000. Debré himself argued that tourism development
was a logical step to take, given the poor soils, but escalating prices
are a strong deterrent to tourists.[26]

Not only has Réunion's government failed to provide climate and amenities that today's tourists expect after they arrive; it has done too little to preserve the attractions on which the island must depend to lure tourists in the first place. Two kinds of problems exist: preservation of the island's fabulous natural heritage and of its historic features. The latter problem is by no means a fault of the government alone. Inadequate private philanthropy has existed to provide funds to protect the unique and picturesque Creole architecture of old Réunion houses, an architectural type not unlike the French colonial houses of New Orleans. These are frequently torn down in favor of "modern-functional" apartment houses and imposing government and school buildings. One must sympathize with the visiting French geographer who scolded: "What an odd way to encourage tourism: to surround the future tourists with a scene analogous to that which they will meet with everywhere, with the same posh-carpeted night clubs and the same air conditioned brassy-looking bars."27

Informed Réunionnais are increasingly conscious of the imminent losses to the island's natural and historic heritage. Public pressures were partly responsible for the creation of an official Commission des Sites (Historiques), but subsequent disillusionment with the General Council's failure to follow the commission's advice has led, during 1974, to the creation of a private interest group, the Association for Safeguarding Réunion's Inheritance (ASPR).28 This growing interest in historic preservation parallels an even more established concern for preserving the island's natural beauty. From the same basis within the local intellectual community (with the Natural History Museum, the Departmental Archives and Library, and other centers as a launching pad) the Réunion Society for the Study and Protection of Nature (SREPN) was formed in 1970. SREPN publishes an attractive periodical, Info-Nature, and will, hopefully, be increasingly successful in enforcing conservationist considerations.

There are some shared attitudes between the autonomist camp, the island's Socialists and Communists, and these "preservationists." The autonomists concern themselves with what they see as the destruction of the island's inherent productivity through mechanization and monocropism of its agricultural economy. Though the concern of these left-wing circles is apparently more for the human consequences of the adverse environmental changes they decry, at times their press has displayed a keen sense of the ecological interrelationships.29 SREPN, on the other hand, resembles a more typical environmentalist organization, concerned with the preservation ot nature for nature's sake. It is likely that the two philosophies would come into serious conflict over environmental consequences of economic development and industrialization: The autonomists are also, largely, economic reformists and welfarists.

Tourism development emerges as a complex and interesting issue in such surroundings. If managed in order to provide jobs and create widespread income effects, while simultaneously being controlled to produce its best features as a "clean" industry, environmentalists and economic reformists alike may be able to support it. As we shall see, however, other forces exist that are less friendly to tourism's development.

To conclude this section on Réunion's major economic and political issues, we can say that the basic difficulty with the island's economic system is that over centuries of French rule Réunion has been turned too completely into an arm of the French economy. The principal money-making parts of the perfume, sugar, and spice industries that use Réunion geranium essence, sugar, vanilla, and other crops are located in France, and the temptation to retain this situation has not been overcome. Concentration of sugar refining into eight factories (from 13 in 1965) has not allowed the refining capacity of the island to surpass 43 percent of the crop. This has meant that much of the sugar refining is still done in France, and the island's economic system is immediately open to the usual accusations concerning "colonial economic exploitation." Autonomists have made this economic argument one of their major points of attack. [30] In their view, agricultural diversification would decrease the cost of living, which has recently skyrocketed, by allowing the island to produce necessary foodstuffs. Most consumer goods, from food to durables, are now imported, too expensive, too fancy, and too French. The visible Frenchness of the goods available to local people serves to remind them of their reliance on a faraway country. It did not soften this image to have only Air France allowed to serve the island (at least until recently when South African Airways received permission to schedule flights to Saint-Denis). Nor did the opening of Hypermarché, the island's first American-type shopping plaza, in 1973. Departmentalists tout such accomplishments, while autonomists use them as evidence of Réunion's colonial economy. [31]

Most damaging of all to the French position economically are the cost of living and growing inflationary imbalance of the island's economy and the rapidly growing employment problems. Some goods not imported from France, such as rice, have undergone significant price increases because of world market pressures. This hurts Réunion particularly because the burgeoning Creole population has become increasingly dependent on imported rice as a food staple as agricultural land has been turned toward export crops and as the self-sufficiency of the island decreased. Thus a 94 percent price rise in the cost of table rice, such as occurred in April 1973, is a very unpopular event and is viewed as at least partly a function of monopoly. [32]

Protection from imported French goods is severe. It is difficult to find goods that are not French; cheeses and wines (in spite of cheaper Kenyan and South African products) and even bottled water are shipped from Marseilles. In spite of the fact that a French automobile purchased in Saint-Denis costs twice that of the same model bought in the metropole, one sees few non-French cars. [33] According to the Catholic journal Croix-Sud:

> The crude integration of Réunion, tropical colonial island, as a sugar monoculture into the industrial metropole, has provoked certain economic, psychological, and social disorders. Réunion is underdeveloped, but this underdevelopment is original. Since 1946, the aid of the Metropole has been considerable. It has favored consumption much more than production and has expanded the tertiary much more than the productive sector. [34]

Trade data confirm the impression that the economy of Réunion (as with the other three DOMs, is closely tied to France. Table 5.3 shows the steadily increasing trade deficits all DOMs have experienced To some extent the deficits are made up for by investment capital coming to each overseas department from France, both from private sources and from FIDES, but it is obvious that the trade data give strength to the argument that France is sytematically "beggaring" the DOMs. Figure 5.1 shows, however, that the percentage of French domination of the trade, however great, has been decreasing in favor of growing trade with countries outside the franc zone. The decline in the proportion of Réunion's trade that is committed to France does not support the argument of intentional colonialist economics.

One impact of this "colonial economy" is that France's inflation automatically becomes Réunion's—more so, as one must add the inflationary effects on costs that intervene between production in France and consumption in Réunion. The inflation rate between February 1973 and February 1974 on Réunion prices was 15.7 percent. Even the more moderate commentators were calling for mandatory controls, a solution the departmental prefect was apparently loathe to employ. Suspicions were increasing during 1974 among the general public that pressure from those in the commercial imports sector not to intervene was determining the issue. The Chamber of Commerce acknowledged the "imported" nature of Réunion's inflation and considered it in a quite matter-of-fact way, but preferred to lay the blame on the rising cost of the natural resources imported to France, increases that were merely being "passed on" to Réunion. They argue that these aspects of inflation are inevitable and that labor, welfare, medical, and other support costs are important

TABLE 5.3

Trade Deficits: Réunion and Other Overseas Departments

Department	1964	1966	1968	1970
Guadalupe				
Value of trade deficit (millions of French francs)	220	286	317	500
Deficit as percent of island's total trade	39%	45%	46%	55%
Guyana				
Value of trade deficit	76	120	240	228
Deficit as percent of island's total trade	93%	78%	88%	83%
Martinique				
Value of trade deficit	224	237	341	644
Deficit as percent of island's total trade	46%	35%	46%	66%
Réunion				
Value of trade deficit	255	323	394	612
Deficit as percent of island's total trade	41%	46%	46%	52%

Source: Computed from figures given by Institut National de la Statistique et des Etudes Economiques (INSEE), Bulletin de Statistique, Supplement to no. 24 (July 25, 1971, pp. 33-34, and Supplement to no. 32 (August 27, 1973), pp. 31-32.

119

contributors to inflation, but that, basically, inflation "is a sickness which Réunion cannot remedy by herself."[35] (It is a fact that old-age compensation, for example, increased by 21 percent during fiscal 1973/74.) This dampens the inflation-impact argument further.[36]

All of these economic problems are made more galling by the constant comparisons Réunionnais tend to make with the situation on neighboring Mauritius. Réunion's "sister island" certainly has its own problems, but at least prices are lower and Mauritian export goods are competitive. As Albert Ramassamy, professor of Economics at the University Center and Reformateur Party leader, put it, "Each time competition opposes our neighbor and ourselves, it is [Mauritius] which prevails because of her competitive prices."[37] But it is the Communists who make the most out of Réunion's "economic enslavement" to France. They despair for their island as a land invaded and overrun by two types of metropolitan French. The first group are functionaries who come on short contracts to enjoy the tropics, make easy money, or (in the case of younger officials, teachers, and so on) to carry out their military-deferment service.[38] Although the remuneration scale for civil servants is slowly moving downward along a generous scale of "hardship post" compensation, the French civil servant will eventually receive 140 percent of pay for equivalent grades within France. A frequent pattern is the life of comparative ease: servants; beach house at Saint-Gilles-les-Bains; four-month vacation in France (with travel paid) following each two-year assignment; perhaps most curious of all, the system of "making CFA," deferential exchange rates, which translate into twice the savings accomplished locally when the money is transferred to France.[39] The total effect is to create what the PCR calls two worlds on one island: "a minority who enjoys an European way of life (California style), and the great mass of workers which suffers exploitation, low salaries and misery."[40]

Second, there are French immigrants of a more permanent nature. Many were forced to flee Algeria, but they could not stand the cold in France and came to Réunion as a last resort. The presence of increasing numbers of metropolitan French, or "Zoreils" as the Creoles call them (a corruption of les oreilles or "people whose ears are very noticeable") introduces two other key issues in Réunion politics: cultural conflict between Creole and French, and migration and population problems.

REUNION'S CULTURAL CONFLICTS

Réunion serves France as a launching platform for French cultural penetration of the Indian Ocean region. The historical fate of the island as the sole remaining authoritative French presence has guaranteed that Réunion would be thrust into such a role. The

FIGURE 5.1
Trade between Reunion and Other Countries
(percents)
Imports

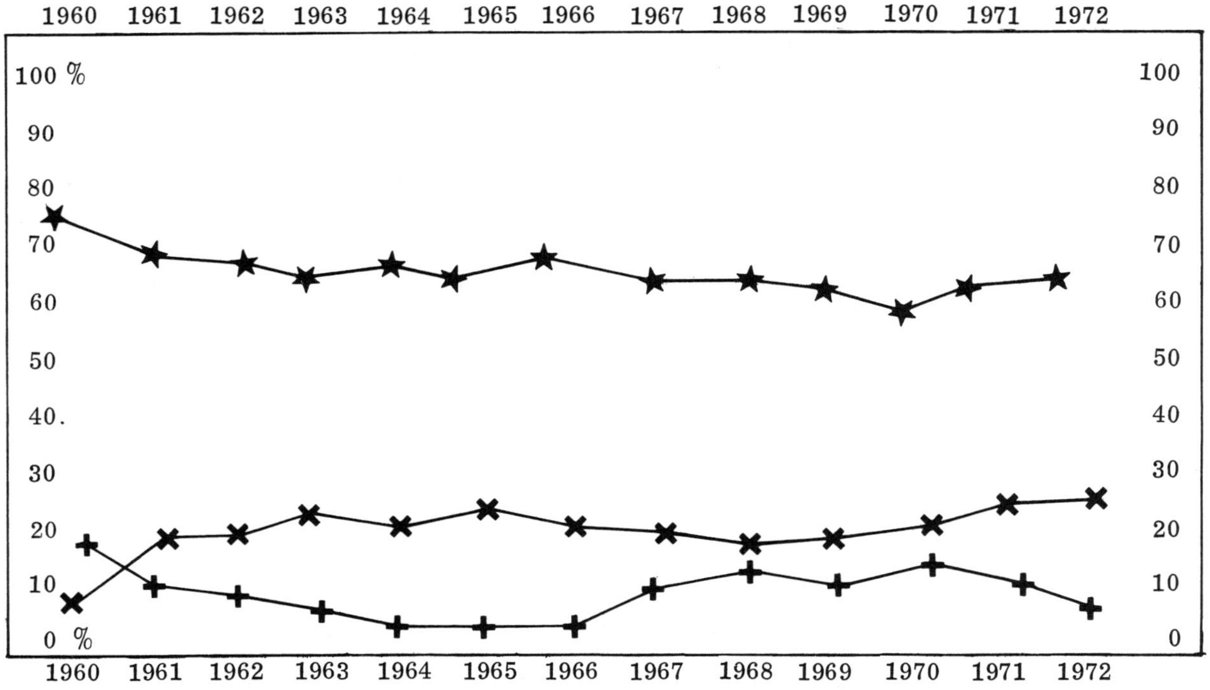

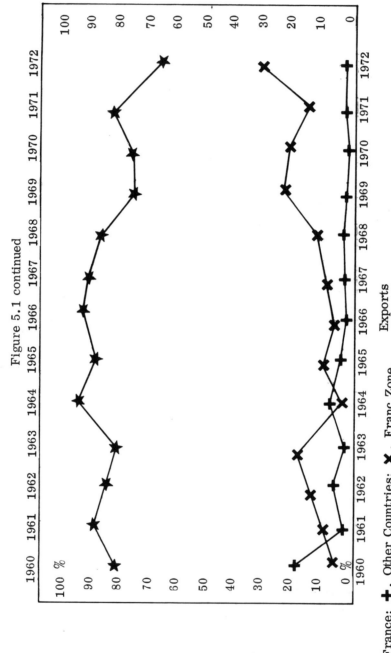

Figure 5.1 continued

★ France; ✚ , Other Countries; ✘ , Franc Zone.   Exports
Source: Compiled by the authors.

122

techniques of ensuring the importance of French culture throughout
the region show some ambivalence, however. On the one hand, there
are obvious programs designed to acquaint the peoples of the region
with the French presence and to spread its influence. The University
Center in Saint-Denis serves as a francophonic research center for
the region: Scholarships for students from Seychelles and other islands
draw future elites to Réunion for extended periods. French Radio and
Television ORTF-Réunion transmits not only to Réunion, but for a
population of at least 7 million French-speakers on the various
islands.[41]

In spite of the strong cultural role Réunion is expected to play in
the Indian Ocean, it is in the island's internal politics that "cultural
oppression," as the PCR calls it, is politically explosive. Advocates
of Creole culture point to the deemphasis of local news and Creole-
related items in ORTF programing and in the government-supported
daily paper Journal de l'Ile as proof that the islanders are being consistently and purposefully propagandized. In 1973, Journal de l'Ile
had three reporters busy collecting news around the island, but the
effect on the paper's coverage of local culture was minimal; the
paper's last page (usually of eight) might cover some uncontroversial
local items. Officials explained this lack of local emphasis by stating
that the only thing the Creoles wanted to read about was the gory
details of the murder trials in the Court of Assizes column. Attempts
by ORTF to broadcast Creole programs are attacked on the grounds
that the Creole used is too archaic, ethnic, and demeaning, not
illustrative of the language's flexibility and beauty in the modern
sense.[42]

The communists and other promoters of Creole culture argue
that their society is being killed by silence: failure to convey a sense
of worth for Creole language, customs, celebrations, and so on.
The French administrator typically answers, "There is no such thing
as Creole culture." In accord with this derogatory French view of
Creole, the Sega dance and other Creole customs are officially
frowned upon, and sometimes persecuted.[43] But, in spite of the
autonomists' "conspiracy theory" concerning the French treatment
of local culture, the truth is probably less sinister. It is likely that
the French approach toward public information in Réunion draws
more from their way of viewing the world than from any conscious
attempt to "subdue" Creole culture. To the French, Creole is simply
not a culture.

The educational system adds to the impression that France is
actually working to destroy local culture, although this effect is
probably more a function of the great centralization of French education than of conscious planning by local administrators of the
school system: The curriculum and reading materials are determined
in Paris, and the inflexibilities of the system have earned it epithets

such as "pedagogical monstrosity" from those who see it as a stifling force snuffing out Creole culture.[44] Even at the university level, where a survey of student attitudes showed a deep social cleavage between metropolitan and Réunionnais students, the relevance of the instructional program for Réunion's problems has been hotly challenged.[45]

Underlying these cultural issues is the gnawing presence of racial animosity, at least from the autonomists' perspectives. The French mastery over Réunion is definitely interpreted by many Réunionnais as "white" dominance. The PCR employs this theme, an ironic situation in view of the fact that this researcher interviewed at least one white adviser (sent from the PCF) among Vergès's entourage. The racist theme may be more polemical than deeply felt, and it is surely an easy problem for an American to overemphasize.

MIGRATION POLICY

Aside from the usual thorniness of the population issue in Catholic France, Réunion's problems are intensified by its underdeveloped condition. While metropolitan France experienced a 17 percent increase from 1955 to 1972, Réunion's population expanded by over 60 percent during the same period. The 1972 growth rate was 2.6 percent, and by 1974, two-thirds of Réunion's population were under 25 years old, indicating even more trouble ahead. Birth control leaves even Réunion's environmentalists and economic reformists cold.[46]

Debré and others decided in 1960 on a policy of emigration by Reunionnais, and the BUMIDOM (Bureau for Migration from the DOM) was founded in 1963.[47] Most of these emigrants have gone to France, where cultural maladaptation has made many of them ripe for radicalization; the Réunionnais workers' organization in France is strongly autonomist.[48] Besides this difficulty, the emigration policy has made only modest inroads on the problem, as Table 5.4 shows. But the official figures published by BUMIDOM are somewhat deceiving. There is a notable discrepancy between the numbers who emigrate each year under BUMIDOM's program, and the net outflow of people from Gillot airfield and Le Port. After very elaborate statistical analysis, French INSEE statisticians concluded that many of the "emigrants" of previous years have been returning to the island.[49]

In spite of problems, officials are still convinced that the answer to Réunion's demographic dilemmas lies in emigration. But projections indicate that even by holding birth rates constant while continuing the emigration program, and assuming no success for other types of birth control programs, Réunion's population will

TABLE 5.4

Emigration from Réunion
(data in numbers of individuals)

	1963	1964	1965	1966	1967	1968
Emigration organized by BUMIDOM	623	920	1,897	2,577	3,011	3,103
Net total migration	n.a.	n.a.	-1,019	-1,886	94	-942
	1969	1970	1971	1972	1973	1974
Emigration organized by BUMIDOM	2,466	3,719	4,021	4,401	4,722	5,400
Net total migration	-305	-1,260	-2,277	n.a.	n.a.	n.a.

Source: INSEE, Bulletin des Statistiques: Supplement to no. 36 (July 9, 1974) p. 4; Supplement to no. 27 (March 25, 1972); Bulletin no. 36 (July 5, 1974) p. 7; and second Supplement to no. 36 (July 29, 1974).

reach 687,000 by 1987. Without the emigration policy, 811,000 would trample the island by that date.

France's population policy is viewed by the autonomists as another technique of control. Creoles are taken to France where they are out-numbered politically and supply cheap labor. Besides this, the opinion that the plight of the 40,000 Réunionnais who have gone to France is far from pleasant is widespread. The leftist Témoignage Chrétien summarized their condition as follows:

> The situation of the emigré is, in nearly all cases, that of
> a young person who will never see, in work, salary, or
> housing, the promises that were made to him. To these
> one must add all the bad surprises of climate, racism,
> loneliness, lack of adaptation to another lifestyle; a
> climate of alienation and repression. . . . [50]

Meanwhile, metropolitans flock to Réunion to take all the good jobs. The French could go far to defuse many of these problems with some political skill. Some positive orientation toward Creole life—vigorous sponsorship of the Creole customs and life-styles and reportage of island affairs—would rob the communists of their less ideologically committed supporters. Couple this with some economic reform based on more open import policies and less institutional use of the island as a market for French goods, and the centrist-conservative group could regain the firm position in Réunion politics it enjoyed during the 1960s by removing the causes of alienation. But to be done honest-ly, these changes would require sincere recognition by the French that there is some value in the life-style the islanders have developed. At this point, French officials would only concede that whatever value Creole life has is owed to the degree in which it has become French.

ELECTORAL POLITICS

Interviewed in April 1973, Paul Vergès, PCR leader, spoke confidently of taking over soon as the majority party on the island. Were the PCR to form a majority, France would be forced to negotiate a new relationship with Réunion, and Vergès wants that relationship to be one between independent nations. Table 5.5 supports Vergès's prediction, in part: The left has become stronger each year, but this does not necessarily mean the Communists are closer to taking power in Réunion.

In National Assembly elections (Table 5.6), the voter shift from 1968 to 1973 from UDR to PCR has been 7 percent in the Third Constituency, 12.8 percent in the First (Debré's), and 12.4 percent

TABLE 5.5

French Presidential Elections: Réunion
(percent)

	1965 (73.9)		1969 (55.4)		1974 (65.2)	
First round	De Gaulle	91.3	Pompidou	82.2	Mitterand	47.8
	Mitterand	4.9	Poher	7.5	Chaban-Del.	29.3
	Tixier-Vigan.	1.5	Duclos	5.6	Giscard	17.7
	Lecanuet	1.0	Deferre	1.7	Others	5.2
	Others	1.3	Others	3.0		
				(63.7)		(75.2)
Second round	De Gaulle	83.5	Pompidou	88.9	Mitterand	50.5
	Mitterand	16.5	Poher	11.1	Giscard	49.5

Source: Compiled by the author.

TABLE 5.6

French National Assembly Elections: Réunion
(first round only; percent)

	1968	1973
The left	24.2	40.2
The center	5.0	8.0
Gaullist and right	70.8	51.8

Source: Compiled by the author.

in the Second (where Vergès won the first round, but lost the runoff).
Also significant is the large number of abstentions and null and void
ballots, which in the March 1973, election totaled 52,379 of the 173,600
total voting potention of the island.[51] When this figure was published,
the PCR cries on the two election Sundays of fraud and terror tactics
took on new meaning.

Electoral politics has centered around the issue of autonomy,
perhaps unfortunately. In this researcher's analysis, autonomy is
an issue only because of the inflexibility of French Government and
the failure to deal with key internal economic, social, and cultural
issues. Both major electoral blocs—the Gaullists, who have equated
calls for internal reform with sympathy for the autonomists, and
thus with treason; and the Communists and their allies who see the
solutions to all problems in autonomy—were avoiding the issues. It
is unfortunate the Reformateur Party and other possible alternatives
that might come closer to discussing the real issues lack adequate
leadership and organization to bring their message before the public,
in the face of the more glamorous (and extreme) themes championed
by the two major parties. There are some signs that a political center
(willing to admit that there are problems, but anxious to look for
their solution within a contect of continued attachment to France) is
developing. Both electoral blocs in the presidential contest of 1974,
second round, included voters who stopped short of the extremism
of both Communists and Gaullists. Most Gaullists supported Jacques
Chaban-Delmas, who lost in the first round, and shifted to Valery
Giscard d'Estaing in the run-off, but the first-round support for
Giscard was significant. His campaign in Réunion had been lively
and well led by the president of the General Council, Dr. P. La-
gourgue, and Giscard's vote came to 17.7 percent, compared with
Mitterand's 47.8 percent, Chaban's 29.3 percent, and 5.2 percent
for the eight minor candidates. This represents a considerable
growth for any movement outside the Gaullist or Socialist-Communist

ranks. In addition, the MSP which favored the Edgar Fauré wing of the Gaullist movement, was exerting pressure on Debré's organization from within. [52]

The electoral blocs present the election contestants, formally speaking. But beneath the surface, the party system is more varied than one might expect for such a small society. Because of the pre-eminence of Debré, Gaullism had been a strong force uniting the center and right. But that part of the political spectrum is now split among the metropolitan leaders—there are the "giscardiens," Independent Republicans, and the Gaullists. The competition for the two Senate seats in September 1974 showed rapidly growing strength for the Independent Republican leadership of the island. Also, it was significant that one of the two victors, Louis Virapoulle, called for self-determination for Réunion. [53] Debré's candidate won the other seat, but very few votes separated the top three in the indirect election.

After the various elections of 1973-74, the left on Réunion was still searching for a mutual understanding, meeting under a Committee of Coordination. [54] The large measure of electoral cooperation emerging in metropolitan France among Socialist-Communists will be harder to accomplish in Réunion because of the issue of autonomy. The gyrations among Socialists during 1974 are evidence that Réunion's politics were undergoing a rather unstable period during the mid-1970s. The Gaullist decline and the readjustments among centrists and rightists further this impression.

The general movement of Réunion politics is unmistakably leftward in the 1974 presidential, as in earlier Legislative Assembly elections. While Francois Mitterand, the Socialist compromise candidate of the left, lost by a scant 1.6 percent margin throughout France, he won in Réunion, as Table 5.5 shows.

THE AUTONOMY ISSUE

The autonomy issue, born in 1959 with the PCR's decision to press in that direction, began to polarize seriously Réunion's politics after 1963. The issue has increased in important with the growth of leftist electoral strength. It was becoming an open topic by 1974, rather than a seditious, unmentionable idea, as it had been during the era of Gaullist dominance. On May 30, 1972, the first conference on self-determination was held in Paris. Thirty delegates from six DOMs and TOMs met with representatives of the parties of the French left. The main purpose was to establish the right of the overseas populations to employ the provisions for self-determination that already existed in 1958. Chapter VI of the 1972 Common Program of leftist parties included the principle of self-determination in their preparations for the National Assembly elections that were soon to be held. If the left were elected, their government was pledged to "recognize the right to self-determination of the people of the Overseas Departments and Territories. New laws will be discussed with the representatives of the concerned populations and these should respond to their hopes."[55]

In Réunion, the issue clearly split the electorate. Besides the PCR, other organizations that were autonomist were PSR, TCR (Christian socialist workers), CGTR (communist workers), UFR, and FJAR (communist-run youth and women's organizations). Opposed to these groups were, of course, the center and right parties, but to fight the autonomy issue, a special organization was formed, the ARDF (Association Réunion Département Francais), which claimed a membership of 12,000 in May 1972.

The left's candidate for the presidency in 1974, Francois Mitterand, repreated the Common Program's vows of self-determination, and the fate of overseas French possessions was automatically an open issue on the national level for the first time in recent years, but it was certainly not valid to argue that the signatories of the Common Program held identical views on the question, for they differed on the completeness, and perhaps even on the desirability of a breakaway from France. Faraway islands, though important to many French as reminders of world greatness, were not the most important issues on the minds of the leftist leaders in Paris. In Réunion, where the PCR is committed to the independence they feel would result from self-determination, the differences between Communists and Socialists were greater than, for example, in Antilles, whose Communist Party is more interested in remaining French. Consider the gap between Vergès's separatism and Mitterand, who wrote: "this history of French overseas departments is intimately linked with that of France, and I know how much our country is present in the hearts of the majority of their inhabitants."[56] Thus the gap between Mitterand and Vergès exceeds that between Mitterand and the French Communist leader, Georges Marchais, for whom the question of overseas departments was but one of the issues between socialists and communists in the coalition. It is very unlikely that all Réunion voters for Mitterand in May 1974 desired autonomy from France; many assumed that self-determination would mean a chance for Réunionnais to reaffirm their ties to France.

Socialist campaign literature supported Mitterand on the grounds that he had "solemnly assured the maintenance of aid. This expression of National Solidarity is the indispensable condition that will allow Réunion to extricate itself from a state of serious crisis."[57] In spite of these appearances of desiring to remain French demonstrated by Socialist supporters of Mitterand, one must remember that the

Communist autonomists participated less equivocably in the 1974 coalition of the left than at any time previously during the history of the
Fifth Republic.

Nor could one be entirely certain that a vote for Giscard was a
vote for continued "Réunion Francais," for Giscard was quoted as
having said, when minister of Finance in Pompidou's government,
that Réunion was "too expensive a dancing partner for France to prop
up."[58] It is likely that neither the Independent Republicans nor the
Gaullists were actively considering casting Réunion off, but the statement showed that there were at least some arguments that could convince them to discuss the issue. In fact, it sometimes appeared, in
the midst of these conflicting statements by Giscard and Mitterand,
that the autonomy issue had caused a reversal in the images·of the
two major blocs. Giscard was feared by many Réunionnais because,
as a "hard-headed" economist, he might well decide against supporting uncompetitive Réunion exports, just as he had supposedly chosen
to import Malaysian pineapples rather than import those from French
Antilles. In support of Giscard's hesitations, a report published by
the Economic and Social Council of the French Government before
the 1974 presidential contest brought new publicity to the failure of
DOMs generally to live up to their projected agricultural growth rates
in the Fifth Economic Plan.[59]

In Réunion, the effect of these incorporations of the issue of
self-determination (leading to possible autonomy) into major party
statements was, as has been stated, to legitimize the issue. In three
years, self-determination and even independence had gone from un-
mentionably treasonable ideas to open discussion topics with the
participation of minister of DOM and TOM. The non-Communist left
has been weak in Réunion, leaving such issues to a Communist Party.
Thus, keeping Réunion French has been easy to defend with arguments
that there is little to be gained by exchanging the domination of Russia
(or China) for France. Non-Communists who mentioned the idea were
called "Vergèsiste."[60] In addition, Réunion's being a religious society
added weight to this attitude. The result, as seen with Minister of
DOM and TOM Olivier Stirn's visit to Réunion late in 1974, was a
growing tendency to argue that there was no issue of complete independence. The French left (as well as the right) is, above all, French,
and what must be done is to face the real economic issues.[61]

In one sense, the result of the de Gaulle constitution's bifurcation
of French politics has been a desirable forcing of the communists to
cooperate with other reform-minded groups. In the Réunion context,
the shrill PCR cry for separation was, by itself, politically unviable.
It was too easily neutralized by Debré's scare tactics of insisting
that there was no substance to the communists' charges, only international conspiracy. By 1974, a far healthier picture was emerging:
Reformists of the center-left, Catholic, and Socialist tendencies

were coming forth to insist that there was something really wrong
with France's relationship with Réunion. [62] Reforms were necessary,
and while Debré's influence was waning, these non-Communist elements
of the left were insisting that their criticisms be taken seriously. One
hesitated to question their commitment to France, but they were, nonetheless, critical, without subscribing blindly to the slogan of separatism. The Reformateur leader Ramassamy spoke for many non-
communists when he wrote, in 1973:

> Departmentalization can only be saved by modifying its
> constitutional status, and it is up to us to determine
> whether we want to save it. One thing is certain: the
> majority of Réunionnais will not forever accept the
> role of silent partner to the excessive consumption
> by a minority more and more indifferent to its [Ré-
> union's] fate. [63]

The problem facing reformists who defined their philosophies
as neither Socialist-Communist (in agreement with the left's 1972
Morne Rouge Program) nor rightist (able to cooperate with the
Gaullist-Independent Republican outlook) was made insurmountable
by the very electoral process that was causing the Communists to
temper their ideas. Ramassamy called a return to straight proportional representation the "only way" to avoid polarization with its
excessive and unrealistic solutions.

As the moderate Croix-Sud expressed it,

> The separatist danger is not, today, coming from Réunion.
> The Réunionnais have taken the test and have come out of it
> strengthened in the deep feeling of their French national
> identity. . . . In this respect, the pledge taken by the
> left for the Presidential election (to decide nothing with-
> out consulting the Réunionnais first) would seem to be a
> worthy promise. [64]

Writing about the "foreign relations" of a French department is
rather like describing the foreign policy of Hawaii. Officially, there
is none. But, perhaps Quebec is a better analogy to Réunion, although
the French are, in that case, on the opposite side of the issue. The
strength of the autonomist movement guarantees that Réunion will
have an international life of its own regardless of its official status
as an internal part of France. Réunionnais opposition leaders visit
conferences attended by other radical elements in the region. For
example, Paul Vergès led a delegation to the Tananarive conference
on "The Indian Ocean, Zone of Peace" during October 1974. This
conference resulted in a strongly worded condemnation of neo-colo-
nialist designs on the Indian Ocean. Réunion's delegation surely

represented a movement of comparatively large significance in the politics of the island concerned; definitely not a "fringe" element. [65] In fact, with the sudden move of Seychelles's governing Social Democratic Party (SDP) toward independence, the defusing of autonomist opposition from the PASOCO and MOLINACO parties of Comoros, the persecution of the Militant Mauritian Movement, and military rule in Madagascar, Réunion possessed the most significant "leftist" movement in the area.

It seems very possible that the growing dominance of the third-world bloc over United Nations' General Assembly affairs may kindle a new fire under the Decolonization Committee, and such pressures may bring into question the whole relationship between France and the overseas departments, as well as the overseas territories that remain after Comoros leaves the French fold. It is up to French administration to head off the growth of autonomism by vigorously carrying out policies that meet the needs of Réunion.

NOTES

1. G. Gerard, Guide Illustré de l'Ile de la Réunion (Saint-Denis: Gerard, 1970), p. 7.

2. André Scherer, Histoire de la Réunion (Paris: Presses Universitaire, 1966) is the best source. In English, T. L. Stoddard et al., Area Handbook for the Indian Ocean Territories (Washington, D.C.: Government Printing Office, 1971) and, for a broader treatment, Auguste Toussaint, History of the Indian Ocean (Chicago: University of Chicago Press, 1966).

3. A list of what has been accomplished, from the Gaullist perspective, was offered by presidential candidate Jacques Chaban-Delmas, in Journal de l'Ile de la Réunion (May 2, 1974). Figures on travel were published in INSEE (Institut National de la Statistique et des Etudes Economiques) Bulletin des Statistiques, Supplement to no. 34 (December 27, 1973).

4. On Debré as an example of multiple office-holding, see Roy Pierce, French Politics and Political Institutions, 2d ed. (New York: Harper and Row, 1973), p. 256. Debré's accomplishments are catalogued in Le Créole (February 23 and 27, 1973). On the loi Debré as it appeared to Réunionnais, see Le Progressiste (April 3, 1973), Le Créole (March 28, 1973), and Cri du Peuple (April 5, 1973).

5. Le Monde (June 6, 1972), p. 19.

6. Journal de l'Ile (May 16, 1974).

7. The French administrative system is described in L. Favoreu, "Droit et Institutions de la Réunion" Cahiers du Centre Universitaire de la Réunion (December 1971), pp 9-19. Favoreu deals with the question of adaptations of Article 73 for Réunion.

8. A session of the General Council was reported in Croix-Sud (July 26-August 2, 1974), p. 1.

9. For analyses of the French local-national administrative system, see Lowell G. Noonan, France: The Politics of Continuity in Change (New York: Holt, Rinehart and Winston, 1970), Chap. 4.

10. See D. J. Orsini, L'Equipement Sanitaire et Social des Collectivités Locales à la Réunion (Saint-Denis: Centre Universitaire, 1972).

11. Croix-Sud (October 4-11, 1974), p. 6. For a further example, the fishermen, see ibid. (June 28-July 5, 1974), p. 6.

12. Croix-Sud (July 12-19, 1974), p. 1.

13. An example of this criticism is found in Le Progressiste (March 10, 1973).

14. As examples of the French official's statements, see Pierre Messmer, minister of DOM and TOM, "Une Place Incontestée dans la Nation," Le Monde (June 6, 1972), and Michel Debré, "La France dans l'Océan Indien," in the same issue.

15. On the levels of subsidies, see Croix-Sud (May 24-June 6, 1974), p. 3. On fertilizer shortages, Croix-Sud (May 10-17, 1974), p. 2. A discussion of the sugar-pricing system occurs in Croix-Sud (May 24-June 6, 1974), pp. 10-11; (June 21-28, 1974), p. 2; (June 28-July 5, 1974), p. 2. On French sugar beet subsidies, see Témoignage Chrétien (July 1974) 1, p. 5.

16. Croix-Sud (July 12-19, 1974), p. 3.

17. A similar Communist analysis for geraniums is in Témoignages (March 29, 1973). See also Témoignage Chrétien (June 1974) I, p. 2.

18. Le Progressiste (September 11, 1972).

19. For the Communist view, Témoignages (March 31, 1973), p. 2. A Gaullist defense is presented in Le Combat National (May 1, 1974), pp. 15ff, and Journal de l'Ile (March 1, 1974).

20. Debré, "La France dans l'Ocean Indian," Le Monde (June 6, 1972). The Communist argument, particularly comparing Réunion's feeble efforts with those of the Mauritian support for its indigenous tuna fishing fleet, is found in Témoignages (April 13, 1973), pp. 4-13. "La Pêche Artisanale," Croix-Sud (July 9, 1972), and "La Pêche Lointaine à la Réunion," Croix-Sud (July 30, 1972). See especially p. 4, comparison of local production with fish imports (more than twice as much).

21. These difficulties are reported in Croix-Sud (August 16-23, 1974), and more broadly in (June 28-July 5, 1974), p. 6.

22. The gains are reviewed in Louis Cotten, "l'Industrialisation Est Bien Partie," Le Monde (June 6, 1972), and "l'Industrialisation à la Réunion," Croix-Sud (January 7, 1973). A very detailed analysis of the subsidies offered for home-building is found in Le Progressiste (January 23, 1972).

23. Croix-Sud, citing a rise in jobless from 2,150 in December 1970, to 8,097 two years later, called unemployment Réunion's "number one" problem (June 14-21, 1974).

24. Témoignage (March 29, 1973), p. 2. Témoignage Chrétien (May 1974), I, estimated the "real" unemployment level of 60,000. A detailed analysis of the present employment situation is found in Pierre Eiglier, Problèmes et Perspectives de l'Emploi à la Réunion (Saint-Denis: Centre Universitaire, 1972). See also "Le Chomage à la Réunion, Une Plaie Qu'il Faut Guerir." See also "Le Chomage (September 3 and 17, 1972); "Une Société Coloniale: La Réunion 1946-1970," Croix-Sud (February 7, 1971); for two academic treatments of this problem, see Bernard Parisot, "Le Colonat Partiaire à la Réunion," Etudes Réunionnaises (Aix-en-Provence, 1965), pp. 77-106, and J. Mas, "Droit de Propriété et Paysage Rural de l'Ile Bourbon" (Paris: University of Paris thesis, 1971). Also see "De Quelques Problèmes Agricoles Réunionnais," Croix-Sud (February 6, 1972).

25. In the best overall Marxist treatment of Réunion's situation, Jean-Claude LeLoutre deals with fishing industry and all other sectors of the island's economy: La Réunion: Departement Francais (Paris: Maspero, 1968), p. 45. An argument on the necessity of import substitutions, an important facet of this "colonialism" theme, is found in Daniel Lallemand, "Le Declin Angoissant des Productions Agricoles Animales et Forestières de la Réunion," Les Cahiers de la Réunion (November-December 1972), pp. 28-37. Many of the same criticisms are found in Croix-Sud, special section "La Réunion Agricole" (April 18, 1971).

26. Lack of effort to develop tourism in Réunion and Comoros is a source of concern to coordinators of tourism in the entire Indian Ocean area. (Interview with Jean Caradec, director of Alliance Touristique de l'Océan Indien, Tananarive, April 25, 1973). Some Réunion sources on the topic of tourism: Le Créole (January 17, 1973) concentrates on the meager facilities at Le Port, (April 11, 1973) argues that there is a policy to promote tourism, but that "little things hurt." Further, Journal de l'Ile (March 8, 1974) describes Mauritius's impressive tourism policies. For figures on Réunion's tourism development, see Croix-Sud (June 28, 1972).

27. Croix-Sud (October 4-11, 1974), p. 5; also September 6-13, 1974, p. 3.

28. Ibid (September 20-27, 1974), p. 3.

29. See, for example, Témoignage Chrétien (April 1974) I, p. 8.

30. Some statements of this facet of the autonomy argument, argued by the Communist Party of Réunion, are "La Réunion Demain," Réalités et Perspectives Réunionnaises (July 1969), pp. 46-58; Opposition Marxiste (October 1972), p. 5. See also "Du Sucre pour le Marché Europen," Le Monde (June 6, 1972).

31. A defense of Hypermarché in Le Creole (April 11, 1974). On SAA's new flights to Réunion, see Témoignages (March 9, 1974). The Communists did not appreciate that the first break in Air France's monopoly should be made by racist South Africa's SAA.

32. Croix-Sud (May 24-June 6, 1974), p. 3; Témoignages (April 5, 1973), p. 1. The defense against these attacks typically accuses consumers of having no sense of product choice: for example, Le Créole (April 4, 1973) on potatoes and (April 11, 1973) on rice prices. See also Lallemand, op. cit.

33. INSEE, Bulletin des Statistiques, Supplement to no. 28 (November 30, 1972).

34. "L'Artisanat," Croix-Sud (November 12, 1972).

35. J. Desbenoit, in Croix-Sud (July 19-26, 1974). The Chamber of Commerce view is reported in Croix-Sud (September 13-30, 1974).

36. INSEE, report of May 6, 1974.

37. Hebdo-Bourbon (April 12, 1973).

38. For example, LeLoutre, op. cit., Ch. 7, describes how French officials combine generous allowances for working overseas with currency-conversion idiosyncracies from Fr. Francs to CFA Francs in order to amass small fortunes. For a more unbiased treatment, "Situation des Fonctionnaires Exercant à la Réunion," Croix-Sud (March 19, 1972). Réunion does have many "metropolitans" serving their "VAT." André Oraison, Les Volontaires de l'Aide Technique, reported in Cahier du Centre Universitaire, no. 1 (December 1971): 19.

39. On the odd exchange rate that allows metropolitan French to "double," see "La Réunion: 1946-1970," Croix-Sud (February 7, 1971), p. 4. On the system of duties, see A. Baylongue-Hondaa, "L'Octroi de mer à la Réunion" (Aix-en-Provence, university thesis, 1972). See also, Croix-Sud (September 20-27 and September 6-13, 1974), p. 1.

40. Témoignages (April 10, 1973).

41. The university center's role is treated in L. Favoreu, president of Centre Universitaire, "Avant-Propos," Cahier du Centre Universitaire de la Réunion (December 1971).

42. For an example, see Le Créole (January 24, 1973).

43. Témoignages (April 6, 1973) and Le Monde (June 6, 1972).

44. Le Progressiste (September 11, 1972). See also Réalités et Perspectives Réunionnais (July 1969), pp. 3-17, which links the French Creole conflict with "class struggle" theory. Creole culture is receiving some study by academics; see Cahier du Centre Universitaire (December 1971), pp. 61ff and 81. An example of curriculum is the very French social studies sequence, J. Leif and C. Valot, Instruction Civique (Paris: Fernand Nathan, 1970). This is a seven-grade sequence to which students were asked to bring local

examples. For a Communist view of the effects of "French" education on Réunion society, see LeLoutre, op. cit., Ch. 6.

45. Le Progressiste (January 15, 1972). For more on the educational system as a political issue, see Témoignage Chrétien (September 15-30, 1974), p. 4, and Croix-Sud (October 11-18, 1974), pp. 5, 8. On racial themes, see Témoignages (March 9, 1974) and Le Progressiste (November 4, 1972).

46. For example, see Le Progressiste (March 17, 1973), in which Bertile says birth control is not the answer.

47. For background on BUMIDOM, see the long article by J.-E. Vie, President of BUMIDOM, in La Gazette de l'Ile (March 16, 1973), p. 4. See also M. Debré, "La France dans . . ." and "Demographic Migration, et Contraception," also in Le Monde (June 6, 1972), p. 23; Croix-Sud (December 5, 1971 and January 23, 1972). For two academic analyses of the migration system, see Wilfred Bertile, "Le Sous-Développement Réunionnais l'Emigration en Metropole, Somnifère ou Rémède?" Etude du Centre Universitaire (Saint-Denis, 1972). Ph. Hubert-Delisle, "Le B.U.M.I.D.O.M." (Paris: Bureau pour le développement des migrations intéressant les département d'Outre-mer, June, 1971). Mimeographed, in collection of Centre Universitaire.

48. "Ceux de la Metropole," Le Monde (June 6, 1972), p. 23. Activities of Creoles in France include the publishing of Nous Créoles, the journal of the Union General Travailleurs Réunionnais in France. Headquarters: Clichy-sous-Bois.

49. INSEE, Bulletin des Statistiques, Supplement to no. 31 (April 12, 1973), and Supplement to no. 24 (July 25, 1971).

50. Témoignage Chrétien (March 1974). See also Le Progressiste (March 10, 1973) on the emigrés' not being allowed to return if they wish. This article also mentions an Ordinance of 1960 under which, supposedly, Réunionnais can be "deported" to France for causing trouble. Severe criticisms of BUMIDOM occur in Cri du Peuple (March 1, 1973), and LeLoutre, op. cit., Ch. 8.

51. Election figures were obtained from various sources.

52. For example, see MSP Le Créole's impatience with local Gaullists Jean Fontaine and Marcel Cerneau, while Debré is praised (April 16, 1973). See also Le Créole (January 31, 1973). An example of a possible third-force program are the five preelection issues of Comité Pour le Soutien du Progrès (Saint-Denis: Reformateur Party of Réunion) Bulletin de Liaison, 1972-73.

53. Croix-Sud (October 11-18, 1974). See also ibid (September 20-27, and October 4-11, 1974).

54. Journal de l'Ile (May 13, 1974).

55. Témoignage Chrétien (May 1974). For the May 1972 Paris Conference, see Témoignage Chrétien (June 1974), and Le Progressiste (June 10 and 24, 1972). The first includes the text of the Common

Declaration and a list of Réunion participants. For background of the growth of the autonomy issue, see Hebdo-Bourbon (April 12, 1973).

56. Journal de l'Ile (May 1, 1974). Other pertinent statements by Mitterand were reported in ibid (May 10, 1974).

57. "Les Elections Presidentielles et l'Avenir de la Réunion" (Saint-Denis: Imp. REI, 1974).

58. Le Monde (April 26, 1974).

59. Reported in Le Progressiste (May 1974).

60. Le Créole (January 24, 1973) brought up the issue of a Vergès trip to Moscow in order to rekindle these fears. Also see Le Combat National (May 15, 1974) for an article on Czechoslovakia's Coalition experience, 1945-48, probably directed at Réunion's socialists.

61. Croix-Sud (October 11-18, 1974).

62. The Church is officially nonpolitical: Journal de l'Ile (May 18, 1974), but for a good example of Church-connected political commentary, see Croix-Sud (July 23, 1972).

63. La Réunion: Les Problèmes posés par l'intégration (Saint-Denis, 1973), p. 15.

64. Croix-Sud (July 19-26, 1974).

65. The conference was reported in The People (Seychelles) (November 6, 1974), and in Témoignage Chrétien (November 1-15, 1974). Most of Témoignage Chrétien (December 15-31, 1974) was devoted to a New Delhi conference on the same topic.

6

**THE MALDIVES
REPUBLIC**
M. Adeney
W. K. Carr

For the Maldives Republic, 2,000 coral islands strung like beads down the Indian Ocean 400 miles west of Sri Lanka, stategic isolation from the sprawling states of the Indian subcontinent has bestowed a historic importance disproportionate to their size and wealth.[1] With a tiny population of 120,000 and a per capita income that puts the Maldives among the 20 least developed nations in the world according to the United Nations Development Program (UNDP), the Maldives maintains an international bargaining power denied to most small and poverty-stricken states.

The islands are close enough to both Sri Lanka and the South India mainland to be a convenient haven for merchants or military in the area, yet far enough away to be easily defensible and largely unaffected by the immediate political influences of the mainland. From this position, the Maldives have successively been used as vantage points by outsiders desiring to influence the subcontinent's affairs, by Arab traders, and by Portuguese and British empire-builders. The same isolation nowadays lures tourists, particularly from Italy and Sweden.

Strategically and economically, another major influence on the Maldives has been military: the British base of Gan situated in Addu Atoll in the extreme south of the chain. Its deep water made it an important naval rendezvous during World War II. More recently, its importance has been as an airfield and communications center, a major staging post on the way from Europe to Southeast Asia and Australasia.

Under the British defense cuts outlined in a government white paper in March 1975, the Gan staging post will be shut down when British forces pull out of Singapore, as planned for April 1976. Competition for use of the base or some kind of landing rights is

MAP 6.1

The Maldives

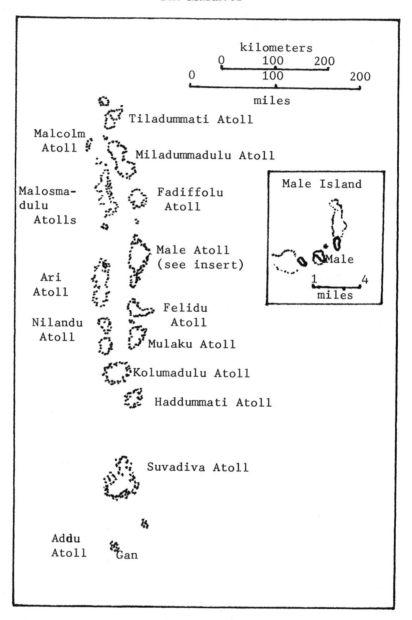

kilometers

0   100   200

0   100   200

miles

Tiladummati Atoll

Malcolm
Atoll

Miladummadulu Atoll

Malosma-
dulu
Atolls

Fadiffolu
Atoll

Male Atoll
(see insert)

Ari
Atoll

Felidu
Atoll

Nilandu
Atoll

Mulaku Atoll

Kolumadulu Atoll

Haddummati Atoll

Suvadiva Atoll

Addu
Atoll   Gan

Male Island

Male

1   4
miles

Source: Adopted from Stoddard, Theodore L. et al. Area
Handbook for the Indian Ocean Territories, p. 22.

likely to be a major diplomatic objective of a number of countries and will bring the Maldives more into the center of South Asian politics.

THE MALDIVIANS

The inhabitants of the Maldive Islands are descendants of Vedda, Sinhalese, Dravidian, Arab, Negro, and Indian ancestors. The Vedda, Sinhalese, and Dravidian peoples came to the islands from Ceylon near the beginning of the Christian era. The Arab and Negro settlers appeared first about the 9th century, and the Indians came in the 17th century.[2]

Except for the Hindi-speaking Indians who have remained apart, miscegenation has blended these several peoples into one, although physical characteristics of the original populations are apparent to varying degrees. The Maldivian in the northern atolls tends to have darker skin, curlier hair, and a shorter stature than does the inhabitant of the southern atolls.

During the 12th century, the islanders became adherents to Sunni Islam. The Indians who arrived some 500 years later were of the Shiite branch of Mohammedanism. The mutual incompatibility of Sunnite and Shiitic religious laws and customs may explain why the Indians remain an unassimilated part of the Maldivian population.

POLITICAL HISTORY AND DEVELOPMENT

From the 12th century until 1968, the Maldives were governed as an hereditary sultanate. During the period of British hegemony (1887-1965) the islands were ruled indirectly through Ceylon. The Maldivians, in effect, governed themselves and so remained largely untouched by Western political and legal institutions.

Following the example of Islamic countries of the Middle East, the Maldives adopted a written constitution in 1932. There was, however, no provision for an elected legislature. The traditional form of Islamic autocracy continued. In 1953 the Maldivian state was nominally changed from a "sultanate" to a "republic." Seven months later, the Maldives were again a sultanate.

In preparation for the anticipated abolition of British rule over the islands, the 1932 Maldive Constitution was revised in 1964. The new Constitution stipulated that the sultan, as head of state, was to be elected by a special convention. A prime minister, as head of government, was to be appointed by the sultan. The Majlis, Maldive's first national legislature, was also provided by the Constitution, as was a cabinet of ministers.

In 1968, three years after the withdrawal of British suzerainty, the present Republic of Maldives was established by national referendum. The 1968 Constitution abolished the sultanate and made statutory provision for a nonhereditary presidency.

THE FUNCTIONS OF GOVERNMENT

At the time of writing (August 1974), the Maldivian governmental system was as devised in the 1968 Constitution, which was amended in 1973. The president of the Republic of Maldives was elected to a four-year term by the 54-member national legislature, the Majlis. Serving as chief of state and head of government, the president appointed his cabinet ministers, ambassadors, and eight members of the Majlis. The president also held veto power over bills passed by the legislature.

Excepting the eight appointed members, the Majlis is composed of relected representatives of each of the republic's 19 administrative districts. Male Island, the site of the capital city of Male, was allocated eight representatives. The remaining islands of Male Atoll were allowed two members, as were each of 17 other atolls. Election to a five-year term in the Majlis was by universal suffrage, women having the right to vote but not the right to hold office.

Following the 1968 reorganization of the government, a presidential cabinet was established, consisting of ministers of External Affairs, Justice, Education, Health, Finance, Public Safety, Agriculture and Fisheries, Home Affairs, and Trade and Development, and an attorney general.

Because of the Maldives' heavy dependence on goods and services from other countries, the minister of External Affairs held a crucial post in the government. Through the Colombo Plan in the early 1970s, the republic received technical equipment, medical supplies, and schoolbooks from Australia, India, Japan, Libya, New Zealand, Singapore, the Soviet Union, and the United Kingdom. Several of these countries also provided educational opportunities for Maldivian students in science, the humanities, and various technical subjects.

In addition to maintaining good relations within the Colombo Plan, the Ministry of External Affairs has been assigned the special task of ensuring a continued favorable trade agreement with Sri Lanka (Ceylon). The Maldives' chief source of foreign revenue has been exported fish, which has regularly been sold to the Sri Lanka Government. The Maldives' most important dietary staple, rice, has been imported primarily also through Sri Lanka. Until recently, the Maldives had depended on the Central Bank of Sri Lanka to handle foreign accounts.

As of mid-1974, the Republic of Maldives had established diplomatic relations with 14 countries, including only one communist nation. These were the Republic of China, the German Federal Republic, India, Israel, Italy, Japan, the Republic of Korea, Malaysia, Pakistan, the USSR, the United Arab Republic, the United Kingdom, the United States, and Sri Lanka. None of these foreign contacts had, at that time, embassies in Male. Maldivian foreign relations have been handled by proxy through the foreign embassies in Sri Lanka.[3]

The legal system of the Maldives is derived from traditional Islamic judicial procedure in which religious law and social law are synonymous. In an attempt to bring the Maldivian judicial system into conformity with contemporary social and economic changes, the minister of Justice and the attorney general have been faced with the problem of taking the interpretation of law out of the hands of Islamic theologians and putting it into the hands of secular officials.

The Ministry of Education, like the Ministry of Justice, inherited a tradition of religious values that excluded an interest in technology. Although the Ministry of Education seems to have recognized the need for modern education, social conservatism and a lack of funds have hindered the government's announced program to provide education for all.

Since there has been no higher education available in the islands, and almost no opportunity for technical training, schooling of any kind beyond the secondary level must almost always be attained abroad. Nevertheless, the Ministry of Education reported that only 90 students were enrolled in foreign schools in 1971. The ministry also reported many children were not in school, even at the primary level, due to insufficient government funding.

Health services in the Maldives are still provided by native practitioners of folk medicine, and sometimes by Western-trained specialists under the auspices of the UN World Health Organization (WHO). Individual medical care has been largely restricted to clinical treatment because of the scarcity of doctors. With the assistance of the WHO, the Ministry of Health has been devoting a major effort to public health problems.

A Ministry of Public Safety exists to oversee the welfare of a population that has been, at least until recently, little given to violence. Other than the short-lived "Suvadivan rebellion" of 1959 and its related anti-British demonstration in 1963, the estimated 500-man police force has had few problems in maintaining law and order among the republic's population. (A major test of the force's loyalty came in 1975, when the prime minister was removed from office by the president and banished to a remote island.)

In addition to the police force, the Maldives have maintained a sea patrol solely for domestic security, but there has been no military establishment designed to counter hostile foreign forces. Furthermore, as the Maldives chose not to become a member of the British Commonwealth, the British air base on Gan Island cannot be expected to be automatically responsive to external threats against the republic. Thus, no treaty-based defense against aggression has protected Maldivian sovereignty. [4]

Clinics have been established in most of the atolls for the primary purpose of controlling malaria, filariasis, tuberculosis, and leprosy. The sole hospital, built in 1960 from funds provided by Britain, has received equipment and supplies periodically from the WHO, the United Kingdom, Australia, and the Republic of China. The Ministry of Health has also depended on foreign-aid fellowships for the training of health technicians.

The main source of revenue for the Maldivian Government has consisted of the tariffs charged on exported and imported products. As there has been no personal income tax, the Ministry of Finance has had to rely on licensing fees, sale of postage stamps, land rentals, telecommunications receipts, and transportation charges, in addition to export-import duties, for the bulk of its internal revenue (Tables 6.1, 6.2). These incomes have been supplemented by Colombo Plan grants, the lease of the British military air base on Gan, and foreign aid in the form of goods and services.

The Maldives' principal foreign earnings have come from exported fish, while the country's supply of essential rice, wheat flour, and milk products have depended on importation (Tables 6.3, 6.4). To ensure the continued import and export of these items, the Ministry of Agriculture and Fisheries and the Ministry of Trade and Development have had to work hand in hand. External trade of fish and the incoming flow of dietary staples were placed under the control of the Government Trade Agency in cooperation with the Ministry of Agriculture and Fisheries, which has maintained programs to explore the possibility of growing new grains as well as the feasibility of expanding and modernizing the fishing industry.

The government has defined the production of food to be an official responsibility rather than a challenge to private enterprise. Public expenditures by the ministries in question have been severely restricted, however, due to lack of adequate revenues.

Matters of demography, employment opportunities, and wages were placed under the jurisdiction of the Ministry of Home Affairs. According to figures released by the ministry for 1970 and 1971, the Maldivian population was increasing by approximately 3 percent a year. [5] But, despite this increase, the government reported continuing shortages of both skilled and unskilled labor.

TABLE 6.1

Selected Economic Data: Maldives and Other Colombo Plan Countries

	GNP Growth Rates (percent) 1960–69	Exports (millions of dollars) 1971	Imports (millions of dollars) 1971	Tax Revenue (percent of total revenue)	Indirect Tax Revenue	Population Growth 1971	World Bank Estimate of Average Annual Growth Rate (percent), 1960–69
Afghanistan	2.3	92	81	75	71	17.48	2.0
Bhutan	2.0	–	–	58	52	–	2.0
Burma	3.9	123	126	82	44	28.20	2.1
India	3.4	2,108	2,520	79	61	550.37	2.3
Indonesia	3.2	1,247	1,174	96	61	124.89	2.4
Iran	8.0	2,642	1,871	39	27	29.78	3.0
Khmer Rep.	3.8	15	78	77	60	7.00	3.3
Korea Rep.	9.2	1,068	2,394	66	44	31.92	2.6
Laos	2.6	2	157	89	77	3.03	2.4
Malaysia	6.9	1,636	1,434	87	61	11.31	3.0
Maldives	2.9	6	5	32	30	0.11	1.8
Nepal	2.2	–	–	94	71	11.29	1.8
Pakistan	5.7	666	917	78	–	116.60	2.7
Philippines	5.1	1,104	1,315	89	75	37.96	3.1
Singapore	7.0	1,755	2,828	59	30	2.11	2.4
Sri Lanka	4.6	327	334	67	50	12.67	2.4
Thailand	7.9	833	1,287	90	78	35.34	3.1
Vietnam, Rep.	4.5	7	442	–	–	18.80	2.7
Total		13,631	16,963	Based on 1970/71 budget estimates for most countries		1,037.86	2.5

Source: Colombo Plan, Nineteenth Annual Report (New Delhi, 1972), pp. 23ff.

TABLE 6.2

Government Receipts and Expenditures: Maldives
(millions of Maldive rupees)

	Fiscal Years		
Receipts	1969	1970	1971
Revenue			
a. Taxes			
i. Income tax	—	—	—
ii. Customs	4.181	3.524	4.668
iii. Excise	—	—	—
iv. Others	0.260	0.290	0.304
b. Net receipts from			
public enterprises	2.682	20.317	10.095
c. Other revenue receipts	0.276	0.658	0.318
	7.399	24.789	15.385

	Fiscal Years		
Expenditure	1969	1970	1971
Nondevelopmental expenditure			
a. Internal security	1.414	1.406	1.472
b. General administration	3.546	4.123	3.542
c. Debt servicing	—	—	—
d. Others	1.736	2.034	2.007
Developmental expenditure			
a. Agricultural and fisheries	0.346	0.164	0.582
b. Economic services	6.546	6.294	5.852
c. Transport and communications	1.013	0.896	0.697
d. Education	1.533	0.990	1.070
e. Health	1.261	0.860	0.838
f. Others	1.231	0.522	1.147
Total expenditure	18.626	17.290	17.207
Excess of expenditure over revenue	11.227	—	1.822

Source: Colombo Plan, Nineteenth Annual Report (New Delhi, 1972), p. 257.

TABLE 6.3

Principal Imports: Maldives
(thousands of Sri Lanka rupees)

Import	1970	1971
Rice	3,812	4,876
Wheat flour	429	1,011
Sugar	1,847	2,215
Textiles, drugs, luxury items, sundries	5,524	11,022
Milk foods	178	1,422
Total	11,790	20,546

Source: Colombo Plan, Nineteenth Annual Report (New Delhi, 1972), p. 255.

TABLE 6.4

Principal Exports: Maldives

Export	1970 Hundredweights	1970 Rupees	1971 Hundredweights	1971 Rupees
Maldive fish	93,304	21,892	106,087	24,897
Other varieties of dried fish and its products	9,399	852	4,731	597
Cowries, red stones, tortoise shells	1,232	117	516	30
Copra	1,538	125	–	–
Total	105,473	22,986	111,334	25,524

Source: Colombo Plan, Nineteenth Annual Report (New Delhi, 1972), p. 256.

LEGAL SYSTEM

Islamic peoples have traditionally governed themselves by Koranic precepts. Civil law was religious law applied to secular problems. The Muslim world has come to know, however, that the complexities of modern society require legal codes more specific than the guidelines offered by the Prophet.

The legislature, the Majlis, has broken with tradition by taking civil law out of the hands of Islamic judges (qadis). Since inauguration of the Democratic Constitution in 1932, Maldivian law gradually became more a function of a political state and less a prerogative of the mosque.

Perhaps the greatest pressure for change in Maldivian society has come from outside. Now that the islands are no longer a British protectorate, Maldivians have had to deal with the rest of the world directly. Membership in the Colombo Plan and in the WHO has required modifications in local customs and traditions. International agreements in commerce and diplomacy have necessitated the discarding of parochial views of human interchange: To meet these new demands, the Maldivian legal system, like other aspects of Maldivian culture, has become more cosmopolitan.

The Majlis, the Ministry of Justice, and the attorney general's office represent a new legal system in direct opposition, however, to many traditional Maldivian beliefs. In addition to the traditional role of Islamic legal specialists, there remains a vestige of the pan-India caste system, under which new occupations are discouraged and old inequities are preserved. Reformation of the legal system depends upon public acceptance of change in many areas of Maldivian society.

POLITICAL ACTIVITY

The Maldivian national electorate was defined by the Constitution as all adult citizens of the republic. In anticipation of becoming independent of Britain the following year, the Maldivians amended their Constitution in 1964 to provide women's suffrage, although the right to hold public office was denied.

As of this writing, no formal political parties around which voting could be patterned have emerged, and there were no ethnic, religious, or economic factions in the society that could have been considered political entities. Maldivian political power has tended to remain in the hands of a small, unrepresentative group of men who inherited their position from the sultanate system, abandoned formally in 1968. Policies have typically been resolved within the precincts of that

traditional power system and afterward presented to the electorate
for confirmation. Government business has proceeded more by
referendum than by public initiative.

At the local level, public administration is performed by appointed
officials. Each inhabited island has a headman (kateeb) and each atoll
has a chief (atoll verin). These officials have been advised and assisted
by elected committees, but they are ultimately responsible to the
national government.

CONTEMPORARY POLITICAL PROBLEMS

Because the Maldives represent not only a small but also a rather
"closed" society, information on the domestic political setting does
not pour forth for the benefit of outsiders. This analysis of current
political development will thus deal more with foreign affairs, touching
on domestic problems where appropriate.

Maldivian affairs have been dominated by relations with Sri Lanka
and the Colombo Plan programs and by the existence of the British
base at Gan. The base remains under British control until December
1986 under the provisions of the 1965 treaty. One of the clauses of
the agreement (Article 3) specifically provides that, without British
Government consent, the Maldives will not permit armed forces of
any other nation to enter its territory or air space or establish any
other base there.

Nonetheless, as the Indian Ocean has increasingly become a
sensitive military area, the agreement with Britain has not deterred
other powers from courting the Maldives. Its relations with the Soviet
Union, whose ambassador visits from Colombo, and particularly
with India, which maintains a naval base in the Laccadive Islands north
of the Maldives, have assumed growing importance. Traditionally the
Maldives have looked toward Sri Lanka, with almost all trade and
financial links in that direction, but over the past two or three years,
Maldivian leaders have made a determined effort to avoid over-depen-
dence on Sri Lanka, and a major shift has begun toward India.

This same strategic isolation, which largely cuts off the republic
from mainland connections—there are only occasional steamer services,
and until a year or two ago there were no regular air flights—coupled
with the wish of external powers to win favor with the government,
has had clear implications for the internal politics of the country.

It has meant that the government has been as secure from any
challenge from outside influences as it could hope to be. An exception
was the attempted secession in 1959 by the southernmost atoll of Addu
as a result of the development of Gan and the consequent improvement
of living standards. At the same time, the international leverage the

Maldives can exert on powers concerned with their positions in the
Western Indian Ocean enables the republic to bring in benefits to
the population through development aid.

The British decision to abandon the Gan base in 1976 will greatly
increase pressures on the Maldives from neighboring and extraregional
powers for friendly links and arrangements that would provide some
use of the base. Sri Lanka's interest in declaring the Indian Ocean a
"zone of peace" will be balanced by economic arguments for leasing
the base as well as the interests of India, and possibly Russia, the
United States, and even China in having some arrangement about its
use.

The government's internal position is strengthened in more direct
ways. It controls almost all external trade. All exports and imports
are handled through the government. The Maldivian Government
Trading Company acts as external purchasing and selling agent both
for the government and private traders. In Male, the government-
owned Bodu stores act as the import and export agency.

Furthermore, more direct methods are employed to ensure strong
government control. Within the country, the government maintains
a relatively large internal security service—the Maldive Regiment,
a force of about 500 men that is based in the capital, Male, but that
can be sent to other islands. Expenditure on internal security officially
has exceeded what is spent on either health or education and amounts
to about 7 percent of the budget: In 1972, according to the report to
the 23d meeting of the consultative committee of the Colombo Plan,
the government spent 1.478 million rupees on internal security compared with 1.126 million on education, 0.896 million on health,
0.857 million on transport and communications, and 0.720 million
on agriculture and fisheries.

In spite of all this, and despite laws that make it a crime to speak
against the government, politics in the Maldives has not been smooth.
As stated above, there was fighting in the attempted succession of
the southern atolls in 1959. Troops were sent to the north islands in
1973, and in June 1974 there appears to have been an attempted coup
in the capital, Male. As all communications are controlled by the
government and there is little outside contact with the islands, information is particularly unreliable and hard to come by. But it
appears that riots occurred that may have been connected with food
shortages and rising prices. The jail was broken into, some people
were killed, and a number of arrests were made including that of
the Agriculture minister, Farouk Ismail. This last, very significant,
event appeared to be confirmed by the fact that shortly afterward,
Ismail's name disappeared from the official list of Maldive Government ministers.

An understanding of Maldivian politics must start from an appreciation of the central power of the president, and under him his

ministers, over the life—and particularly the commerce—of the
country. "Commercial despotism" is not too strong a description
of the situation. Power resides, as it has done since the end of the
last sultan's reign, in the president, Amir Ibrahim Nasir, who was
reelected in 1973 for a six-year term. He has always maintained a
tight grip on the government. The Majlis meets merely to approve
government policy, though it has the power to vote on the office of
prime minister. Proceedings usually last less than an hour.

It is also true that during the two or three years before mid-
1974, a countertrend could be identified. The president's rule was
softening in some respects. The prison island off Male was emptied
and is being used for tourist accommodation. Increasingly the day-to-
day running of the country was being carried out by the prime minister,
Ahmed Zaki. This trend reached a climax in 1973 when the president,
while building a new palace in Male, departed with much of his
furniture for an extended stay in a comfortable home in Colombo, the
Sri Lanka capital. This softening of President Nasir's rule was
dramatically reversed in February 1975 when only 12 days after being
reappointed to office, Zaki was removed by the president and banished
to a remote atoll, along with the chief of protocol. The action was
taken under Article 37 of the Maldives Constitution, which allows the
president "in the event of emergencies confronting the state to pro-
claim temporary orders that do not contravene the Constitution."

Second, one must take into account the way the whole of Maldives is run for the benefit of one atoll, Male. An island half a square
mile in area with a population of 12,000 has all the government offices,
the only hospital and doctors, and the majority of the country's schools,
including all those at secondary level. Half a mile offshore is the
country's airport, while the street lights burn electricity all night
long to light the way for the 30 or so cars on the tiny island. Small
wonder that a sort of "internal passport" system exists: Outer islanders
need jealously guarded permits to remain on Male. Outside Male,
conditions are poor. Only four atolls have electricity, there are no
government schools, and yet not all atolls have the rudimentary health
centers being established with locally trained nursing auxiliaries.

Not unnaturally, the politics of the Maldives Republic has consisted basically of the politics of Male—or to be more precise, of the
great and loosely connected family of Male. The 54-member People's
Majlis is dominated by Male, and although most of the island chiefs
come from the islands they administer, all but two of of the atoll chiefs
came from Male.

The commercial hold of the government over national life has
already been demonstrated. Coupled with this is a close financial
involvement by the president himself in a number of important money-
spinning activities. A number of the islands on which tourism is being
developed with the building of chalets and the flying in of package tours

are owned by the president. 6 He also has a large share of Crescent
Travel Agency, the principal tourist agency. Furthermore, he owns
Blue Haven, the guest house in Male at which official visitors stay
at government expense.

Like a number of underdeveloped countries, the Maldives pursue
extra foreign exchange through such devices as the minting of thousands
of colorful stamps for collectors and the sale of air time on the
government broadcasting station. Incongruously for a fiercely Muslim
state, this time is principally bought by an American Christian sect
that broadcasts to Southern India.

The most remarkable success for the Maldives, however, has
been its far-flung merchant fleet, few of whose vessels call regularly
at the islands. From eight or nine ships in 1969, this has grown to
over 40 ships. It is managed from Singapore by one of the president's
closest aides, Ali Manikoo. Financial details of the activities of the
shipping corporation, most of whose vessels trade on routes that do
not call at the Maldives, are difficult to obtain. They do not occur
in the reports to aid organizations. But with 40 ships trading they
should be expected to make a major foreign exchange contribution—a
lot more than the 317,000 rupees given in one report for earnings
other than exports of fish.

Ali Manikoo's name does not appear on a list of the Maldivian
Government. But Manikoo is, next to the president (to whom he is
closely connected), the most important person in the Maldives. He
spends most of his time outside them as the manager of the Maldivian
Government Trading Corporation (MGTC), which deals not only with
the growing fleet but also with all external trade. His base is now in
Singapore, although the MGTC (formerly the Maldivian National
Trading Corporation), was formerly based in Sri Lanka. The change
to Singapore followed not long after a major diplomatic incident with
Sri Lanka: Manikoo was found in Sri Lanka with several thousand
dollars worth of hard currencies.

The country's external trade is vital. Just how much importance
it exercises can be seen in the case of the fishing industry. The economy of the Maldives has always depended on catching the fish that
jump and swim in profusion on its coral shores. Until the early 1970s,
there was one market, Sri Lanka, to which something over 60,000
hundredweight was dispatched every year. Dried, cured, brown, and
stinking, "Maldive fish" was the vital trimming for a good Ceylonese
curry. The Maldives, in return, depends on export of the fish, which
brings in the currency to pay for the rice and other imported vegetables. During World War II, when the absence of shipping halted
exports, the population declined, as people died of starvation.

Now the situation has changed, bringing with it new fears of local
starvation. Foreign exchange pressures on Sri Lanka led to the changing of the agreement, considerably reducing the amount of fish taken.

In part replacement, the Maldives made an arrangement with one of the largest Japanese fishing combines in April 1972, providing for four large freezer trawlers to be stationed at strategic points throughout the atolls along with four smaller 20-ton vessels. Fresh fish caught by Maldivians with their traditional sailing craft are then ferried to the waiting foreign ships.

In the first seven months of the scheme until the end of 1972, just over 2,000 tons of fish were exported this way. This compares reasonably with the old Sri Lanka commitment of 3,000 tons, which was usually exceeded. But for the fisherman, the new system had one major drawback: The processing of fish for the old market meant that it could be stored and transported over an extended period. The new fresh fish arrangement means that any catch must be quickly taken to the waiting freezer ships. If they are not in the vicinity for any reason, or if the weather prevents loading, then the catch spoils. As a result, there are recent reports of the reappearance of malnutrition in some of the outer islands. This is clearly a very serious development.

The report by the Maldives to the 16th session of the UNDP Governing Committee in June 1973 puts the importance of the fishing industry starkly. The economy, it says, is almost wholly based on fishing. Of the foreign exchange earnings it quotes (a total of 20.4 million rupees), 19.8 came from the export of fish.

The government's principal objective, says this report, is to increase foreign exchange earnings, with the intention of creating further resources for its development program. The short-cut to this, as seen by the government, is the helter-skelter development of tourism. As the report puts it, "The most promising prospect and one with perhaps the greatest growth potential is the field of tourism." The basic attraction of the Maldives is the unspoiled perfection of its coral lagoons, which, with their white sands and waving palms, are everyone's ideal vision of a South Sea Island. For the tourist they offer magnificent swimming and underwater fishing.

So far, tourists numbering up to about 300 a week have come to the Maldives on package holidays spending a week in Sri Lanka and a week in the Male atoll. They fly into the airport concreted across the coral of Hulele Island in Male harbor and live in chalets on neighboring islands, some owned personally by the president. The UN report talks of two 60-bed tourist centers well-equipped with speedboats. This contrasts with the almost total lack of any motorized fishing boats in the Maldives at large.

The size of the airstrip has prevented larger aircraft such as the Boeing 707 from calling at the Maldives, and the government has been discussing a major lengthening of the runway, or even the use of the Gan facilities, in an attempt to bring tourists directly from Western Europe cutting out the week's stay in Sri Lanka. The British

withdrawal from Gan opens up the chance for the Maldives to develop the
base as a major tourist center, and this is bound to prove attractive
to the government. However, if this were to be decided, the country
would need to draw heavily on outside resources and expertise.

The energy crisis and economic stringency in the West is already
slowing down the growth of tourism generally, and this may have some
effect on the Maldive plans. But because they cater to relatively
wealthy travellers, the slow-down will probably be less marked.
But this advantage, drawn from the uniqueness of the tourists Maldives
lures, may be offset by a longer-range problem. The arrival of
well-heeled tourists in the cause of foreign exchange provides, however, an ironic comparison with the subsistence poverty of the mass
of Maldivians, who are preserved from the sight of most visitors,
diplomatic and otherwise, by the lack of easy communication between
the different atolls.

DEVELOPMENT ASSISTANCE

The Maldives were admitted to the United Nations on September
21, 1965, an event that was swiftly followed by a request three months
later for a UN survey of economic and social conditions to indicate
the "type and content of assistance that could be sought from the aid
programs of the United Nations." The mission visited the Maldives
in April 1966 and produced a 124-page report.

As a result of this, a variety of UN assistance has been provided.
It includes a WHO team, which is engaged in malaria eradication
throughout the country and training assistance to produce auxiliary
nurses who can man health centers in the atolls, plus the services
of a Food and Agriculture Organization (FAO) agricultural expert
to investigate the agricultural possibilities of the islands. He has
reported that there are 8,000 acres available for cultivation, but
because of saline conditions only a quarter of this is available for
production of rice, which together with fish is the Maldives' staple
food. But, he says, with modern methods (a major qualification), such
vegetables as tubers, onions, maize, and so on are practical possibilities. This is not too encouraging a report, and the main agricultural development recently has been the clearing and replanting
of areas of coconut under UN advice. Breadfruit and coconut grow
profusely in the islands.

The poverty of the Maldives is measured by the UNDP by their
inclusion in the list of 20 hard-core least developed countries that
have been earmarked for a special, though very limited, program of
assistance. Factors determining this position include per capita
gross national product—estimated to be $90 for the Maldives—population

per doctor, and literacy. The Maldives' two doctors (both based in Male) provide it with a score on UN figures of 50,000 population per doctor. Only seven countries in the world do worse, and five of those are around the 60,000 mark, which is probably the true Maldivian figure. As for literacy, the Maldives report to the 16th UNDP session ventures that "literacy in the younger generation can be placed at a little over 50 percent." This may well be overestimated.

The five common characteristics identified among the countries seeking the special assistance all apply to the Maldives. They are (1) subsistence agriculture, (2) a pervasive weakness of administration, (3) an acute shortage of trained manpower at all levels, (4) inadequate transport and communications, and (5) a very narrow industrial base. In the Maldives case, this should read "the complete absence of an industrial base."

The main sources of development aid so far have been Britain, the United Nations and its agencies, and the technical assistance program of the Colombo Plan, which has largely provided scholarships and training abroad including some in Asian countries. Other countries such as Russia and Libya have played a relatively minor role. Unusually among underdeveloped countries, if realistically, the Maldive Government has avoided loans and the burden of debt repayments and has only taken grants.

Outside Male and the atoll of Addu, which benefits from the financial fall out from the British base, the country is almost untouched by development. Among the major problems that face the islands, apart from the lack of health and educational facilities, are deep structural difficulties: the cost of importing rice (one of its basic foodstuffs) and other foods and the grave difficulties in expanding agriculture; a rising population with a 3.5 percent annual growth rate a year and not a hint of a birth control campaign; the lack of adequate powered transport between the atolls; the absence of an effective administrative machine; and finally the grave shortage, which is endlessly harped on in official reports, of trained personnel in any field one cares to name.

Most of these have been or are at present the subject of development negotiations, but there are some surprising omissions and inclusions within the development priorities. For the fishing industry, for example, the acknowledged mainstay of the economy, it has frequently been suggested that the introduction of simple powered craft, enabling fishermen to reach shoals quickly and then to stay with the fish longer, would be valuable. But the Maldive Government has shown less enthusiasm than willing foreign donors have to the prospects of introducing them. The government points to difficulties of servicing and repayment, which may be realistic but are not insuperable. Finally in its latest submissions to the United Nations after a fact-finding trip by Fisheries Minister Milmy Didi to look at other Asian experiences, it has proposed, as a result of a Japanese study in the islands, to ask for $100,000 for a few vessels with fiber glass hulls.

Inter-atoll communications are another odd case. Communications are so difficult that visiting delegations are usually told it is impossible for them to go outside the Male atoll. The harbor at Male has in it, however, a significant number of powered craft of some size including a "sea-bus" donated as a gesture of Islamic brotherhood by Libya. Of course, these vessels may not be suitable for the purpose, but surprisingly little practical concern has been shown so far about inter-atoll communication by the government. However, in its latest submission to the UN, the Maldives Government claims that it has one vessel available, but that that one has been out of order for two years because of engine breakdown. It therefore asks for new engines costing $30,000. The report speaks of "a serious shortage of fast inter-island vessels between Male and the Atolls which is hindering all development activity and particularly the implementation of WHO and other UNDP assisted operations."

The program of assistance the Maldive Government was discussing with the UN during 1973-74 would cost about $750,000 and would largely benefit Male.

Apart from the items already listed such as fishing boats and new marine engines, the aid request included a second telecommunications link between Male and Colombo at the cost of $99,500, night landing facilities for Hulele airport off Male priced at $30,000, and a new water supply and sewage scheme for Male at a cost of $183,000. The request explained that "gastrointestinal diseases, the enteric group of fevers and intestinal parasites constitute a major threat to the health in the republic. Male, the capital city and the principal administrative and cultural center acts as a major link in the spread of these diseases within the republic."

The report proposed further money be spent for an adviser on coconut agronomy and for a $72,500 nurse auxiliary training program, which was due to end in 1974. This would extend the program to 1976 at the cost of another $210,500. Maldives also requested more overseas scholarships for doctors at a cost of $87,900, and it suggested a short-term adviser on tourism.

In 1960, a grant of $2.1 million was agreed with Britain and a further $1.4 million in 1971. Among the expenditures in the first grant was the 40-bed hospital in Male (the first in the country), training for personnel, equipment for the harbor, for Hulele airport, and for the power and broadcasting stations, and some assistance with boatbuilding. The 1974 discussions centered around further improvements, including dredging of Male harbor, fire-fighting equipment for the airport, a hydrographic survey of the Male harbor, and mapping of the island, the provision (agreed to) of a tug, two barges, and a crane

for the harbor, and the possibility of another inter-atoll launch. On
a smaller scale, medicines for the atoll clinics, and books and equipment for the three government schools in Male were under discussion.

FOREIGN RELATIONS

Because so much of Maldivian foreign relations have been concerned with aid and much of the information about the country is
prepared for these discussions, it may be easy to overestimate the
importance that development aid plays in the Maldives' foreign policy,
but it is clearly the central theme.

The republic has been cautious in its foreign policy, having an
ambassador in Sri Lanka only. There was, for a while, a Washington
representative, who also represented the country at the UN, but this
appointment was withdrawn, presumably on the grounds of cost. The
only country that has ever maintained an embassy in Male was
Nationalist China, presumably in hopes of securing the Maldives' vote
to retain its UN position. But this "embassy" was closed about four
years ago.

The Maldives' "caution in international affairs" is shown in their
voting at the UN General Assembly. They were one of only three
countries—the others being Oman and Nationalist China itself—not to
vote on October 25, 1971, when the Peoples' Republic of China was
admitted. In fact, no Maldivian representative attended the General
Assembly that year or in the 1973 session. In 1972, an analysis of
the voting record finds the Maldives always on the majority side with
the mass of the uncommitted Afro-Asian states.

Among motions it supported were those called for a zone of peace
in the Indian Ocean,[7] a world disarmament conference, the suspension
of underground nuclear tests (on which the nuclear powers abstained),
and on self-determination for the Palestinian people. The Maldives
voted firmly for equal rights for women and for the ending of capital
punishment even though many brother Muslim countries such as Iran,
Iraq, the United Arab Republic (UAR), and Libya opposed this.
Curiously, the Maldives appeared absent in the vote dealing with
sovereignty over natural resources on the sea bed.

There are signs, however, of an emergence of Maldivian foreign
policy in a more active role. In early 1974, the prime minister, Ahmed
Zaki, who was also the External Affairs minister, paid the first official
visit of a Maldivian leader abroad when he went to India. There was
a chance that this visit would be returned later during 1974 by Indira
Gandhi, the Indian prime minister. A further official visit, in autumn
1974, to London, was being discussed but never took place.

The major shift in Maldivian foreign policy has been away from exclusive economic ties with Sri Lanka, with whom traditionally its trade and communication and education has been closely linked. The special relationship with Sri Lanka, which at times has lapsed into the ill-feeling to which such ties are prone, has been modified by the removal of the headquarters of the Maldivian trading company to Singapore and the cultivation of friendship with India, the Maldives' next nearest neighbor. But strenous efforts to forge closer relations have been made by the Sri Lanka Government with some success. The Sri Lanka prime minister, Mrs. Bandaranaike, was to pay an official visit to the Maldives toward the end of 1974.

Relations with India were improved by the amicable settlement over a disputed island north of the Maldives. Zaki appeared to go some way toward accepting Indian concern about foreign military bases around her coast when he said during his visit in February 1974 that Gan was an "environmental anachronism." Zaki seemed to suggest that the lease would not be renewed after 1986.[8]

The State Bank of India (rather than Sri Lanka) has been chosen to set up the first banking facilities in the Maldives, and discussions have been held about a possible telecommunications link and air services with Southern India, paralleling those with Sri Lanka. Relations with Britain remain warm, and Queen Elizabeth II paid a visit in 1972 during a world tour.

In the immediate future, there are a number of imponderable questions that hang over the Maldives. The most immediate is the future of Gan, which has very important economic consequences for the country as well as the strategic and diplomatic ones. Addu Atoll has benefited enormously from the economic fallout from the base. Of scarcely less importance is the future of the fishing industry and the consequences of the switch to fresh fish export, with the attendant risks and apparent suffering to the fishermen who comprise most of the islanders. Not far behind this is the cost of living. Prices, in spite of official Maldivian statements, have risen markedly. The statement to the 1973 Colombo Plan meeting that "as prices are controlled by the Government, the prices of essential foodstuffs are fluctuating more or less in accordance with the world market" actually conceals a situation of growing hardship, in which even United Nations gift milk powder has appeared for sale.

The revolution of rising expectations is also becoming a reality for the Maldives. With some 90 students annually gaining knowledge and techniques abroad, and incidentally having their eyes opened to wider horizons outside Male, dissatisfaction with Maldivian provincialism and backwardness will be an increasingly important factor. There are not many jobs to be had in the Maldives, and most of these are with the government. Some Maldivian students have stayed in the countries where they have been studying and have shown little

wish to return. One proposal being discussed by the government is
the establishment of a technical training institute within the Maldives.

Finally there is the question of foreign exchange and the impact
of the oil crisis on the shipping fleet, on prices, and on the development of tourism. This will continue to be a major cause of concern.
At the time of writing, however, the French Elf company was carrying
out exploratory sea-bed oil drilling in Maldivian waters. If they find
oil, the economic picture of such a small country would be greatly
altered. But even in that event, basic questions of Maldivian priorities—how to use the money—would remain.

NOTES

1. This historic importance is not reflected in any measurable
quantity of modern writing on the Indian Ocean area. The Republic
of Maldives has been ignored in modern research to a remarkable
degree. Major Congressional hearings on the Indian Ocean completely
fail to refer to the Maldives (U.S. House of Representatives, Committee on Foreign Affairs, Subcommittee on National Security Policy
and Scientific Developments, The Indian Ocean: Political and Strategic
Future, Hearings, July 20, 22, 27, and 28, 1971 [Washington, D.C.:
Government Printing Office, 1971]. Sparse mention occurs even in
the major academic symposium published to date: Alvin J. Cottrell
and R. M. Burrell, eds., The Indian Ocean: Its Political, Economic,
and Military Importance (New York: Praeger Publishers, 1972).

2. Further background on Maldivian history can be found in T.
W. Hockley, The Two Thousand Isles: A Short Account of the People,
History and Customs of the Maldive Archipelago (London: Witherby,
1935), and Alan Villiers "The Marvellous Maldive Islands," National
Geographic Society (June 1957), pp. 829-49.

3. Maldivian negotiations with the People's Republic of China
during 1973 are discussed by Guy de Fontgalland, "Maldives: Real
Delight for Tourists," Christian Science Monitor, January 29, 1974.

4. A description of life at the base on Gan appears in "The Island
of Not Having," Time (May 17, 1971).

5. United Nations estimates of the Maldivian population growth
rate, cited here, differ from the World Bank's projections, which
are nearer 2 percent. Colombo Plan, Nineteenth Annual Report (New
Delhi, 1972, p. 30).

6. A report on Maldivian efforts to stimulate tourism appears
in "Isolated Maldive Islands Now Letting the World In," New York
Times (April 9, 1972).

7. As evidence of increasingly close Indian-Maldivian relations, a six-day visit by Maldivian premier Ahmed Zaki to India ended in a joint communiqué supporting the "zone of peace" concept for the Indian Ocean. "Former DoD officials Say Atoll to Be Major Base," China Post (March 16, 1974).

8. In a three-part series on "The Indian Ocean Contest," Hanson Baldwin referred to the Gan base in the "politically sensitive" Maldives. New York Times (March 22, 1972).

7

INDEPENDENCE POLITICS
IN THE SEYCHELLES
John M. Ostheimer

During 1976, or soon thereafter, a tiny island country of 55,000 people will enter the world of independent nations. With such a small population, few resources, and a land territory of about 100 square miles, the Seychelles will never rank high on the list of the world's most important states. Nevertheless, other Indian Ocean countries seem to be aware of the importance the Seychelles have inherited from their geographic location. As the Mauritian Ambassador to the United Nations expressed it, the Seychelles, "minute as they may be . . . have a paramount role to play in international affairs from within our world organization, particularly in the best interests of the Indian Ocean as a zone of peace free from great power rivalry."1/

The growing strategic significance of the region will undoubtedly assure a measure of attention to the archipelago's rapidly changing political situation. The governing party's recent advocacy of independence, after years of arguing that continued colonial attachment was both admirable and fruitful, has also ensured a new measure of interest in the Seychelles. This chapter examines current Seychelles politics for indications of how Britain's colony is adapting to its sudden emergence onto the world scene.

The Seychelles archipelago numbers over 80 islands, but three are particularly important to internal politics. Mahé, Praslin, and

This chapter is a substantial revision of "The Seychelles: Politics in the Islands of Love," which appeared in Journal of Commonwealth and Comparative Politics (July 1975).

MAP 7.1

Mahé Island: Seychelles

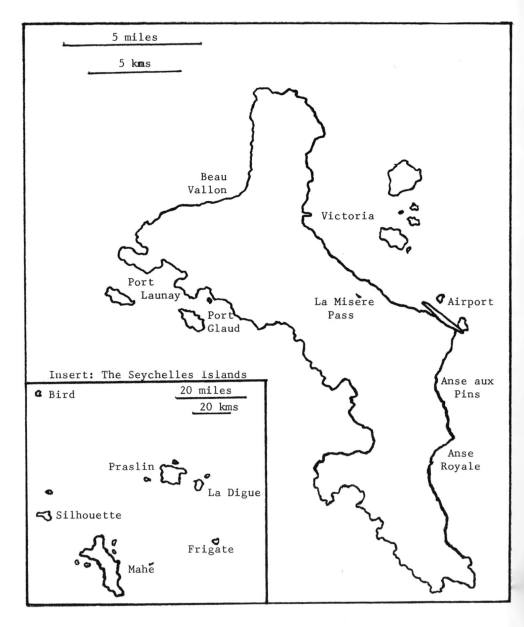

5 miles

5 kms

Beau
Vallon

Victoria

Port
Launay

Port
Glaud

La Misère
Pass

Airport

Insert: The Seychelles Islands

Bird

20 miles

20 kms

Anse aux
Pins

Praslin

La Digue

Anse
Royale

Silhouette

Frigate

Mahé

La Digue rate this arbitrary status because they are sufficiently populated to merit representation in the Legislative Assembly, but Mahé is by far the most important (see Table 7.1).

TABLE 7.1

Seychelles Demography, 1971

	Total Number	Percent
Victoria	13,736	26.1
Rural Mahé	31,684	60.2
Mahé	45,420	86.3
Praslin	4,244	8.1
La Digue	1,985	3.8
Other inner islands	474	0.9
Total inner islands	52,123	99.0
Outer islands	527	1.0
Seychelles	52,650	100.0

Source: Seychelles Government, Provisional Census Results (Victoria: Government Printer, May 1971).

The Seychelles are very poor, although during the early 1970s the agricultural economy has rapidly given way to tourism and tourist-related cottage industries. Energy consumption levels per capita are comparable to countries like Ecuador, Jordan, and the Philippines. The island population is about 25 percent urban; by 1970 there was one motor vehicle for each 36 Seychellois. Demographically, Seychelles represents an odd mixture of underdevelopment characteristics. The population is relatively young: 53 percent of the people are under 20 years of age, which is a typical characteristic of underdevelopment. But literacy is increasing rapidly, and the medical health of the Seychellois is remarkable for such a poor country. Life expectancy is now greater than 60 years. Perhaps the Seychelles' small size has made the impact of British medical and social policy more complete than in larger colonies. One unfortunate feature, however, is that the combination of poverty and dominant Catholicism renders population control difficult: The annual growth rate has been as high as 4 percent but dropped steadily to about 3 percent by 1970.[2] Overpopulation is acknowledged to be a problem, but unlike Réunion, there seems to be no coherent policy to deal with it. Quite probably no population policy has been pressed in recent years, because, with the tourism and construction boom, a labor shortage developed. Before 1970, however, some 7,000 Seychellois had moved to Australia. It is possible that emigration will pick up again should economic growth level off after 1974. [3]

Creole is the native language for 94 percent of the Seychellois, while 5 percent speak French and the remainder speak English and other, mostly Asian, languages. French and English are spoken widely as second languages: English is the language of educational instruction. Creole culture is mainly Catholic in religion, although the Anglican church had an earlier start in the islands as an organized faith and has been active throughout the Seychelles' civilized history. The 90 percent of Seychellois who are Catholic have been long known for their ability to mix traditionalistic cults with Catholicism, but this syncretism should not be interpreted as having caused any weakening of the Church's influence. The incredibly high illegitimacy rate and the islanders' rather "flexible" value system may embarrass the Church, but the Seychellois are a devout people, and the Church's influence has been strong. Until recently, the Church has been a conservative influence. It is now divided between conservative and reformist elements.

GOVERNMENTAL STRUCTURES

During the concluding colonial years, Seychelles has been administered formally by the Hong Kong and Indian Ocean Department of the United Kingdom's Foreign and Commonwealth Ministry. [4] The local "governor and commander in chief" has resided in Port Victoria, the capital city on Mahé. Everyday administrative problems have been handled since 1970 by the deputy governor, who, with his senior staff, was responsible to a Council of Ministers. Deputy Governor John Todd's difficult role under Sir Bruce Greatbatch, who was replaced as governor in November 1973, combined too great functional responsibility with ambiguous final authority. The deputy governor's position (which may not last much longer in any case) may be more compatible with the comparatively vigorous role being played by the new governor, Colin Hamilton Allan, former resident commissioner of New Hebrides.

The division of responsibilities within the Seychelles Government as it was in 1974 is shown in Figure 7.1. Council of Ministers posts 4 through 8 were held by Seychellois who were leaders of Seychelles Democratic Party (SDP), returned to power in the 1967, 1970, and 1974 elections. The three other posts were filled by British officials.

FIGURE 7.1

Governmental Structure in Seychelles

A. The governor and commander in chief

B. The Council of Ministers (8 members)

1. Chief minister: development coordination, tourism, lands, commerce and industry, local government, public relations, cultural activities, immigration policy, census, surveys

2. Minister of Agriculture, Natural Resources and Marketing: land settlement, cooperatives, cold storage, outlying islands, national parks, and conservation

3. Minister of Aviation, Communications, and Works·

4. Minister of Housing, Labor, and Social Services: film censorship, employment, public health, sports, youth, education

5. Minister without Portfolio

6. The deputy governor
Reserved subjects: prisons, immigration, procedure for Council of Ministers and Assembly, elections, allocations of offices and quarters, technical assistance, ceremonial and naval visits, information

7. Financial secretary: finance, accounting and statistics, customs and excise, income tax, currency and banking, price control

8. Attorney general: legal affairs, public prosecution, civil status

C. The Seychelles Legislative Assembly
15 members elected for five-year terms, 5 of whom hold posts B, 1 through 5 above. They may pass a motion of censure of Council of Ministers and force resignation

---

Source: Compiled by the author.

165

The Council of Ministers seemed to be more reliant on the civil servant heads than is seen in larger systems. The directors of departments, equivalent to the "permanent secretaries" in Britain, had impressive degrees of latitude to carry out the work of their departments. Ministerial portfolios were obviously extremely multifunctional, but, according to one SDP minister, this presented little problem because the five ministers were working as a team, frequently covering each other's areas of responsibility.[5] Some department directors offered a more pessimistic evaluation, commenting on how little the ministers knew about what was going on under their jurisdiction.

A spread of subjects such as those for which the Social Services Minister was responsible must inevitably result in a superficial approach to specific problems. The tendency of SDP ministers to travel abroad frequently intensified this problem, leaving important matters in the lap of Secretariat civil servants. "Travel fever" was also, very definitely, a political issue: Opposition leaders (who enjoy traveling themselves) continually lambast the governing party for their extensive (and expensive) junketing. As the opposition paper once put it, "The Chief Minister is still on holiday in Seychelles. He has not yet resumed his duties abroad."[6]

Local government has not existed in Seychelles since 1971. Defensible from a demographic point of view, the decision to do away with it was highly questionable from the perspective of political education and development. However, local government has been a subject for which neither Seychellois politicians nor British administrators have shown much sympathy. Previous experiments, such as the District Council system (1948-71), are remembered as expensive and fruitless, even trouble-causing, because of the false expectations they promoted. Fortunately, this subject has again been under discussion; recent studies of aspects of Seychelles' social development suggest that channels for demand are necessary in order to involve the people more fully in development projects.[7]

Complaints about the inefficiencies of government are probably no more frequent in Seychelles than elsewhere, but the type of criticism is interesting. In 1973, several key British civil servants were considered highly competent, but there was a growing tendency among supporters of both parties to stress the availability of able Seychellois who could carry out the expatriate-held jobs. On the other hand, to a remarkable degree, the opposition Seychelles Peoples United Party (SPUP) supporters attributed governmental failings to the political party in power, rather than to any inherent difficulties in the tasks involved or to the lack of effort by the people generally. Conversely, those who supported the governing SDP saw no failures at all. What was striking in Seychelles was the total politicization of virtually all affairs, public and private. Anything was possible, if you knew a minister (and a high proportion did), while for those with oppositionist views, _everything_ was explained by the fact that the SDP must have been involved in some sinister way.

The British Government encouraged this development by the abstemious use of its power to guide political change. Britain and the United States apparently decided in the 1960s that the preservation of some influence over the greater Western Indian Ocean area was all that really mattered. Setting up the British Indian Ocean Territory (BIOT), described elsewhere in this volume, realized this interest. At the time of the BIOT's formation, Seychelles was secure because the leading politicians saw no advantages in separating from England. They, in return, were given a free hand (in 1970) over major areas of internal affairs in exchange for support for the British strategic presence in the region. Britain's policy toward decolonization of small territories was explained to the United Nations Decolonization Committee by a British official:

> We will respond to the wishes of the people concerned, if it is their wish to proceed to self-determination and independence in the exercise of their inalienable right to do so, so be it, we will help them on their way. But let me say equally categorically that it is not our intention to impose independence on those who do not desire it. [8]

Britain was committed to doing whatever the elected Seychellois leadership desired but did want to retain some strategic leverage in the region, on uninhabited islands if nowhere else. As if to symbolize the relationship between BIOT and the SDP's growing constitutional internal power, the first administrator of BIOT, in 1967, was to take over as the first deputy governor in 1970.

After 1970, SDP leaders became increasingly jealous of those internal powers that remained in British hands: powers over the political process and over the structures that ensure democratic liberties. SDP ministers undoubtedly would have taken stronger actions against the opposition were it not for British presence. For example, the chief minister, SDP leader James Mancham, advocated increased control by his cabinet over the island police force. The British replied that any greater devolution of police power would necessitate granting full independence to Seychelles, which Mancham had insisted he did not favor. [9] By March 1974, he had decided that independence was the only alternative.

Governmental structures are bound to change somewhat under the Independence Constitution. These changes were already under way during 1974. For example, the Financial secretary's real powers were formally turned over to the Legislative Assembly in July 1974, in preparation to being handled by an elected Finance minister. [10]

Mancham appointed a constitutional adviser, from the University of Sussex, in May 1974. The Constitutional Conference was to be held in London in the fall of 1974, although the opposition argued that because of the expenses of travel and the benefits of public information and input, the deliberations ought to have taken place in Seychelles instead. [11] Mancham's hope was that Independence Day would be celebrated by June 1976.

ELECTIONS AND POLITICAL DEVELOPMENT

In 1948, the first contest for 4 elected seats in a Legislative Council of 13 members marked the beginning of organized electoral politics. Only the "grand blancs" (important white people) of the islands were represented. Mass political party organization was nonexistent, and the franchise was restricted to literate taxpayers. Fewer than 2,000 people were eligible to vote. Elections in 1951, 1954, and 1957 did not change this pattern, and even in 1960 (the year that saw a flood of newly independent African states join the international scene), when the number of elected members was raised to 5, the franchise remained unchanged. [12]

Political change intensified during the early 1960s, as new urban professional and middle class candidates emerged to win seats, and formed new alliances in the Legislative Council. The issue of what type of relationship Seychelles should have with Britain was not new. Several Legislative Council members had called for greater autonomy before 1963. Up to that time, the principal political force had been the Seychelles Farmers' and Taxpayers' Association, used by the planters to defend their interests in matters related to crop marketing and other policies. But during 1964 some of the new Seychellois elite were joined by a young lawyer, France Albert René, under whose leadership the SPUP was formed. Self-government was SPUP's main issue, and in a 1965 byelection René was elected to the Legislative Council.

SDP was also formed during 1964, by other young educated Seychellois who thought, along with René, that popular political organization was required to counter the vested interests of the Farmers' and Taxpayers' Association. James Mancham and the other SDP organizers were apparently motivated, as was René, by desires to have access to political machinery through which they could press their claims to a part of the prosperity that seemed about to dawn in emergent Seychelles. Personal rivalries were probably as much the cause of separate SPUP and SDP organizations as were any differences in philosophy although both parties tend today to stress the intellectual differences present during their formative years. [13]

Under a new Constitution adopted in 1967, election battles in eight constituencies were fought by the SDP (along with one independent ally), opposed by the SPUP. The simultaneous introduction of universal adult suffrage resulted in an expansion of the electorate from 2,500 to 17,900. In this contest, Mancham's SDP emerged with a 4-3 majority of the 8 elected members, and the one independent member sympathized with the SDP's antiindependence views. Also, for the first time, the elected members (8) outnumbered the official (4) and nominated (2) Legislative Council members.

By 1970, another round of constitutional revision had placed power in the hands of Seychellois for the first time. With the formation of a Council of Ministers, a small-scale model of the British parliamentary system emerged. Seychelles became a crown colony with a Council of Ministers (see Figure 7.1). The new Legislative Assembly included 19 members: 15 elected, 3 ex-officio, and an impartial speaker. Constituencies were identical to the 8 of 1967, but the 7 largest were given 2 seats each; the SDP won 10 seats to the SPUP's 5, and the electorate increased to roughly 40,000.

Further constitutional revisions were imminent. Partly for political reasons, the SDP needed a change in its relations with Britain. Independence had proved more viable an issue for SPUP than Mancham's SDP had expected. SDP still desired close association with the United Kingdom through Commonwealth membership. The flow of investment funds had begun to slow down while the European tourism corporations awaited indications of Seychelles' future political development. According to Mancham's "independence" radio speech on March 18, 1974, "Her Majesty the Queen of England will remain our Queen forever." Mancham also asked the governor to dissolve the Assembly, and new elections were held on April 25. It was inevitable that, with SDP's strong election showing, Mancham would ask for Seychellois control over a Civil Service Commission and over the existing police structure, now under the deputy governor. Election violence was certainly not widespread, but there was sufficient unrest, particularly on Praslin Island, to justify strong reaction by security forces. SPUP claimed that the arrests showed SDP's oppressive tendencies, while the very existence of unrest tended to substantiate SDP's views about the dangerousness of their opposition. According to SPUP, their post-election effort to interest the International Commission of Jurists (ICJ, in Geneva) was a success: ICJ had agreed to study the alleged injustices of the April 25 election.[14] Also likely was a move toward greater control over the media, again directed by the deputy governor's office. Radio Seychelles and the Bulletin had tried to present both sides of important issues, under governmental management.

SURVEY OF THE POLITICAL PARTIES

The governing party, SDP, was, in 1974, a curious amalgam of politicians who seemed to have only one thing in common: For a variety of reasons they had, at least until 1974, concluded that Seychelles gained from its association with Britain. The SDP leaders were Mancham, chief minister—a lawyer; David G. Joubert, minister of Housing, Labor, and Social Services—an ex-British solider and schoolteacher; Chamery Chetty, minister of Agriculture, Resources, and Marketing—a businessman, landowner, and planter; Robert Delorie, minister without portfolio—a businessman and landowner; Justin Pragassen, minister of Aviation, Communication, and Works—a teacher. This cabinet remained intact after the formation of the postelection government in April 1974.

The SDP leadership had business and real estate interests but also had strong connections with some Seychellois labor unions. Robert Moulinie, Gonzague d'Offay, Nicolas Stravens, and Joubert are all past or present Union officials. Thus, it is quite difficult to generalize about the social background difference between the two main parties. Survey data, allowing comparisons of party preference with other data, do not yet exist. Furthermore, the past elections show no clear party differences of a rural-versus-urban or economic nature. Rivalries between personalities and their local power bases explain much of the growth of the parties. For example, intervillage rivalry produced a patchwork-quilt effect on the east side of Mahé: Anse Royale and North Victoria are SDP strongholds, while their neighbors, Anse au Pins and South Victoria, developed as SPUP strongholds. As ideological differences between the parties have crystallized, it is tempting to look for the expected social groups that would underpin SPUP as the "party of reform" and SDP as the "party of order," but, without survey data, any such emerging partisanship pattern is hard to substantiate.

Some observers have argued that there were no differences between the parties ideologically, but this researcher does not agree. Indeed, there seem to have been a list of divisive issues. Before March 1974, self-images were unmistakable. Referring to the debate over the value of tourism, the SPUP avowed "today in Seychelles we have a capitalistic Government [SDP] in power, tomorrow we may have a socialist Government [SPUP]."[15] SPUP's self-image as a "socialist" and "progressive" party seemed, if anything, to strengthen after the 1974 elections deprived the party of the long monopolized issue of independence. Its 10th-anniversary statement emphasized that the differences between the SDP and SPUP have not disappeared. The SPUP "believes in political and economic independence."[16] For the SDP, socialist priorities were utterly unacceptable:

> Little Seychelles . . . fully endorses Kenya's stand that
> private investment should be welcomed not only for the
> capital it brings with it but also for the transfer of tech-
> nology, managerial, and technical skill it facilitates.
> In brief, the Seychelles government wishes to promote
> the free enterprise system . . . and does not accept
> the so-called "Tanzanian Experiment" as being com-
> patible to the wishes and interests of the people of
> Seychelles. [17]

Certainly the interparty differences were not as clear-cut as
this in practice, but as the section on political issues will show, they
may still be significant. It will be interesting to watch the strains
on party unity caused by the clear statements of principle that some
leaders have made. In the case of SDP, one backbencher, A. Uzice,
had already shown that revolt was possible, objecting that social
security legislation by his party's government was not sufficiently
generous or popularly administered. [18] Also this same member virtually quit the party in the past over what he considered the chief
minister's "personal excesses."

SDP organization was not at all well developed. It resembled
a "party of notables" in Maurice Duverger's sense. There were
locally designated parish agents, but they operated mainly as a sort
of party fire brigade, active in noticing "who the enemy is" in areas
where the SPUP was strong. The SDP organizationally suffered from
having always been in power and was only well-developed in areas
where it had lost or was in danger of losing. Financially, the party
was narrowly based and generally feeble. [19] As members of the party
in power, some SDP ministers had expectedly developed a strong
"favor system" in their districts. For example, strong control over
Praslin reflected the increasing "political machinery construction"
of its representative, the minister of Social Services.

The main SPUP leadership in 1974 was France Albert René,
president of SPUP—a lawyer; Guy Sinon, secretary general—a unionist;
Matthew Servina, publicity secretary—ran the SPUP office in Dar es
Salaam and was the general secretary of Cable and Wireless Staff
Union; Karl St. Ange, a planter and estate owner; Philibert Loizeau,
organizing secretary—a labor leader and former copper-miner in
Uganda; Rifnid Jumeau, editor of The People. During 1974, Dr.
Maxime Ferrari, a physician, emerged as vice president.

Like the SDP, the SPUP had some difficulty holding itself together, and rumors of intraparty strife were widespread. One of the
five Legislative Party members, M. J. Green, left the party because
of its strong stand after 1970 in favor of independence. [20] Also there
were those who believed that St. Ange was unhappy with the party's
socialist-sounding statements and that St. Ange and René (both white)

disliked the obsession of Sinon and Servina (both black) with Africa.
In spite of all this, it would be wise to take SPUP unity, and therefore
intentions, at face value.

According to René, his party had always espoused independence,
although for tactical reasons the issue was deemphasized during the
1968-70 period. René stressed that the party's original talk of "association" with Britain was used during 1968-70 because "independence"
seemed so unpopular that to stress it would threaten the SPUP with
political suicide. With the benefit of hindsight, he later insisted that
this was a tactical blunder; education of the masses on the merits of
independence had to begin someday, he argued, and the SPUP would
have been even closer to power by 1973 if it had made public its views
on the issue before 1970. In 1973, René was confident that his party
would gain power soon, although there were obviously many reasons
for calling his view overoptimistic.[21] But in March 1974, the SDP
announced its reversal of policy regarding independence. Elections
were called for April 25, in a surprise move by SDP leader Mancham.
As he announced his new pro-independence policy, the SPUP's prospects appeared bleak, and the election resulted in a predictably strong
SDP victory, as Table 7.2 indicates.

By December 1974, it was still premature to say what SDP's
cooptation of the independence issue might mean to the party system.
One possibility is that the SPUP, having no strong issue left, might
simply fade away. At first glance, the April election results appeared
to confirm this. However, 47 percent of the voters still chose the
SPUP although the party won only 2 of 15 seats. And, in spite of at
least two meetings between Mancham and René, SPUP's determination
to offer vigorous opposition appeared undiminished. The party newspaper argued consistently after Mancham's March 1974 turnabout
that the chief minister's moves were completely opportunistic and
that the superficial "deal" he could be expected to make with the
British would not hide unchanged policies toward the BIOT and other
key issues.[22] On socioeconomic issues, the SPUP was firmly to the
left of the SDP, consistently critical of failures to finance programs
adequately or to ensure egalitarian distribution patters. But it would
be a mistake to label the SPUP leadership "communist." Some of the
SPUP leaders make very questionable socialists. René argues issues
quite pragmatically, and his opponents alternate between calling him
a communist in one breath and an opportunist in the next. Generally
speaking, SPUP members do not appear to be atheists; one of their
five basic policies is "upholding and respecting religious institutions
without fear or favour," and they have supported the right of Catholic
priests to be active commentators on social, economic, and political
injustice.[23] This trend was strengthened with the arrival in 1972 of
a new acting bishop, Father Gervais Aeby, whose sympathies cor-
related well with those of the SPUP on many social issues. Generally,

TABLE 7.2

Seychelles Election Results under Universal Adult Suffrage
(percent)

	1967	1970	1974
Victoria North			
SDP	63.0	65.3	67.2
SPUP	37.0	31.2[a]	32.8
Victoria South			
SDP	43.0	45.0	51.2
SPUP	65.1	52.1	48.8
North Mahé			
SDP	0[b]	55.6	53.1
SPUP	41.4	39.5	46.9
East Mahé			
SDP	37.4	34.3	34.3
SPUP	62.6	63.5	65.7
South Mahé			
SDP	61.5	60.8	56.4
SPUP	38.5	37.0	43.7
West Mahé			
SDP	42.7	58.7	57.6
SPUP	40.0	38.1	42.4
Praslin			
SDP	54.8	57.8	58.1
SPUP	45.2	40.0	41.9
La Digue and outlying islands			
SDP	37.9	44.6	52.3
SPUP	62.1	52.3	48.7
Number of votes	(17,900)	(35,917)	(41,833)
Percent of electorate voting	72	82	84
SDP	51.5	52.8	52.4
SPUP	45.5	44.1	47.6
Other	3.0	3.1	0

[a]Percentages may not add up to 100. The residual is accountable to independent candidates and minor parties.

[b]In the North Mahé election of 1967, an independent candidate ran with SDP support, polling 58.6 percent of the votes.

Source: Compiled by the author.

the SPUP's tendency is to defend its "socialistic" policies by identifying their origins as religious not Marxist. [24]

By 1973, the SPUP organization began to reflect its leftist ideology and its struggle for power. A "branch" system, the typical organizational form of European democratic socialist parties, was to have been completed by early 1974, according to René; 16 branches were planned, which would encompass every legislative district.

SPUP financing was rather similar to that of the SDP's, depending in part on the private funds of the party leadership. But the SPUP balanced the SDP advantage drawn from the salaries and influence (bestowed by being in power) by its connections with the Liberation Committee of the Organization of African Unity (OAU). The experience and personal contacts of Sinon and Servina opened the door to large amounts of OAU support since that body defined SPUP as a "genuine liberation movement." There is argument about the exact amount, but at least 12,000 pounds had come into SPUP's possession from OAU by 1973. Mancham referred repeatedly to these "unfair" contributions as justifying, in part, his change of heart toward independence.

MAJOR EVENTS SINCE THE 1970 ELECTION

The most unsettling event of the 1970s was the series of bombings and the extended "treason trials." Following the 1967 elections, four bombings occurred in Seychelles, but no one was convicted. Then in February 1972, there were two separate bombings, one at a new tourist hotel and the other at the shop of an Asian merchant, and a certain Guy Pool was arrested in connection with one of these events. [25] Pool was a little-known associate of SPUP organizers, and many people concluded that higher SPUP leaders were implicated, although there was no proof of complicity. SPUP President René, did, however, pay for the services of a Nairobi lawyer to defend Pool, who was eventually convicted and sentenced to a 12-year prison term.

The SDP found one aspect of this situation to be quite humorous, believing that a large part of SPUP's OAU funds were used to pay Pool's lawyer. SDP leaders were in earnest, however, when they stated that they were jealous of the power retained by the British Crown over police and internal security. To SDP minds, René and all SPUP leaders were guilty by association; their supposed motive was to create chaos in time for the Queen's visit to the Seychelles in March 1972 and to embarrass the Seychelles just as the tourist boom was intensifying. This view was reinforced by the statements of people who were probably in search of clemency. [26] The most important result of the trial was a "law-and-order" mania which certainly threatened the demise of democratic institutions in Seychelles as the SDP entered a period of negotiations toward full independence.

Aside from the moral question of what the SDP would do with more internal power, its analysis of the bombings was probably partly correct. Just before the bombings, the SPUP's party paper, The People, announced "tougher tactics," and SPUP leaders echoed this theme up to the day of the explosions.[27] Proof may be missing, but it is hard not to conclude that SPUP leaders, like President Richard Nixon in Watergate, at the least failed to control their overzealous underlings.

A second key event, less sensational but important in stimulating opposition to the SDP regime, dated back to January 1971, when the Government Workers' Union turned in a claim for a 40 percent wage increase. Negotiations dragged on for months as government and management argued that raises ought to be tied to productivity increases. During that period, construction and tourist-related economic development was causing serious inflation. When the union received no satisfaction by April 1972, a strike was called, with marches and demonstrations.[28] Several arrests occurred; potential martyrs were created,[29] and sympathy for the workers extended far beyond the SPUP offices. For example, certain of the younger Swiss Catholic clergy, who possess the most disciplined "reform-socialist" ideology to be found in the Seychelles, came to the strikers' support by marching with them. Furthermore, they championed the strikers in their journal, L'Echo des Iles.

Early in 1972, Father Alain, one of these activist priests, had taken over the editorship of that paper, and its approach to church-state relations changed drastically from that time.[30] As the Seychelles are at least 90 percent Catholic, and as L'Echo des Iles is surely the most professional of the Seychelles' journals, these events ought not to be underemphasized. By August 1972, at least one section of the Catholic Church, traditionally a conservative force in the Seychelles, was heavily committed to reformist and oppositionist politics.

Other events were directly related to all this. During 1972, Dr. Ferrari, government gynecologist, was released from his duties at the Government Clinic and Hospital in Port Victoria. The priests obviously felt this to be a politically inspired blow at the Church. Ferrari was a longtime supporter of Catholic family planning and other programs, but the SDP also knew that he was enamored of SPUP ideas. In any case, the government never explained the dismissal. L'Echo des Iles took up the cause of Ferrari, and a heated press war ensued, with the SDP Weekly opposed by a strange press alliance: the reformist Catholic and SPUP papers and the conservative Nouveau Seychellois, which saw the issue as a challenge to freedom of the press.[31] In 1974, Ferrari became SPUP vice president.

These events, with others of shorter duration or less glamor, explain what had become, by early 1974, a dangerous situation, a general decay of the political process including a radicalization of the oppositional elements and a hardening of the attitudes of those in power. This analysis of politics in the Seychelles concludes with surveys of the less structurally formal aspects: the system of pressure groups, political attitudes, and a survey of the major issues that will supply the raw material for future political debate.

POLITICAL CULTURE, ATTITUDES, AND ACTIVITIES OF GROUPS

During the early 1970s, the political style of the Seychellois developed in quite unpleasant directions, perhaps confirming some of the theoretical writings on the effects of isolation and small size on island politics covered in Chapter 2. Personal vendettas, rumor-mongering, and seeming avoidance of constructive, problem-solving politics are nothing new to observers of small towns. This is a question of degree: At least in the small American town, one can find diversions from petty issues and personal rivalries by focusing "up" to the state or national level. Seychelles is like a small community in search of some larger arena to take peoples' minds off local matters. Unfortunately, there is a total fixation with Seychellois personalities and problems that extends into the "prepolitical" age levels. There hardly exists a youth of 14 years who cannot name at least five leaders of both political parties (see Table 2.1). For Seychelles the consequences of lacking a supralocal political level were, in some ways, distinctly undesirable. Even insignificant events seemed to lose their perspective and become momentous, and people's sense of humor was weak. This is not to belittle the Seychelles' real problems but only to point out that without a variety of problem levels, local politics can become an unhealthy obsession. Furthermore, because it is difficult in such a place not to know at least one government minister personally, politics must become a "personal" activity.

In Seychelles, this trend has been worsened by the newness and intensity of the competition between two parties and also by certain unfortunate tendencies of British administration. One expert labeled the Seychelles public information system "nonfunctioning."[32] It is hard to tell who was more at fault, the Seychellois politicians who tried to misuse it or the British administrators. The office walls of the New Secretariat building displayed slogan cartoons such as "Telephone Talk Is Not Secure," "Keep Our Secrets Secret," "Does He [the messenger] Need to Know?" and "If You Can Read It, So Can He." Siege mentality abounded; it sometimes looked as if the British colonial staff had left London in 1942 and had not been back since. In such an atmosphere it is no wonder that Seychellois politicians tended to justify their stinginess with information with paternalistic logic shared by many of their British civil servants: "Our people are new to all of this, and we must guide them and introduce them slowly to modern politics." In this environment the rumor mill grinds constantly, because many people know just enough to "have a suspicion that. . . ."

The results of these trends seemed by 1974 to include a growing disillusionment with democratic politics, and possibly, along with this, a climate of readiness to accept some future alternative to democracy as palatable. During the early 1970s, SPUP politicians by and large abandoned the more constructive forms of legislative participation in favor of a combination of more bizarre tactics: legislative walkouts and motions to eliminate the budget for the governor, deputy governor, and chief minister on grounds of their inadequacy. Furthermore, the SPUP was convinced that the constituency basis was unjust and that the SDP would try to keep power through electoral fraud. The SPUP announced that it would not compete in the next election, which was suddenly called for April 1974, unless there was adequate reapportionment. The legislative session of 1973 refused any reapportionment, and SPUP's disillusionment deepened. The SPUP did enter the April election, but their attitude remained cynical afterward, as one comment by René to the governor makes clear: "No matter what the last farcical General Elections indicated we consider that the [SPUP] represents the majority of the people of Seychelles."[33]

For varied reasons, the vicious circle intensified during 1973 and into 1974 as SDP sensed some support slipping away among the more organized and vocal sectors of the electorate. An example was the labor movement. Both parties had been actively organizing parts of the Seychelles' labor movement for years. These political party initiatives had proven to be quite destructive for the development of labor organization itself. Labor unity was made impossible, and serious divisions hindered even the development of specific, craft-based unions. When government sought help from outside to organize unions more effectively, the International Confederation of Free Trade Unions (ICFTU) officials who visited the Seychelles were astonished to find such a strong degree of political party involvement in the union movement, and they declined to provide any aid for labor education and organization programs until union leadership less attached to the parties could be found.[34] Some progress on this front was made, and the Afro-American Labor Center was apparently ready to start negotiations with a newly formed National Labour Education Committee.

The Trade Union Movement appeared to be moving in the direction of the SPUP, which was perhaps to be expected with SDP heading government. The award that followed the strike of 1972 convinced many that the workers had a legitimate complaint. But SPUP argued that the award was negated by inflation during the interim. Hotel workers were an increasingly disgruntled group. This was perhaps inevitable, considering the frustration of suddenly seeing the great wealth that the tourists manifested. This certainly explained some of the swing toward Sinon's Hotel and Allied Workers' Union.

Taxi Owners' and Drivers' Association (TODA) members also typified some of the adverse effects of tourism on SDP power. Previously, this group was strongly SDP, as it was Mancham's policies that encouraged Seychellois to enter this occupation: The chief minister himself suggested that people purchase taxis and "get ready for the tourists." But since then, TODA leaders felt government was far too lenient in allowing European package tour companies to bring in their own small buses to Mahé.[35] The enraged taxi drivers were being forced to move aside in favor of these buses at the airport. Growth of car rental firms (in one of which Mancham had invested) further hurt them.

Recent work to expand the cooperative movement to other producer and consumer areas was hurt by the same forces that divided the labor movement. The failure of an attempt to form consumer cooperatives is a good example. At a meeting of those concerned with the idea, Albert René was elected president. His opponents automatically discounted the new cooperative as another vehicle for his political ambition, ignoring the possibility that the SPUP president was genuinely concerned with cost-of-living problems. Once René's name was attached to the East Mahé Consumer Movement, the SDP government fought the whole idea vigorously. René has been confronted by the same problems in his attempts to establish a credit union. These are examples of the costs of the lack of numerous, competent leaders in little Seychelles, and although some progress in expanding the cooperatives movement was being claimed during 1974,[36] the movement of the Cooperative Department under the Agriculture director may have represented government disenchantment with its vigorous efforts.

INDEPENDENCE, SEYCHELLOIS IDENTITY, AND RELATIONSHIPS WITH THE OUTSIDE WORLD

The independence issue has been dealt with briefly in reference to the parties' ideologies, but, looked at separately, the issue throws light on several related questions. Seychellois find themselves asking "Who are we?" There are cultural pulls that serve to beg such a question but that confuse the answers. Racially, there is no doubt of the strong African ethnic contribution to the islands. But there have been enough other sources, including European, Chinese, Indian, and

Arab, for a thorough racial mixture to have occurred.[37] Color has
been traditionally a status determinant, but visitors from England or
America are impressed by the racial mixture and harmony as compared to our own societies. After several weeks in Seychelles, a visit
by the U.S.S. Noah reminded this researcher of this difference as I
watched the American sailors with their strict, although informal,
system of segregation. The historical circumstances that produced
the racial mixing of Seychellois were unique, but the islanders have
a lesson to show the world today in which they justly take pride.

The independence issue touched raw nerves because of its association with Africa and that continent's comparatively race-conscious
politics.[38] The SDP and the SPUP have struggled for Africa's support.
The SPUP had earlier contacts in Africa on which to draw. Its initiatives began some time ago with a successful 1971 campaign to persuade the OAU Liberation Committee to recognize the SPUP as a
genuine liberation movement. The SDP was forced to enter the contest, realizing that a continued British rule over Seychelles might be
hard to defend in the face of international opprobrium. Thus, in
February 1973, Chief Minister Mancham toured several leading OAU
countries to advocate the untimely concept of the benefits of colonial
rule, arguing that a people should be allowed to choose their own fate,
even if that fate were colonial status. Mancham continued this campaign
with a strong cable to the Liberation Committee in August 1973. The
March 1974 shift of policy on independence made the SDP more palatable to the OAU, and Mancham's June mission to the OAU meeting in
Mogadishu, Somalia, appeared to have been a success. It would
obviously be difficult for the OAU to continue to finance the SPUP once
it had admitted the SDP government as an observer to the OAU Summit
Conference.[39] The OAU has virtually assured membership for the
SDP independent government of the future.

Beyond Africa, Mancham indicated that he hoped Independence
would also bring full UN membership (Seychelles would replace Equatorial Guinea as the smallest UN member) and affiliation with the
Commonwealth and the European Economic Community. He stated his
argument with the "zone of peace" concept as applied to the Indian
Ocean. If vigorously advocated, this policy would dull the political
success of the SPUP's criticism of the further development of BIOT
by Britain and the United States. The SPUP's defense against SDP
cooptation of yet another opposition issue was to insist that Mancham
could not be trusted to be genuinely "nationalist" in his approach to
these problems. On BIOT, the SPUP argues "that these islands should
be returned to us and we feel confident that the British Government
will have no serious objections to this—particularly as they have continually denied that these islands are used for military operations."[40]
As Anglo-American plans took shape, however, Diego Garcia emerged
as the probable location of any base. That atoll had originally been

taken from Mauritius. Thus, the issue seems more important to SPUP for polemical reasons than for any other: Indeed it is possible that Britain will return the other, comparatively useless parts of BIOT to Seychelles as a good-will gesture.

To this complicated situation, one must add the presence of a small but articulate segment of francophile opinion that chipped away constantly at the psychological reserve of attachment to Britain. The radical reformist priests who edit L'Echo des Iles are joined in a new effort by Alliance Francaise and Union Culturelle et Technique de Langue Francaise affiliates, through a French language journal, Seychelles Culture. A French consul arrived in Victoria in early 1974. Old plantation-owner families complete this odd mixture.

Literacy data indicate that these efforts to sustain French should not be interpreted as a "cultural offensive." French has been declining in popularity as a written language (see Table 7.3). As a spoken language, French is claimed by 37 percent of those over 15, but by only 19.7 percent of those under 15. During the early 1970s, the francophile segment was also, not coincidentally, SPUP oriented. But Chief Minister Mancham has been quite successful in also stressing French as a part of the Seychelles' cultural heritage. One has to wonder whether the lure of French aid is in part responsible.

TABLE 7.3

Proportion of Literacy by Language, Seychelles, 1971

Age Group	Total	Literate in English	Literate in French and Creole
15–29	8,135	86.2	12.9
30–44	4,424	67.4	30.5
45–59	2,710	56.1	42.1
Over 60	1,772	42.6	54.7

Source: Seychelles Government, Provisional Census Results (Victoria: Government Printer, May 1971).

These varied elements worked against British rule, perhaps not in all cases actively or specifically, but each added its share. The issue of Africa was by far the most important. The two parties offered their contending views of Africa in a constant propaganda war. The SDP painted the continent as ruthless, actively racist, antidemocratic, and, with a few exceptions (such as Kenya), unconstructively "Socialist-oriented."[41] The SDP line was that those African states who pushed the OAU to accept SPUP as a "genuine liberation movement" must have had aims of their own in view. Either they wish to embarrass their former colonial masters for psychological reasons[42] or they wish to resist Western military bases in the Indian Ocean. In any case, SDP argued that the OAU was misled by René, Sinon, and Servina into believing SPUP represented a majority of Seychellois. In the SDP view, the OAU ought to have examined the Seychelles more closely, identified correctly the majority view, and then followed its own precepts of self-determination.

" Why should the Seychellois not be allowed to pursue their wish and remain British?"[43] Chief Minister Mancham worked hard after SPUP's African success became apparent, to build stronger relationships with Africa's more "moderate" states, through the Afro-Malagasy Mauritian Common Organization (OCAM). During 1973, Mancham claimed success for this counteroffensive. However, the SDP's sudden move in 1974 toward independence was at least partly explained by a growing sense of failure on this issue.

Even after the OAU decided to acknowledge the SDP government, the SPUP has used the issue of Seychelles-South African relationship to discredit Mancham's rule. South African tourists are increasingly among those lured to the islands, and in September 1974, South African airways began service to Seychelles. SPUP delighted in pointing out that this SAA air service began soon after Mancham had declared at the Mogadishu Conference that Seychelles would observe the OAU policy of embargo against South Africa. SPUP was likely to encounter ever increasing difficulty in using this issue to embarrass SDP, for Southern African events moved so fast in 1974 that it became hard to be certain that either policy emphasis—the "confrontation" espoused by more radical Black African governments or the bargaining posture adopted by regimes such as Malawi and Ivory Coast—was more appropriate. In any case, Mancham's policy toward South Africa was certainly not out of step with that of the more accommodationist African governments. Sounding very much like Malawi's H. Kamuzu Banda, he argued, under the UN Decolonization Committee's questioning, "We have no sympathy for and cannot but condemn in the strongest possible terms the policy of apartheid as practiced in South Africa or anything else which resembles it in any part of the world." But the proper tactics toward South Africa, as seen by Mancham's party newspaper, include contact and example:

What is wrong, therefore, in allowing South Africans who are prepared to pay for sunshine to discover in the process the falsity of their Government's doctrine? Cannot the editor of The People imagine the impact on the mind of the average racially indoctrinated South African when he comes to Seychelles and discovers the smile of happiness all over our multiracial faces?[44]

The other Indian Ocean islands have also provided lessons and/or reasons for despair for the Seychellois. The SDP had called attention to the autocratic practices of Maldivians in order to show that the British umbrella had been a good idea there. On the other hand, the SPUP used Maldivian independence to legitimize the idea for Seychelles. SPUP's weekly, The People, welcomed Queen Elizabeth's 1971 trip by pointing out, "It is significant that on the way to the Seychelles she will be visiting former British colonies including Maldive Islands which like us are small islands. . . ."[45] The SDP argued that Réunion's association with France produced beneficial economic attachments with the Common Market, and Mancham even voiced envy at the Réunionnais' status as French, free to come and go to the metropole, in contrast to Seychellois, who must obtain permits and pass through special formalities to visit the United Kingdom. SPUP tended to dismiss these claims with its view that Réunion will not be a French Department much longer: The SPUP predicts that French maladministration will soon produce an electoral majority for the autonomists. "In this sense, Britain is wiser than France. It is true that Réunion is a 'part' of mother France. But for how long? The Indian Ocean is stirring and Réunion will stir along with the others, so the policy adopted by France of integrating some of her colonies is a short-term one and everyone knows it."[46] The SDP criticized recent anti-French events in Madagascar. As a final example, SPUP championed the Comorian moves toward independence, but SDP put more faith in her hesitant statements by the conservative Ahmed Abdallah, the Comorian prime minister, who seems to hope that Comorian independence will not progress too hastily.[47]

Underlying all of these polemics about political progress and the value of independence in Africa and in islands of the Indian Ocean are the inevitable psychological questions that accompany colonialism. Seychellois have been taught that they are not capable of managing their own affairs, but there are many who resent this, a group far larger than the top leadership of SPUP. At some stage nearly all educated Seychellois—civil servants, leaders of both parties, businessmen such as the few local hoteliers, in short, all who find themselves in competition with expatriates for jobs and income—have felt this way. Seychellois capability has really become a nonpartisan issue, but the SPUP was more able to capitalize on it than the SDP, at least until SDP's own recent move toward independence.

SDP had equated continued colonial status with "common sense." In explaining its government's successful "foreign policy," the Seychelles Weekly argued that Chief Minister Mancham has discovered a

> new method of international diplomacy . . . under the
> protection and auspices of British Embassies every-
> where our diplomats can move with relative ease to

conduct the affairs of our country. This saves the
cost of establishing representatives in foreign
capitals. The relatively speedy communications
between Seychelles and other capitals of the world
have enabled Victoria, small in comparison, to be
as important as they are. Perhaps this is the sign
of a new movement towards a new form of Nationhood which does not include the prerequisites inherent to the big nation states. After all the small
colonial territories are seeking a form of National
existence which will ensure their integrity and freedom now that Associated Status is proved to be a
failure after the recent incident in Anguilla.[48]

Not much reading between the lines is required to see that SDP leaders
were as aware of the psychological requirements of nationhood as were
the SPUP. Like the SPUP, they have little love for the British. Nonetheless, SPUP's arguments have always gone further, questioning
the financial "common sense" of colonial status. They have argued
that the Seychellois must take over the tasks of running their own
islands; the SPUP links the values of independence with the immediate
demands that local people accede to the good jobs. In SPUP's view, the
annual subvention (on which the SDP has insisted Seychelles depends)
would not be necessary were it not for the overinflated pay scales
and allowances of expatriate staffing. (See Table 7.4 for British
budget support.)

TABLE 7.4

Annual British Budget Support: Seychelles
(approximations, pounds sterling)

Year	Support	Year	Support
1966	None	1971	1,845,000
1967	325,000	1972	n.a.
1968	540,000	1973	n.a.
1969	285,000	1974	4,338,000 (roughly
1970	1,208,000		80 per Seychellois)

Source: Compiled by the author.

Finally, to realize the seriousness of this issue, one need only recall that recently the issue of expatriate employment has divided SDP membership from their leader, and the SDP itself from the British.[49] The Civil Service came under the authority of the deputy governor, and the SDP stressed its dissatisfaction with the dominance of expatriates.[50]

To summarize, the SDP has given up trying to argue for continued colonial association. The Seychelles are not attached to England in any cultural sense, and the more the SDP realized that the recent gains of tourism and development could be retained without formal British rule, the easier it was to acquiesce in the inevitable. In the final analysis, there were at least four reasons for the SDP change of heart on the issue of independence: (1) the British did not care deeply whether Seychelles remained under their wing, and took no real action to perpetuate their rule; (2) the OAU pressured for independence; (3) during 1971-74 the United Nations had also seemed unsympathetic to Mancham's pro-British stand; and (4) SDP needed greater power over internal security: The British would not use it sufficiently in SDP's behalf, while the OAU and UN role gave support to the SPUP.

KEY INTERNAL ISSUES

Tourism has for several years occupied an important place in the Seychelles development effort.[51] Air travel is primarily responsible, but Seychelles officials anticipated a cruise ship boom with the reopening of Suez. On the surface, government appears to appreciate the need to control this activity:

> Government has accepted the view that every encourage-
> ment should be given to an orderly growth of tourism
> which will not outstrip resources in manpower, materials,
> and the skills which will be necessary to achieve a balanced
> and viable industry. At the same time it will be necessary
> to provide for the attractions which tourists will seek, and
> above all to protect the natural beauty of these islands . . .[52]

In addition to this evidence that the Seychelles Government does not intend to allow uncontrolled tourism development, at least two aspects of the administrative process work to enhance regulatory power. The director of tourism exercises control over restaurant and hotel rates and policies, and the director of planning issues construction permits only after study of the economic and environmental impact of the proposed facility.[53] Tourism's growth has been

spectacular. During 1971, a total of 3,175 visitors arrived in Seychelles, but by 1973 the figure had climbed to about 20,000. Officials
find themselves in a difficult position. In spite of the attempts to
keep tourism development at an orderly and controlled pace, "disas-
ters" have occurred: Unfinished hotel space was sold to a package
tour. Bad publicity from experiences like this, coupled with pro-
hibitive travel costs, could leave Seychelles in the "overdeveloped"
position that some Caribbean islands now find themselves.[54] Seychelles does possess a small but vocal conservation-oriented group
that is searching for effective ways to remind the development-oriented
regime of the necessity for environmental common sense. There are
signs that their message is not entirely lost.[55]

The governing politicians exhort all Seychellois to strive to
make tourism a success. But the SPUP has clearly found this emphasis distasteful, in spite of protests that the party does not oppose
tourism per se.

> SPUP has <u>NEVER, REPEAT NEVER</u> been against tour-
> ism. It is true that it has served the purpose of certain
> individuals to accuse SPUP of being against tourism, but
> from the beginning, even before the airport was built,
> SPUP had been for TOURISM.
>
>   The difference between SPUP and the present SDP
> government lies not in whether a TOURIST INDUSTRY
> should be established in Seychelles but rather in (a)
> the way a TOURIST INDUSTRY should be run and (b)
> What kind of TOURIST INDUSTRY the Seychelles should
> have.[56]

While there is little proof, accusations that the SPUP has tried to
sabotage the tourism industry have been common. SPUP obviously
disliked the moral impact of the European tourists, the menial status
and low earnings of most Seychellois work contributions, and the
cases of discrimination that have occurred against Seychellois in the
hiring of staff of the new hotels and restaurants.[57] Above all, SPUP
leaders have expressed dismay over the picture of Seychellois that
has been painted in the foreign press—that of a primitive, lazy
people still to be found in this last isolated "paradise."[58] SPUP
buttresses their claim that Seychelles has been humiliated before the
world with complaints about Mancham's "playboy" image.[59]

The "Seychelloization" theme intrudes on the subject of tourism
also, as the legislative session of December 11, 1972 demonstrated.
A majority voted against continuing to allow expatriate firms to control the car and boat hire business.[60]

CONCLUSION: THE RETREAT FROM
DEMOCRATIC POLITICS

Politics in Seychelles has been extraordinarily intense, and the combination of deep concern over a few crucial issues, the great importance of personalities, and the novelty and resulting lack of sophistication with politics as an activity could well jeopardize the the future of democratic procedures. SDP leaders have been very quick to define oppositional activity as treason and have made statements indicating that SPUP dealings with OAU countries were unconstitutional and illegal. Civil servants were admonished to be loyal to Mancham's government. Seychelles Weekly warned those "who are noted for their antigovernment attitudes and make it a point to sabotage all Government efforts. Luckily the country is small enough and sooner or later those people get to be known, and now we hope they are being kept under watch."[61] As the SDP solidifies its power, there is no reason to believe SPUP leaders will remain free for very long if any "treasonous" events occur to equal those of 1971-73. The chief minister obviously resented the British Government's failure to deal more harshly with matters of internal security. The Church would probably not be allowed, under conditions of increased SDP power over internal security, to continue its current role as social critic.[62] Nor would any opposition press be so assured of continued freedom; according to one SDP backbencher, L'Echo des Iles should have already faced court action for an article dealing with the bomb trial.[63]

In response to this, and at least as a partial cause of it, SPUP's tactics may radicalize in the future. SPUP's argument now allows a ready-made excuse for not participating in future elections if support looks disappointing. The party was on record in 1973 that unless redistricting occurred they would not compete in the election.[64] In spite of their frustration, René's party did choose to compete in April 1974. But after the election, their criticisms arose anew with calls for a change to proportional representation replacing the previous requests for reapportionment.[65] (The SPUP won 14 percent of the seats with 47 percent of the popular vote.) The SPUP also criticizes undemocratic activities by SDP leaders, such as alleged spying on personal mail by the chief minister, complaints that SPUP leaders are searched and harassed at the airport, and criticisms of SDP's attempt to keep René and other SPUP leaders from meeting a visiting Kenya trade mission. The SPUP had moved toward the tactics of marches and demonstrations to show the depth of their alienation. Their conclusion was, increasingly, that participation in democratic procedures will not pay off, and they feared repression from a more powerful, independent SDP government. [66] By 1974, Seychelles politics was showing very unfortunate tendencies, but it is not yet clear where these trends will take the picturesque "islands of love."*

NOTES

1. United Nations, Committee on Decolonization, proceedings of May 17, 1974.

2. Some economic data are available in United Nations Demographic Yearbook (annual), and UN Statistical Yearbook (annual); Barclay's Bank International, Ltd., An Economic Survey of Seychelles and British Indian Ocean Territory (London, 1972), and Seychelles Government, Provisional Census Results (Port Victoria, 1971). Key data such as gross domestic product and per capita income were not available.

3. Seychelles Bulletin (August 2, 1974); Seychelles Weekly (November 9, 1974).

4. On current Seychelles governmental structure, see Seychelles Government, Report of the Seychelles Constitutional Conference 1970 (Victoria, 1970). The change of governors is described in Seychelles Bulletin (April 26, 1974).

5. Conversation with the Honorable Chamery Chetty, minister of Agriculture, March 13, 1973.

6. The People (October 23, 1974).

7. Original Ordinances, Title XVIII, Ch. 131, p. 1569f. Although still classified in 1973, the report of Professor Walter James, submitted to Seychelles Government in March 1973, includes proposals for setting up "Community Councils," which might afford the necessary degree of elite-mass political communications. Seychelles Bulletin (March 7, 1973). Discussions will probably revolve around possible contributions of the present Parish Allowance Committee (Social Welfare) with other possible functions to produce a citizen's general "advice and recommendations" committee system. (Conversation with Gilbert Green, Social Development Supervisor, and R. P. Bradley, director of Social Development and Housing.)

---

*At the March 1975 Seychelles Conference, meeting in London, SPUP and SDP agreed to June 30, 1976 as a target date for Independence. The legislature and cabinet are to be enlarged, and SPUP will join in a coalition, holding 4 out of 12 positions.

8. Times (London) (November 8, 1972).

9. See "Sir Hugh to Go, Sir Bruce to Return," Seychelles Weekly (July 1, 1972).

10. Seychelles Bulletin (July 29, 1974).

11. The People (October 9, 1974).

12. For political developmental data, 1948-70, the author has relied on unpublished sources from the Secretariat, Seychelles Government.

13. SPUP and SDP historical development is described (from the SPUP's viewpoint) in "10th Anniversary Issue," The People (July 10, 1974), and from the SDP's perspective in a special anniversary issue of Seychelles Weekly (October 5, 1973).

14. The People (September 4, 1974).

15. "Tourism: How, Why, and for Whom?" The People (April 18, 1973). For a fuller statement of SPUP programs see SPUP, New Horizons, 1972.

16. The People (July 24, 1974). For an analysis by the SPUP of the social class characteristics of the SDP, see The People (October 2, 1974).

17. "Welcome to Our Kenya Friends," Seychelles Weekly (August 5, 1972). On the concept of private property, see the Lockeian statement in "Aftermath of Guy Pool's Conviction," Seychelles Weekly (January 13, 1973).

18. "The National Provident Fund Ordinance . . . ", The People (November 3, 1971).

19. On SDP organization, conversation with the Honorable Chamery Chetty, March 13, 1973. A comprehensive description of SDP finance appeared in "SDP in the Red," Seychelles Weekly (July 22, 1972), and then became the subject of debate: "SDP Is Broke," The People (July 19, 1972).

20. According to The People (August 22, 1971), Green's defection was due to political opportunism solely. For his role in Reef Hotel labor dispute, see The People (October 25, 1972), pp. 11-12. On SPUP backgrounds, see The People (November 10, 1971), p. 2. More SPUP history appears in The People (July 22, 1972). The party reorganization is described in The People (August 17, 1974).

21. Conversation with F. A. René, March 12, 1973. On the associated status policy, see M. Servina, "Looking at the Historical and Political Background of the Seychelles," The People (June 7, 1972), also The People (November 19, 1971).

22. The People (March 3, 1974, June 19, 1974, and particularly May 22, 1974). SPUP sources have had little to say about the meetings between René and Mancham. Mancham has described them as "cordial" but has given no substantive indications of the results. Seychelles Bulletin (May 1, 1974 and July 8, 1974).

23. See strong defense of the priests in The People (August 25, 1971). See also the editorial in The People (January 4, 1972). On

SPUP's belief that the next Pope should be an African, see The People
(April 25, 1973). Basic policies in The People (July 24, 1974).

24. See "Is Pope Paul VI a Communist?" The People (August
17, 1974). Also The People (September 4, 1974).

25. For accounts and polemics on the Seychelles' various explosions, see Seychelles Weekly (August 12, 1972). Harry Bonte
was acquitted in the trial of the second explosion case.

26. Pool stated during the trial that René had showed him how
to make the bomb. Seychelles Weekly (October 14, 1972).

27. The People (February 2, 1972). For the SDP's interpretation
see "René Has a Lot to Explain," Seychelles Weekly (January 13,
1973).

28. Seychelles Government, "Award of Arbitration Tri-
bunal . . . ," 1972. The SPUP considered the final terms of the award
a full victory. The People (June 28, 1972), pp. 6-8. For the SDP's
attempt to salvage some political capital, see postaward interview
with Chief Minister Mancham, Seychelles Weekly (July 8, 1972).

29. See recent account of H. F. Rosalie's prison life in The
People (April 4, 1973).

30. Alain's first issue was headlined "Les Seychelles à l'Heure
du Mouvement Ouvrier," which began the press war. L'Echo des Iles
(May 15, 1972). SDP knew of Père Alain before he took over the official
Church paper. He was one of those producing the less formal paper,
Vie-Action, during 1971. See The People (August 25, 1971).

31. Le Nouveau Seychellois (February 2 and March 7, 1973).
On the Ferrari dismissal, see The People (December 13, 1972).
Ferrari ran unsuccessfully for the assembly under the SPUP's banner in
the 1974 election.

32. Lecture by Professor Walter James, March 5, 1973, to
Seychelles Society; partially reported by Seychelles Bulletin (March
7, 1973).

33. The People (October 9, 1974).

34. ICFTU was represented by Lennart Kindstrom, who
arrived from the regional office in Addis Ababa, May 6, 1972. He
was preceded in December 1971 by Paul Kanyago of the same office.
Afro-American Labor Center's Gerry Funk visited earlier in 1972.
For the SPUP view of lack of labor leadership, see The People (November
8, 1972). For an example of party competition for the unions, see
"Moulinie vs. Sinon," The People (July 22, 1972 and January 17, 1973)

35. Conversation with an official of TODA, March 15, 1973.

36. Seychelles Bulletin (March 14 and 28, 1974). On the difficulties of organizing effective cooperatives, see Seychelles Government, Biennial Report of Cooperative Development, 1969-70 (Victoria,
1971).

37. Descriptions of the Seychellois are found in Benedict, People of the Seychelles (London, 1966); Guy Lionnet, The Seychelles (Newton Abbott, Devon, England, David and Charles, 1972), Ch. 7; and A. W. T. Webb, "The People of Seychelles," The Seychelles Annual (1962), pp. 41-45.

38. As an example of what it sees as a SPUP-promoted black cultural offensive from Africa, the SDP cites the derogatory article in Sunday News of Dar es Salaam (March 23, 1972). Quoted with SDP editorial views in Seychelles Weekly (August 12, 1972).

39. Seychelles Bulletin (June 12, 18, and 22, 1974).

40. The People (September 4, 1974). These foreign policy arguments are also covered in Seychelles Bulletin (March 22 and 25, April 3 and 29, May 20, 1974), and The People (July 3, 1974); New York Times (May 19, 1974). The clearest statement of Mancham's foreign policy views is found in proceedings of United Nations, Committee on Decolonization, May 17, 1974; on BIOT, the most exhaustive local treatment appeared in The People (November 6, 1974), which included the text of the "Indian Ocean-Zone of Peace" conference memorandum, held in Tananarive, October 13 and 14, 1974. Guy Sinon of the SPUP attended.

41. For stories of atrocities on Zanzibar, see Seychelles Weekly (November 14, 1972). For SPUP's mirth when the SDP was later forced to be polite to a touring deputation of Zanzibaris, see The People (September 18, 1974). The SDP gave big play to Amin's ruthlessness toward Asians, in "Points of View on Uganda," Seychelles Weekly (September 30, and November 25, 1972). The SDP on Nkrumah's undemocratic rule in Ghana, Seychelles Weekly (September 9, 1972).

42. East African Standard (October 5, 1972), reporting Chief Minister Mancham's remarks at the opening of the Seychelles Festival. For the SPUP's view, see "BIOT Throws out Islands' Natives," The People (November 3 and 19, 1971 and November 8, 1972). On SPUP discussions with Government of Somalia on Indian Ocean strategy, see The People (February 21, 1973). On NATO role in the Indian Ocean, The People (March 14, 1973). On the SDP view, see Seychelles Weekly (October 17, 1972).

43. Seychelles Weekly (January 20, 1973). For a fuller account of OAU reasoning, see West Africa (January, 1973).

44. Seychelles Weekly (October 16, 1974). Mancham's UN speech is found in Committee on Decolonization (May 17, 1974). For the SPUP's attack on allowing SAA flights, The People (September 18, 1974).

45. The People (September 22, 1971). SDP's view on the Maldives, Seychelles Weekly (July 8, 1972).

46. The People (November 22, 1972). The SDP's view on Réunion, Seychelles Weekly (May 27, 1972).

47. The SPUP's The People has printed long articles on the Comoros situation (November 2, 8, and 15, and December 6, 1972). The Seychelles Weekly report appeared January 20, 1973.

48. Seychelles Weekly (November 18, 1972).

49. As the SPUP puts it, "Our people will go to England to do catering and Englishmen will come here to get the good jobs!" The People (October 20, 1971). Also see the SPUP's view on appointment of assistant Labor commissioner, The People (October 20, 1971) and on the government obstetrician-gynecologist (December 13, 1972).

50. See Seychelles Weekly (November 18 and 25, 1972), on hiring of a public relations officer. On the expatriate management staff at Reef Hotel, see Seychelles Weekly (January 13, 1973). On employing competent Seychellois at hotels generally, see Seychelles Weekly, (September 23, 1973).

51. For statistics on tourism's growth, Safari (December 11, 1972). In 1972 Seychelles joined ATOI (Alliance Touristique de l'Océan Indien) and hosted the 1973 meeting.

52. Government of Seychelles, Tourism Development in the Seychelles (Victoria, 1971).

53. See Land Development and Town and Country Planning Ordinances in Colony of Seychelles, A Collection of Subsidiary Legislation: 1971 (Victoria, 1971).

54. Tatler rated Seychelles 1972's "most fashionable resort," and Chief Minister Mancham stated after the October Seychelles Festival that he would like to see the islands turned into a "festival center." But for an adverse report, see Seychelles Weekly (January 20, 1973), with a reprinted article from the Liverpool Daily Post, reporting the refund of 22,000 pounds to irate guests of the unfinished Coral Strand Hotel.

55. The conservation policies can be studied in John Proctor, Conservation in the Seychelles (Victoria, 1970) and Government of Seychelles, Conservation Policy in the Seychelles (Victoria, 1971).

56. The People (April 18, 1973).

57. See the letter from Regina Mundi Convent students to The People (July 29, 1972). Also the graphic description of degenerate tourists in The People (April 18, 1973), and the SPUP's heavy publicity of an "incident" involving the minister of Social Services and a tourist, Mrs. C. Sinex, The People (July 18, 1973). On wage levels, see The People (October 11, 1972); see also "Hotel Chef Slaps Clerk" (January 20, 1973), and an article on December 6, 1972, criticizing the gains from tourism for foreigners rather than for Seychellois. On discrimination in hiring, The People (August 19, 1972).

58. The People (November 15, 1972). See also L'Echo des Iles (September 1, 1972), questioning the value of continually calling the Seychelles "paradise"—a theme that might lull people into complacency. "Ce'est là de la reclame pour attirer les touristes. . . .

On n'est pas obligé de tout croire! . . . Elle endort l'homme. Elle le rend aveugle et sourd à ses frères."

59. On Mancham's personal activities, see Daily Express (London) (May 11, 1974), and The People (June 26, 1974).

60. The People (December 13, 1972, and January 31, 1973).

61. Seychelles Weekly (December 16, 1972).

62. Seychelles Weekly (May 25, 1972). "In Permanent Opposition" shows that the SDP feels justified in taking any means necessary to deal with the threat of the SPUP. See also letter from Chief Minister Mancham to Governor: Seychelles Weekly (July 15, 1972). After the 1974 election Mancham did make more magnanimous statements concerning the value of opposition: Seychelles Bulletin (June 24, 1974). Regarding the Church, see Seychelles Weekly (June 17 and October 14, 1972, and January 20, 1972). For the Church's rebuttal: L'Echo des Iles (May 5 and February 1, 1972). For the SPUP's view on Church-state relations, see The People (January 21 and October 11 and 18, 1972).

63. Seychelles Government, Report on the Budget Session of the Legislative Assembly (Victoria, 1973).

64. The SPUP's general view on the role of violence in the Seychelles can be read in The People (June 21 and November 15, 1972). On redistricting, see The People (November 8, 1972, and February 2 and April 4, 1973). Each of these articles includes only slightly veiled threats about the alternatives to electoral reform.

65. The People (July 3, 1974). See also June 13 and May 22, 1974.

66. The People (July 1, 1973; August 19, 1973; September 4, 1974); and particularly, S. Bouchereau, "Musings and Amusing," The People (August 17, 1974).

8

MAURITIUS:
THE ILE DE FRANCE
RETURNS
Philip M. Allen

On March 12, 1968, the flag of independence rose for the first time over a lost island plagued with civil strife . . . and settled at half mast. Bitterly resisted by a third of the Mauritian electorate for a decade before 1968, independence appeared destined to compound the Malthusian anguish of an abandoned micro-state in an overheated ocean.

Seven years later, Mauritius promises to set a pace for development of a minuscule monocrop economy, and perhaps even to act as catalyst for the hitherto illusory union of the Western Indian Ocean. Diligent pursuit of markets for the island's sovereign crop of cane sugar, imaginative labor-intensive industrial projects, agricultural diversification, and family planning have encouraged fairly steady growth in a still unsteady social setting. Progress has been registered without entailing solutions to social dilemmas or a coherent international commitment to any side. Relative stability has cost a considerable ransom of civil liberties in a once fairly open society.

While the lids remain fixed over seething cauldrons at home, Mauritian statecraft has bought time and planted prosperity by foraging abroad. Mauritian policy has ventured boldly out over seas of power maneuvers and comparative ideologies. It has been caught on lengthy tangents and often had to digest its own statesmen's words. Enjoying, perhaps, a mini-state privilege of relative irresponsibility among greater powers, Mauritius has evoked flurries of misunderstanding abroad and sustained dissension at home. But the essential domestic conflict has changed subjects, for the time being at least: political controversy has replaced ethnocommunal animosity as the source of division within Mauritius society. If this conversion proves durable, the pragmatic young nation will have provided an answer to its overriding preoccupation: how to chart the trajectory from a heterogeneity of communities into a Mauritian nation.

MAP 8.1

Mauritius

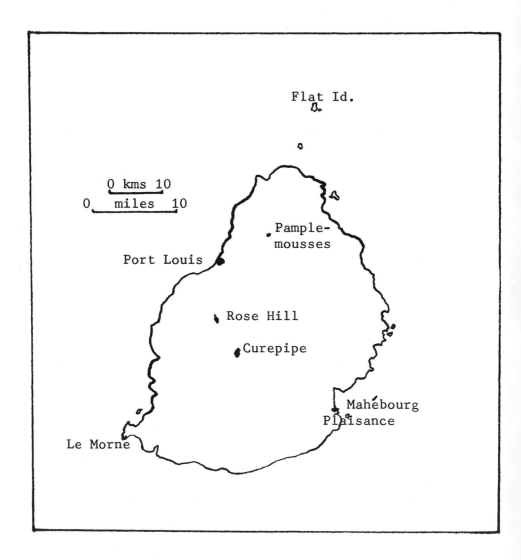

PARADOXES OF HERITAGE

Middle island of the volcanic Mascarene group, lying between Réunion, 200 miles to the west, and Rodrigues, 350 miles to the east, Mauritius nests ovally within a garland of reefs. A half-dozen peaks rise to between 2,000 and 2,700 feet over a central plateau, capturing quantities of rain for ubiquitous canefields and flower gardens. Water torrents and good paved roads interlace over the steep slopes of the island's 720 square miles, down to the torrid coasts. The oval measures 39 miles from north to south, 29 miles at its broadest east-west girth. Madagascar is 500 miles to the west, Mombasa 1,100 miles northwest, India 2,400 miles northeast. The next stop eastward is Perth, Australia.

While Mauritius possesses fertile soils, ample fishing beds, two good harbors, a literate population, and self-evident tourist assets, it has no known mineral resources and no room for expansion. At 1,150 inhabitants per square mile, it represents one of the world's most densely populated agricultural landscapes. Isolation and over-population are the beginning of Mauritius's troubles.

Only isolation, however, at the very beginning: Until Dutch and British sailing ships found it conveniently stationed between the Cape of Good Hope and the East Indies, Mauritius lay neglected by man. It had been flung too far south of the monsoon trade-wind system, too often visited by cyclones (hurricanes), too treacherously wreathed in coral, to interest the Arab, Malay, and Swahili seamen who preceded the Europeans in the ancient Sea of Zanj. Hence, "Dina-robin," as the Arabs called it, cordially welcomed the Dutch refreshment station installed there in 1638, fourteen years before the first Hollanders settled on the Cape. But this Mauritius (named for Prince Maurice of Nassau, Holland's lord) was to rise and fall like a minor star before reaching its present perilous upward pathway as a modern state.[1]

The Dutch bunkering station collapsed in 1710 after maritime technology enabled merchantmen to run from the Cape to the Indies along lower latitudes south of the Mascarene cyclone zone. During that Dutch occupation, from 1638 to 1710, Mauritius lost its population of indigenous dodo birds and giant land tortoises, easy prey for hungry men. Its magnificent forest also ebbed away and now remains only in sylvan tokens around the mountain slopes. Sugar cane had been started by the Dutch, and a few former slaves (maroons) were left in the hills when French shippers and planters arrived from Bourbon Island (Réunion) in 1721 to begin a permanent settlement.

Bringing slaves from Madagascar and East Africa, artisans from southern India, and marginalia from European society, the French East India Company used their renamed Ile de France for

cultivation of coffee, spices, and sugar, as well as a maritime base.
When the French Crown took possession in 1767, the island offered
a haven for corsairs who preyed on foreign shipping (mainly British)
through the end of Napoleonic wars. A romantic 18th century society
bloomed in Ile de France, bred in an alliance of exotic innocence
and the manners of the Bourbon court. Mauritian noble savagery was
celebrated in J. H. Bernardin de Saint Pierre's idyll, Paul et Virginie,
whose purpose was to depict "the moral beauty of a small society." The
more civilized virtues found admirable examples in the illustrious
Governor Mahé de la Bourdonnais, the courtly De Caen, defender of
the island against the English, the corsair Baron Surcouf of St. Malo,
and the great green-thumbed botanist Pierre Poivre.

French power and France's name fell from the island in 1810,
when a British siege put Ile de France out of action for Napoleon. In
the Treaty of Paris (1814), Britain tossed Réunion back, retaining
Mauritius under its restored Dutch name, as well as the dependencies
of Seychelles to the northwest, the Chagos and other small islands to
the north, and Rodrigues. The Seychelles were separated in 1903.
The Chagos archipelago, including Diego Garcia atoll, Pergos-Banhos,
and Solomon islets were removed from Mauritius's patrimony on
November 8, 1965 and combined with Aldabra, Farquhar, and Des
Roches (previously part of Seychelles) as the British Indian Ocean
Territory.

Although semiautonomous Mauritius consented to "sell" the
Chagos (population about 500 seasonal workers), the 1965 UN General
Assembly voted a resolution censuring Britain for "dismembering"
the colony prior to Independence, then scheduled for the following
year.[2] Controversy on the island itself centered less over the
principle of territorial amputation than over (1) the allegedly cheap
price of 3 million pounds accepted by Mauritius and (2) the United
Kingdom's announced intentions, confirmed a year later in an exchange
of notes with the United States, to use the BIOT for defense purposes.
Construction of a joint U.K.-U.S. naval communications facility
began on Diego Garcia in March 1971, and the installation has been
substantially expanded since that time, thus furnishing considerable
grist for the mills of militant neutralism.

Unlike the Chagos, Rodrigues, with 25,000 people on 40 square
miles of sultry, heavily eroded farmland has remained an administrative dependency of Mauritius. So have the islets of Agalega, 580
miles to the north, and Cargados, shoals 250 miles northeast, also
known by the name of their principal component, St. Brandon.

Swashbuckling French Mauritius calmed into doldrums under
the 19th-century pax Brittanica and dropped out of the tighter sea-
lanes created by the Suez Canal. But British colonial sovereignty
proved to be as light-handed on Mauritius as anywhere in the dominions
of "indirect rule." France had begun its insular civilization, and

France's heirs were welcome to continue the job under distant English
eyes. The plantation and commercial institutions remained in the
hands of 70-odd Franco-Mauritian families, although their slaves
were taken away from them in 1833-38. Emancipated Africans,
Malagasy, and mulatto (Creole) plantation workers fled en masse
to the towns, leaving a severe shortage of labor for the rapidly
expanding cane fields. Under British authority, indentured workers
from Hindu Bombay and other regions of India filled the gaps, albeit
at significant demographic and political price. The Hindu laborers
tended to settle in Mauritius and bring their familes after the ex-
piration of their five-year contracts. Some purchased tiny plots for
sugar cane and vegetables; others became sharecroppers. Numbering
about 150,000 before the turn of the century, they represent a 52
percent majority of the island's 863,000 population in 1974.

Sugar cane production amounted to 70,000 tons in 1853, to 150,
000 tons in 1900, to 680,000 tons in 1963, and to 718,000 tons in the
record year of 1973. Mauritius is Africa's second largest sugar
producer. It passed Australia in 1965 as Britain's primary supplier.

Extensive sugar cultivation for English dessert habits made
Mauritius's fortune but, in the process of so doing, converted 93
percent of the cultivated land surface (equivalent of 45 percent of
the entire island) into cane. The final forests gave way to plantations
reaching well up the mountain slopes and crowding the island's road-
sides. Thus the colony became gravely and perhaps permanently
dependent on imports of rice and other vital foodstuffs, timber, raw
materials, and manufactured goods, adjusting its recalcitrant balance
of trade through the help of sterling zone devices.

In addition to the monocrop economy, Britain introduced its
overseas banking system to Mauritius, established an Anglican
cathedral with a sparse attendance in Port Louis, the capital, built
a flower-bedecked road system with wrong-hand drive, instituted
a Crown Colony administration headed by a governor responsible to
Whitehall, and made English an official language spoken only by the
elite (and then only rarely with fluency). English residents of the
island seldom numbered more than 300, most of them on limited
assignments in government, business, and finance.

To this day, Mauritius has remained essentially French in its
"high culture," French creole in its lingua franca, Roman Catholic
in the religion of its so-called general population (Europeans and
mixed bloods), and Asian largely in its underprivileged mass.[3] Trade
and day-to-day government business, secondary schooling, street
signs, a certain amount of elegant poetry and scholarship, and chic
fashions all follow impulses from Paris carried over silent waves
and sounding seas to the former Ile de France. The French consul
and the Alliance Francaise preceded all other foreign representation
on the island. Paris is today a metropole equally as important to

Mauritius as London or New Delhi. Yet, throughout the colonial period and its aftermath, Britain remained for the island's francophone classes a bulkhead against the tides of Asian people with inevitably rising expectations. And the governing coalitions have kept the faith: Giving no sign of a republican spirit, Mauritius has stayed independent under the Queen. Since 1973, Sir Raman Osman, a Mauritian, has been Her Majesty's governor general.

COMMUNITIES IN POLITICS

As in other parts of the post-World War II empire, Britain's relinquishment of Mauritius in 1968 had the earmarks of a flagrant evacuation "east of Suez." Few independent states even at that time were so small, so economically fragile, or so unreconciled to national objectives. The island was isolated, densely packed, volatile, dependent on a monocrop at the ruthless mercy of Indian Ocean meteorology, unable to demonstrate consensus on any major issue, least of all on the issue of sovereignty.[4] Politics were determined by the interests of ethnic communities living in abrasive juxtaposition with nowhere else to go.

Communal pluralism in Mauritius developed over the last century, when thousands of Hindus arrived too late, or under too exceptional circumstances, to join the process of "creolization" among blacks, whites, and earlier Asian arrivals. Unlike Réunion, and particularly the Seychelles, where that slow process pursued its homogenizing way, Mauritius experienced arrested sociological development: A sudden Asian majority occupied the lowest economic ranks by 1900. The erstwhile Creole (colored) proletariat perforce became an ethnic lower middle class, joining the inveterately unassimilable Muslim and Chinese traders in the towns and fishing villages of the island. The white Franco-Mauritian aristocracy, left intact by British authority, retained as much "purity" as it could in this tropical enclave of cultural France.

And so these self-segregated communities subsist today, hierarchically arrayed on a sociological scale, but packed geographically into a minuscule island landscape.[5] Mortgaged to seasons of toil on the fields of cane, the 450,000 Hindus have made up in numbers for what they lacked in privilege. Their political champion since the 1930s has been Sir Seewoosagur Ramgoolam, a high-caste physician with a London degree who began his public career four decades ago agitating for improvements in the treatment of the cane field proletariat. Ramgoolam's moderate but efficacious platform emphasized independence first, social change later. He has had to resist the splintering of his Hindu constituency into factions reflecting castes

or ideologies dedicated to reversing those priorities. His Mauritius
Labour Party has suffered defections over the years but has remained
on top. Now, as the island responds to relatively progressive strategies
in a climate of hopefulness, Ramgoolam sees the Hindus increasingly
divided along generational, rather than ideological or religious lines.

Consistently and alone since World War II, Labour has clung to
nationalist—as opposed to protectionist, communal chauvinist, or
imperial—objectives. From 1947, when limited politics was authorized
in Mauritius, through the advent of universal adult suffrage in 1959,
Ramgoolam and Labour steadily pressed for increased national autonomy under majority rule. Stimulated by the Bandung conference in
1955 and the waves of self-determination in Africa after 1957, Mauritius obtained recognition in 1961 of its right to independence through
successive constitutional stages. Ramgoolam as leader of the majority
party (Labour had obtained 23 of 40 parliamentary seats) became
chief minister with prerogatives of consultation on internal matters
by the governor. The former Executive Council was reconstituted as
a Council of Ministers.

In the elections of October 21, 1963, a controversy mounted
over the implications of independence, Labour's legislative representation dropped to 19, beneath the absolute majority, but the margin
was restored by electoral alliances with the Muslim Action Committee (MAC). The four Muslim MPs helped replace Hindu defections
to the more radical, albeit neo-Gandhian Independent Foreward Bloc
(IFB), led by schoolteacher Sookdeo Bissoondoyal. After a conference
at London in February 1964, Mauritius received the title of Self-Governing Crown Colony, the Legislative Council became the Legislative
Assembly, and Ramgoolam was named prime minister. The Crown
retained powers over foreign affairs and national security, as well
as a legislative veto and the prerogative to appoint up to 15 MPs
above the elected 40 in order to attain political and social equilibrium
in the Legislative Assembly. Final constitutional talks began in
1965 after Ramgoolam had succeeded in forming an all-party governmental coalition to seek a national consensus.

While the hallowed Westminsterian route had been successfully
negotiated to this point, every increment of self-government had
been contested on political and ethnic-communal grounds. The all-
party coalition was to fail, and the ultimate negotiations for independence to extend over almost three years. In fact, Whitehall decided
during late 1965 to continue Mauritius toward independence "without
the benefit of unanimous advice from the [Mauritian] delegates to
the conference."[6] After another year, a British electoral commission
managed to obtain general agreement on a new complex voting system
under which the island was divided into 20 three-member constituencies
(plus two members for Rodrigues) and eight seats for the highest
scoring "runners-up."

Most resistance to independence has come from Mauritius' largest minority, the Creoles, a community wrought over three centuries of cohabitation among Europeans, Africans, Malagasy, and Asians. Their 19th-century ancestors resolutely turned their backs on the bondage of cane, preferring urban trades and fishing to the work they had done until 1833 as slaves. Latter-day politics has brought the Creoles into alliance with their old masters, the Franco-Mauritians, who remain landed proprietors, industrialists, and city bourgeoisie. (See Table 8.1.) The 250,000 Creoles and less than 10,000 whites share a highly literate, Roman Catholic, French-speaking heritage and a venerable opposition movement, the Mauritian Social Democratic Party (PMSD—known as the Parti Mauricien [PM] until 1964 and still occasionally identified without the "Social Democratic" appendage).

Although not so comfortable in colonialism as the European patricians, the Creoles have made much of their cultural opportunities under francophone tutelage. Accepting antitheses of Western versus Asian, Christian versus Hindu-Muslim, urban versus rural, they generally admit few affinities with the Africa of their origins, and they have traditionally feared the vicissitudes of an unprotected state of sovereignty dominated by an Asian ethnic majority. A small but important number of liberal Creoles nonetheless support Ramgoolam's Labour Party. On tiny, poverty-stricken Rodriques island, the predominantly Creole population has occasionally expressed these inclinations by seeking to secede from independent Mauritius.

A Muslim community of 135,000, which gathered on the island at different periods starting in the 18th century remains politically split. Half the community follows Sir Abdul Razack Mohamed's MAC in its alliance with Labour, while the other half supports the PMSD out of an affinity for the artisans and traders of the Creole world. Within these larger political groupings, however, both Muslim factions tend to press in favor of constitutional safeguards and social justice for minorities.

Like the Muslims, smaller minorities of Tamil- and Telegu-speaking Hindus, arriving while the island was still French, adhere more readily to the European-Creole PMSD where their numbers (about 40,000), their professional skills, and their vested economic interests appear better served than in merger with the Hindustani-speaking majority.

A Chinese trader class of about 22,000 occupies traditional positions in the Port Louis import-export structure and local retail commerce. Flexible in their allegiances, the Sino-Mauritians have played as many sides of the Mauritian poltical contests as necessary for survival.

TABLE 8.1

Mauritius Communities and Their Politics

Community	Population (1974)	Percent Population	Economic Position	Traditional Politics
Hindu	450,000	52	Agric. labor, farmers	Labour, IFB
Creole	250,000	29	Artisans, fishermen, service trades, and professions	PMSD, some Labour
Muslim	135,000	15	Merchants, craftsmen, urban labor	Split between MAC and PMSD
Chinese	22,000	3	Shopkeepers	PMSD, Labour
European	8,000	1	Industry, professions, plantations	PMSD

Source: Compiled by the author.

ANTAGONISMS IN SELF-DETERMINATION

This pattern of organized, self-conscious, chauvinistic ethnic communities has plagued Mauritian politics with violence for the past 15 years. Street tactics became a fixture of electoral campaigns by 1963 when the PMSD's young deputy leader Gaetan Duval assumed the sobriquet "King Creole" and donned a modified paratrooper wardrobe to engage forces with rival Indo-Mauritian bully boys. After obtaining 19.5 percent of the October 1963 vote (half the amount scored by Labour) and 8 seats in the legislature (to Labour's 19), Duval's supporters demonstrated impressively in Port Louis against their party's exclusion from Ramgoolam's government. The demonstrations forced postponement of the opening of parliament that December and foreshadowed the unhappy circumstances of Mauritius's turbulent accession to independence over four years later.

As a popular young lawyer in Curepipe, Duval had already attracted Ramgoolam's attention, but the future prime minister was unable to win Duval's urban Creoles away from the bourgeois Parti Mauricien (now PMSD), then led by Queen's Counsel Jules Koenig and other white patricians. Duval's disciplined Creole militants with their flair for quasi-fascist tours de force dominated the sedate PMSD far more easily than Ramgoolam's Hindu-oriented Labour Party. Duval could thus play an important countervailing role to Ramgoolam's within the communal and ideological dialectic. The Parti Mauricien old guard never recovered from this new wave of urban populism. They suffered the addition of "social democratic" to the party name in 1964, permitting Duval to compete for recognition with Labour Party leaders in European-dominated circles.

More important, Duval's choice to transfigure the PMSD and thus to confront, rather than join, Ramgoolam also assured that Mauritius's constellation of political parties would remain congruent with prevailing ethnocentric communal divisions. This lamentable stamp remained fixed over Mauritian politics even after March 1964, when Ramgoolam succeeded in attracting the PMSD and the agrarian Hindu IFB into his all-party government dedicated to seeking independence with minority communal safeguards, a consensus that proved illusory the next year. Duval then served as minister of Housing, Lands, and Planning, and Koenig became attorney general.

Despite Ramgoolam's skillful use of his modest electoral majorities through the 1960s, the pressures building up within Mauritius seemed to represent internal communal antagonisms rather than a Mauritian national sensibility forcing itself against colonialism. Fearful of social upheaval under majority rule and wary of the appetites of international communist leviathans, the island's propertied classes began exporting capital, skills, and families out of the country

well before independence became scheduled. But most whites and
Creoles stayed in Mauritius and fought against the inevitable. Instead
of casting the island adrift, as they saw it, Britain might choose to
relieve its internal pressures first. The 1960 Congo tragedies and
the even closer 1963-64 massacres on Zanzibar stood as warnings
against impulsive grants of independence to unprepared, multiracial,
prerevolutionary societies. In the past, several sage British commissions had predicted violence and misery if the population growth
were not curbed from its 3.5 percent heights in 1963 and the economy
not relieved by job creation and labor emigration. [7]

Property owners repudiated the idea of Mauritian independence
under any conditions. Since it often appeared that the Hindus wished
for sovereignty only because Britain was offering it, the more privileged
Franco-Mauritians and Creoles typically interpreted a British departure
from the island as a concession to ethnic and social radicalism and
only secondarily as the fruit of Mauritian national feeling. Civic dis-
orders, no longer restricted to election campaigns, seemed to support
this jaundiced assessment.

Yet the PMSD "Tories" obtained little satisfaction from the
governor, J. S. Rennie, or the successive high-level British missions
that witnessed the instability of Mauritian communities. Colonial
Secretary Anthony Greenwood visited the island in April 1965 during
an uproar between Hindus and Muslims, which tended to reflect in
microcosm the contemporary international conflicts between India
and Pakistan. On May Day, rioting left three persons dead, and the
governor called for troops from Aden to pacify the island. Yet four
months later, on September 25, a constitutional conference scheduled
independence for no later than the end of 1966, after six months of
self-government. Communal turmoil and the search for satisfactory
electoral formulas prolonged that apprenticeship for more than a year,
and still no real Mauritian consensus had been reached.

Unable to block constitutional change, the PMSD launched appeals
to London for consideration of some sort of adjusted dependent status—
on the "Channel Islands" formula, the Ulster model, or the "departmental" situation of nearby Réunion within metropolitan France.
(Note many of the same examples—minus Ulster—invoked again
fruitlessly by the Seychelles Democratic Party, this time presuming
to speak for a majority.) Although the PMSD spoke as a coalition
member at the 1965 negotiations with three ministers out of 14 and
11 seats (three of them appointive) out of 52 in the Legislative Assembly,
its successive suggestions were rejected. A last-ditch plea to test
the level of self-determination through a French-style referendum
proved equally unavailing. London seemed to be forcing its own will
for decolonization on a partially reluctant territory.

The closing sessions of the September 1965 constitutional conference were boycotted by the PMSD delegates, who also refused to sign
the final communiqué setting 1966 as the year for independence. On

November 13, the PMSD ministerial trio left Ramgoolam's 20-month-old "grand coalition." Reinforced by minority defectors from Labour, the MAC, and IFB, Duval's forces agreed to the Banwell Commission's new election rules in June 1966 and vowed to destroy the specter of independence at the polls. Here, as in other instances, Ramgoolam temporized, hoping to win back the defectors in time to keep the elections from constituting an unofficial referendum. Moreover, 1966 was proving a poor year for sugar cane.

To the outrage of his opposition, which eventually resigned their parliamentary seats in protests, the prime minister managed to postpone the elections until August 7, 1967, entailing a 14-month delay in the original decolonization timetable. Sugar was doing better, and domestic turbulence had quieted. Yet the PMSD still came close to an upset, winning 44 percent of the total vote and 23 seats (out of 62) in the enlarged legislature. Four "best loser" seats brought Duval's party representation to 27 (out of 70). Labour tallied an equal number of seats on fewer votes, but its electoral allies, the MAC and IFB, obtained 5 and 11 places respectively, thus giving Ramgoolam a 43-27 majority, with a combined total of 54 percent of the ballot (2 percent went to nonpartisan candidates). The election was certified valid by British observers, and the date for independence was set for March 12, 1968, six months after the inception of full internal self-government. Had Duval been able to estrange the Hindu IFB away from Ramgoolam, their customary state of relations before and after this period of constitutional crisis, he could have forced London to renegotiate the disputed 1965 accords.

Thus Britain ceded sovereignty, as it seemed, to an irrepressible Hindu proletariat led by an astute party politician who claimed to represent a fictitious Mauritian nation. The deed to independence was wrapped in constitutional fustian designed to appeal to the apprehensions of the minorities, most of them allied with Duval's PMSD. Entrenched safeguards within the new constitution included the elaborate electoral procedure aimed at ensuring proportional parliamentary representation (the so-called best-loser system); an ombudsman for civil rights litigation; rights of appeal to the Queen's Privy Council; the theoretical privilege of legislative veto by the Queen's governor general. Amendment to the entrenched constitutional provisions requires a vote of three-fourths of the entire Legislative Assembly. A defense agreement between the United Kingdom and independent Mauritius permits British intervention in cases of civil disorder, but only on request of the Mauritian Government.

On Independence Day in 1968 Mauritius was the same inchoate polity, the same communal pressure cooker, the same vulnerable economy it had been for a half-century. Rioting resumed in January 1968 and eventually cost 26 lives. The governor again called a state of emergency. Now that the island was free, the solutions to its

Malthusian problems seemed to confront even more powerful odds than before: Crop diversification for food production required sacrificing cane fields; land reform would reduce the efficiency of sugar production and thus weaken Mauritius's competitive position at a time when markets were hard to find; family planning encountered resistance in Hindu, Muslim, and Roman Catholic orthodoxy; emigration applied realistically only to those Mauritians with skills and ethnicity acceptable in Europe, South Africa, Canada, or Australia—hence excluding the overflow Hindu poor. Industrialization had to cope with an absence of raw materials and of skills in the semieducated labor force, as well as a minuscule domestic market and vast distances to most prospective overseas sources of demand and supply. Shipping depended on an Indian Ocean maritime conference addicted to raising rates on any pretext.

Independent Mauritius lacked a firm basis for the creation of a truly national mythology. It had no traditional institutions except those supplied by the departed Europeans. With the communal cauldron at boiling point, the island seemed condemned to seek perpetual overseas protection from itself. On March 13, 1968, the day after Independence, 1,500 Mauritians, mostly Creoles, sailed for a new life in Australia.

POLITICS AS A NATION

Despite these inauspicious beginnings, Mauritius did not follow the unhappy example of Congo or Zanzibar or stagnant Equatorial Guinea or Dahomey. At times the new Mauritius seems on the way to a 20th-century revival of the busy freebooting and big-little precocity of the 18th-century Ile de France. Nevertheless, the nation was born in bloodshed, and it has been kept intact by force. Strikes of critical labor dislocated the economy seriously in 1971, and the resultant social and political confusion prompted a perennial grant of emergency powers for law enforcement. Ethnocentric communities remain hostile to one another. Sugar still dominates the economy through fat years and lean. Only the skilled or well-educated, those whom the island needs most, can find jobs outside Mauritius.

And yet the distinct line of Mauritian political development since 1968 has not followed the old parallelogram of ethnic forces. Nor has government policy been forced to choose between the proverbial camps of pro-Westerns and positive neutralists. Foreign affairs, vital to an economy chained like Mauritius's to external trade, have been remarkably casuistical—pragmatic at best, opportunistic if a ministate can be reproached for "dealing" in favor of its own survival.

Ramgoolam knew well before Independence that his inexperienced team would be engaged in an intricate game of statecraft and power politics.[8] Few optimists could have predicted so brisk a resumption of international free-sailing after 150 years as a quiet colony.

Radicalism on Mauritius used to be identified entirely with (1) unsubstantiated rumors of communist conspiracy, usually whenever any union leader or student accepted a trip to Moscow, and (2) a series of relatively atavistic Hindu movements. A short-lived All-Mauritian Hindu League took part in some of the street brawls of 1964-65, but its leaders overstepped legality and its political audience disappeared when Bissoondoyal's Independent Forward Bloc joined the pre-Independence all-party coalition. The IFB itself has maintained a colorful if ineffective opposition effort toward agrarian reform. Its parliamentary deputies have the habit of walking out on major confrontation.

As the Labour Party neared its main objective, Independence, it was obliged to concede points to the more conservative communities and parties. This process lost Ramgoolam most of the socialists in his movement. Labour proved more "social democratic" than the PMSD, more respectful of property than any of the radical ethnic movements.

Following the first shocks of 1968, the PMSD discovered both the inevitability and the tolerability of Independence. Duval accompanied Ramgoolam on several international tours, and the two leaders sparred toward a new coalition. Reconciled first to a "constructive opposition" role, then to Ramgoolam's refusal to hold immediate new elections, the PMSD agreed to furnish six ministers out of a 21-member cabinet in December 1969.

This apparent opening to the right provoked the defection of the IFB and reinforced a new political movement among intellectual, unemployed, and alienated youth. Several false starts marked the gestation period of the "new left" in Mauritius. All were stimulated by controversy over putative Western military designs in the Indian Ocean. Rumors had circulated since 1963 over British, U.S., and occasionally South African ambitions on Mauritius itself. The United Kingdom has had a naval radar station there since World War II, and the United States operated space tracking facilities on Madagascar (NASA) and Seychelles (Air Force) since the early 1960s. Speculation intensified with escalation in Vietnam and British retrenchment east of Suez. Separation of the Chagos archipelago and the creation of the BIOT focused conjecture on Diego Garcia in Mauritius's erstwhile domains. A petition from one M. Ayaperoumall, purporting to represent an (otherwise invisible) Mauritius Communist Party, alerted the United Nations on November 29, 1965 to the "storm of indignation . . . sweeping through the island."

Most conspicuous of a number of such one-man "secretariats" was the Mauritius People's Progressive Party (PPP), whose representative, Teekaram Sibsurrun, warned frequent international conferences of the imminent nuclearization of the area. Although the PPP received funds from several sources, it lacked a political base and was soon swallowed up by the more dynamic Mouvement Militant Mauritien (MMM). Nevertheless, Sibsurrun's pronouncements represent a prelude to the current serious drama between sponsors of the Indian Ocean "zone of peace" and the intruding great powers.[9]

Organized by Paul Bérenger, South African-born son of an affluent Franco-Mauritian family, the MMM took root in the worldwide convulsions of 1968. It brought the sense of "confrontation politics" and "direct democracy" into a Mauritian political spectrum vacant on the left. And it came at a time when, thanks to Ramgoolam's handling of the independence dilemmas, Mauritius was prepared for political controversy that cut across purely ethnic-communal lines. By 1970, the MMM claimed 20,000 members and had aroused the usual insular speculation regarding supplies of "Chinese weapons." It had successfully replaced dead-wood ideologues and communal chauvinists in a dozen unions among the island's already well-organized labor movement and put Dev Virahswamy into the Legislative Assembly through a byelection in 1971. Successful MMM strikes were staged during 1970 and 1971 in the sugar industry and in the port and commercial institutions. The PMSD-Labour coalition, faced with an MMM threat to its control of urban administrations, abolished elected municipal councils, and replaced them with appointed commissions.

This move was among a number of transgressions of the civil process by a frightened regime during 1970 and 1971. The normally scheduled 1972 elections were canceled by legislative fiat in 1969, as were several byelections and local contests that might have tested the efficacy of government on the first six years of independence. After proscription of the MMM unions, several wage demands at the basis of the 1971 strikes were upheld in court. A Public Order Act passed in December 1970 permits the authorities to control public assembly, resort to preventive detention, and hamstring a lively and usually responsible island press. Fifty MMM political and labor leaders were jailed on flimsy charges during 1971 and 1972. Their unions remained under ban until 1974 and the party newspaper Le Militant outlawed. Ramgoolam was in personal charge of security determinations at this time, and he appeared to be agreeing with many observers that Mauritius was on the verge of revolution.[10]

As in many other new states, the uncertainties of distinguishing national interest from political ambitions caused much of the desperation in which civil liberties were abused. Only in Mauritius the prime minister may be understood for overlooking the distinction, having himself personified the Mauritian nation for so long before it came into existence. Inevitably, power rivalries and corruption afflict the independence parties, including Ramgoolam's remarkably stable Labour-MAC directorate. The MAC chairman since the 1950s, Sir Abdul Razack Mohamed, admitted recently that in any imminent election, "all of us would find our votes reduced. Politicians here are not prepared to open their eyes."[11]

Yet the 74-year-old prime minister will have to find somebody sufficiently awake to receive the mantle of succession before too long. Satcam Boolell, minister of Agriculture and Natural Resources, and Virahsamy Ringadoo, minister of Finance, have strong followings in Labour's ranks, but the former is closely identified with Hindu chauvinism and Ringadoo is said to be in poor health. Neither has the age advantage of Duval, or Bérenger, for that matter, but if Ramgoolam plays true to form, he will hold his cards patiently until something happens, probably well after the contestants have given up.

Ramgoolam is frequently said to be "dickering" with Bérenger, as he did with Duval for years in the 1960s. Yet, the MMM too has had its thicks and thins. When Queen Elizabeth visited Mauritius in March 1972 to inaugurate the new university, her speech (delivered to thousands despite the ban on public assembly at the time) ignored the current state of emergency and the political detention of dozens of MMM activists. The leaders were gradually released and their unions restored to legality; reluctant dockworkers returned to full work days in February 1974 in exchange for a promised government industrial relations code.

But the MMM began to sag, weakened by government pressures no doubt, but also from within. Its lone parliamentary deputy, Virahswamy, resigned from the party in 1973. The Hindu leader Sooresh Moorba and the respected Creole intellectual Hervé Masson (editor of Le Militant) left in March 1973. Doctrinal ambiguities in the "Marxist but non-Communist" party line have complicated the task of Secretary General Bérenger, a self-styled "gradualist" who seeks power electorally while holding together a movement based on radical change.[12] Anirood Jugnauth has become MMM president and Cader Shayat vice president.

FOREIGN AFFAIRS: DUVAL'S RISE AND FALL

The PMSD rode an eccentric course in Sir Seewoosagur Ramgoolam's government from December 1969 to December 1973. Labour and the PMSD had already composed joint lists for municipal elections in March 1969, and they agreed to give the "grand coalition" a chance to mobilize all Mauritius, necessitating, so Ramgoolam persuaded Duval, a prolongation of the original Legislative Assembly beyond its terminal point of March 1972. Their collaboration condemned the IFB to opposition, but by then, Ramgoolam was strong enough to do without their 11 Hindu deputies who had ensured his victory in 1967.

PMSD's machismo champion, Duval, assumed the foreign affairs portfolio (previously held by the prime minister) in December 1969 and soon became identified with the development of strong bonds between Mauritius and France, the French-oriented African member states of OCAM, West Germany, and South Africa. Defending an activist Eur-African constituency at home, Duval proved most congenial in docile diplomacy among conservative powers abroad; whereas the gentle Asian Ramgoolam undertook a somewhat complementary, more "African" course: scrupulous cooperation with the OAU majority and UN African caucus, special cordiality with East African states and African liberation parties, careful attention to commonwealth affairs under India's guidance, and overtures to the USSR and China. However self-contradictory these approaches seemed, Mauritius was operating on a double diplomatic track toward an eclectic portfolio of foreign relations calculated to assure the new nation's security.

Well before Independence, Ramgoolam had struck normal sympathetic chords with India, France, Germany, Pakistan, Madagascar, and the newly emergent East African nations, in addition to attending OAU, Commonwealth, and UN technical agency meetings. The evident purpose of vigorous pre-Independence diplomacy was to begin correcting both the isolation and the obscurity of the fragile island, if not to find markets for sugar and for surplus population. This strategy was readily supported by Labour. The intrepidly pro-Western PMSD proved tolerant of any foreign policy, Duval's, Ramgoolam's, or otherwise, so long as the party's weight could be exerted against any jeopardy to land-holding, labor-industrial relations, the tax structure, and other economic priorities. Although communal prestige always endowed political actions with a tone of its own, PMSD leaders were too sophisticated to see their essential interests threatened by a visit to Peking or the port call of a Russian trawler.

As foreign minister under Ramgoolam, Duval lost none of his verve, but he did assert a new style in Mauritian diplomacy. Leaving bush jacket and paratrooper boots at home, Duval affected a frilled shirt, long-curly-haired, and flowery-necktied dandyism unusual in the buttoned down corridors of diplomacy. [13]

Duval and Ramgoolam disagreed on more than style, and they acted at cross-purposes on occasion. In November-December 1970, Duval resigned (briefly) after Ramgoolam signed a four-year trade and fisheries agreement with the Soviet Union; the foreign minister charged that the accord had alarmed the West and provoked a flight of

capital from Mauritius. He also remarked candidly that his own position had been weakened by the prime minister's meddling in foreign
affairs, acknowledging the defections of PMSD deputies to Maurice
Lesage's new, arch-conservative Mauritian Democratic Union (UDM).
Duval was soon back in the cabinet, but the UDM's Cyril Marchand
swept municipal elections at Curepipe (Duval's bailiwick, although he
had "graduated" to become Lord Mayor of Port Louis) in April 1971;
now it was the UDM's turn to insist, vainly, that Ramgoolam call
national elections on schedule.

Characteristically, Duval abstained from the OAU's 1970 condemnation of British and French arms sales to South Africa, while
Ramgoolam talked African liberation at home in the presence of
Indian Prime Minister Indira Gandhi. In the autumn of that year,
while Duval was courting South African investment, tourism, and tea
purchases, Ramgoolam denounced apartheid at the UN General Assembly. A month earlier, the prime minister had categorically rejected
"dialogue" with South Africa, but at the OAU meeting in June 1971,
Duval voted in favor of Ivory Coast President Houphouet-Boigny's
dialogue program (only five other states supported Houphouet).

Years after criticizing Ramgoolam for acceding to Western
exploitation of Diego Garcia, almost seeming to ally the PMSD with
neutralists, Duval emerged on November 2, 1970 with a public "offer"
of Mauritius itself as a naval base if the British should have to abandon
their Simonstown agreement with South Africa. Ramgoolam had to
deny the "offer" on February 5, 1971. In early 1972 at New Delhi,
the prime minister declared his opposition to any base rights for the
U.S. "interlopers" in the Indian Ocean. The United States was already
using Diego Garcia for communications by then.

Ramgoolam has conducted modest relations with the Soviet Union
without failing to shock Western sensibilities. The 1970 agreement to
provide trawler facilities at Port Louis merely formalized ongoing
relations and expressly limited the advantages Soviet ships might
take. In return, Mauritius received Soviet fishery equipment and
technical assistance. This unspectacular bargain was magnified at
the time in the British, French, U.S., and South African press, for
Soviet trawlers were universally suspected of carrying advanced
electronic detection equipment. Not only did Mauritius evidently have
to worry about being "detected," but also no mini-state could be
expected to manage its affairs harmlessly with the "great red power."
Duval himself (who resigned after the accord was publicized) told a
press conference in Paris on February 6, 1973 that no Soviet abuse
of its trawler rights had been discovered.

Yet the Western press bubbles intermittently with reports of
fictitious strategic concessions by Ramgoolam's government to Moscow.
Most popular among these gifts are the excellent but abandoned harbor

facilities at Mahébourg across the island from Port Louis. During 1973-74, while France was busily denying that pro-Western Duval had donated Mahébourg as a replacement for the Diego Suarez base (see the Madagascar chapter), Ramgoolam and the USSR took their turns refuting allegations that the old port was being turned into a Soviet stronghold.[14]

In the future, Mauritius will doubtless have to weather further trials of international conjecture over strategic issues, especially as Indian Ocean dialectics intensify. Chinese participation in Mauritius has already provided another source of speculation. Despite the implicit attraction of a Chinese community on the island, both "Chinas" have kept on the fringes of Mauritian development, thanks largely to Ramgoolam-Duval stalemates. In 1972, while Duval was cosponsoring the U.S. "two-Chinas" UN resolution, Ramgoolam visited Peking and announced diplomatic recognition. The news was criticized by Duval and embarrassed two other Mauritian ministers who happened to be sojourning in Taiwan at the time. A major new airport project was decided during the Ramgoolam visit, to be financed through a 13 million pound loan from Peking, but execution of the project was delayed for undisclosed reasons until after Duval's departure from the government. Work began in mid-1974 and seems to have had as little ideological or strategic implications as comparable World Bank undertakings.

During extended periods in the four years of the "grand coalition," the prime minister allowed Duval to operate freely from the catbird seat he so obviously enjoyed. The foreign minister was shaken from his perch in 1970; in 1973, Ramgoolam sawed off the limb. While foreign affairs provided a background for the confrontation, the crucial issue was over new taxes and export duties that Ramgoolam had proposed in order to offset the island's 1974 import bill. The new levies charged the commercial classes and upper-income groups for subsidies on imported staple food (rice, vegetable oils, flour, meat), thus benefiting rural and urban working classes who purchase these necessities at subsidized prices. Apprehensive of the effects of the surtaxes on their constituency, the PMSD sought frantically to find alternative sources of financing. In November, Duval made an unauthorized announcement of his efforts to obtain a free gift of 10,000 tons of rice from the European Economic Community, at a time when negotiations for sugar quotas under the new EEC association treaty were becoming critical. Ramgoolam reacted by firing Duval and his three PMSD colleagues from the cabinet. The PMSD returned to opposition benches, along with the UDM (Union Démocratique Mauricienne [Mauritian Democratic Union]) and IFB. Subsequent PMSD defections sustained the Labour-MAC majority.

Although humiliated in this episode, the PMSD had actually successfully prevented until that time any substantial social concessions from the middle classes to Labour's constituencies. The MMM, stripped of its parliamentary representative, remains alone in advocating land reform, public ownership of major industries, and radically improved social benefits. But if it cannot overcome its own internal flabbiness before the 1976 elections, the MMM will have to come to Ramgoolam. Election fever rose in early 1975 as the prime minister began taking domestic political pulse readings well in advance of the constitutional limit for the present parliament, March 11, 1976. He has recently rejected the notion of a one-party system as "retrograde" but has asked the Legislative Assembly to enact changes in electoral representation favoring laborers, artisans, and cooperatives. [15]

During 1974, with Ramgoolam again his own foreign minister, Mauritius's external relations continued their energetic, kaleidescopic course. The usual risks of self-contradiction remained alive even in Duval's absence, particularly in regard to the Indian Ocean strategic controversy. After the Anglo-U.S. announcement early in the year that the Diego Garcia communications facility would be expanded to handle missile-equipped Polaris submarines and other advanced equipment, Mauritius came under pressure to denounce the West's designs. [16] On April 6, its high commissioner in New Delhi threatened publicly that Mauritius would take Britain to the World Court for violating the terms of the 1965 transfer of the Chagos archipelago in erecting a full-scale naval base on the atoll. This bit of bravado came on the eve of Ramgoolam's official visit to India. While it doubtless pleased his expectant hosts, the prime minister was obliged to renounce the opportunity to sue the island's former metropole. He did it with sheepish grace, deploring military intensification in the "zone of peace," but conceding that further protests from Mauritius would be unlikely to have any influence on the great powers.

Ramgoolam has demonstrated in other respects the compatibility of his own and Duval's tendency to "play opposite sides of the street." He has quietly maintained relations with Israel despite the OAU bandwagon of 1973 and has sustained Duval's substantive arrangements with South Africa, albeit with less personal enthusiasm. For several years, South Africa has supplied $7-8 million of vegetable, fruit, and manufactured goods at reasonable prices for the island economy. Since 1969, Durban importers have contracted for the bulk of Mauritius's tea crop. White South African tourists are increasing their vacation attendance on Mauritian beaches, especially as Madagascar and Mozambique become less congenial to them. Mauritius continues to promote tourism from South Africa, although Ramgoolam withdrew the island's participation in the Southern African Regional Tourist Organization (SARTOC) in April 1971 (while Duval was chairman of the organization) following leaks of an alleged South African plan to construct a racially segregated tourist hotel on the island. South African Airways uses Mauritius as a convenient refueling stop on its 5,000-mile flight from

Johannesburg to Perth. An excellent full-scale English-language guidebook to the island was published in Cape Town in 1973. [17]

Continuing along Duval's "beat," the prime minister has reassured France of francophone Mauritius's fidelity. His position was facilitated considerably the change of French regimes in mid-1974. for Duval had been a favorite of the Pompidou establishment. Ramgoolam had countermanded a Duval project for French military advisers in 1971 and was conspicuously displeased with reported improvisations in Duval's Paris contacts, culminating in the foreign minister's ill-fated announcement in late 1973 that Ramgoolam's new tax program could be scrapped if the EEC donated 10,000 tons of rice. Duval had been the architect of recent French education exchange and technical assistance agreements, labor export contingents to French shipyards, an airport expansion project, cooperation in electrical energy development with Réunion (using compatible French equipment), an investment guarantee for French capital, the installation of a 250-bed Club Méditerrannée vacation village on the island's north coast, a luxury tourist complex built originally for OCAM leaders in 1973, and other activities with the usual degree of return benefit to France. The MMM even warned Ramgoolam in 1971 that the French Embassy had offered arms to the PMSD as a guarantee against the spurious communist conspiracy then being bruited abroad.

In reply to this array of achievements by Duval in Paris, Ramgoolam could call upon his seniority in French-Mauritian bilateral relations. Mauritius began adhering to francophile organizations like OCAM and the Francophone International Association well before Duval's incumbency at Foreign Affairs. It remains the only commonwealth state in that company. Ramgoolam had flown from London to attend Pompidou's hasty "summit" convocation of franc zone friends in November 1973 (although Mauritius remains in the sterling zone), and he went to Pompidou's funeral in 1974. Even before Independence, Ramgoolam had encouraged the French consulate to broaden cultural activities on the island.

ECONOMICS: SUGAR AND HARDWARE

To PMSD's satisfaction, the island's economic foundation has indeed remained relatively intact, even while a new industrial dimension becomes grafted onto a far from self-sufficient agricultural base; diversification of cultivation proceeds without diminishing the primacy of sugar cane; labor unions have disturbed but not overpowered the fragile "free enterprise" system. The legacy of dependence on a cane-logged agricultural surface—Britain's imperial bequest—remains both the blessing and the bane of the otherwise free-spirited island. [18]

Far from receding as the mainstay of Mauritius's export economy, sugar has fallen as principal exchange earner only by 10 points in the

past five years, from 70 percent to 60 percent. It now represents
88 percent of export earnings, as opposed to a 1971 high of 94 percent.
The sugar industry has improved its records of cane production,
productivity (ratio of sugar to bulk cane), sugar byproducts, and
export revenues fairly steadily—cyclone weather willing—since Independence. Notwithstanding its social democratic program and respon-
siveness to the Hindu rural proletariat, Ramgoolam's Labour Party
has declined to attack the golden goose. Instead, it has conformed to
recommendations filed by British Labour Party economist Thomas
Balogh in 1963, arguing in favor of progressive taxation, wage councils, government welfare programs, and other moderate devices
instead of nationalization or alternative form of public control over
the sugar industry. [19]

Two-thirds of the cane is cultivated on 22 large estates with
factories, all but one privately owned; 92 percent of the private stock
is in Mauritian hands. Approximately 15,000 small-hold plantations
and a like number of sharecroppers produce the remainder—all supported technologically by an internationally known Sugar Research
Institute. Relatively benign weather conditions in the cyclone belt for
the past decade (except for the "political year" of 1967 and a double
cyclone in 1970) have permitted high cane tonnage as well as extraction
ratios averaging above 11 percent of sugar. The 1973 harvest reached
a record sugar total of 718,400 tons, and the 1980 target is 800,000
tons; even mediocre years should assure about 650,000 tons. Still,
Mauritians shudder at the recollection of the 1960 cyclones, which
reduced their crop to 40 percent of normal and export earnings by
one-third. A freak cyclone hit Rodrigues in 1968, destroying 80 percent of that island's total agricultural production, engendering food
riots, and virtually squelching the "go-it-alone" Rodrigues seces-
sionist movement.

Assurance of long-term export outlets have constantly preoccu-
pied the Mauritian Government, but shrinking world supplies of sugar
in the 1970s have worked to the island's advantage. Commonwealth
sugar agreements ran through 1974, assuring Mauritius a British
market for 380,000 long tons at supported prices (reaching as high
as 79 pounds per ton in 1974). Canada has been a strong secondary
purchaser of Mauritian sugar under the commonwealth agreements,
which have been replaced by equally auspicious EEC association terms.
Signature of a long-term EEC sugar agreement on February 1, 1975
brought genuine sighs of relief from Mauritius, which labored ardu-
ously over years to ensure the accommodation of its sugar export
needs once Britain entered Common Market agricultural structures.
The U.S. sugar quota for Mauritius rose from 15,000 tons in 1965
to 29,000 tons in 1975. Japan and (reportedly) China were also prospective customers. As an extra measure of security, Ramgoolam

single-handedly kept the modest OCAM Sugar Agreement from lapsing in 1974.

Independence-hour pessimists have happily proved incorrect thus far. Mauritius has not been left by the cruel consuming world to wallow in sweet mountains of her unwanted crop. The island's lease on viability depended on a combination of fortunate weather at home and unfortunate weather in other parts of the underdeveloped world. It also needed receptivity from tough-tempered West European agricultural ministries pressed by their sugar-beet planters and their own traditional overseas suppliers. Barring catastrophe, Mauritius is a secure exporter of sugar for another three years at least. But steeply rising costs of production at home and prospects for recovery in competitor countries continue to jeopardize the prosperity of the vital industry, at least while it remains a monocrop.

The optimism of Mauritians regarding the success of their economic policies was of course predicated on maintenance of high production in sugar and continued developmental productivity. These factors were in turn dependent on a number of uncontrollable variables, including the capricious climate of the Mascarenes. On February 6, 1975, cyclone Gervaise dealt the island's hopes a blow unprecedented since the disastrous storms of 1960. Early estimates of the damage mounted in the millions of pounds sterling. Some 1,500 houses were destroyed by winds up to 200 kilometers per hour, eight people were left dead, electricity and water service were cut for several days. About 20 percent of the 1975 sugar crop was said to have been destroyed, representing a prospective loss of well over 10 million rupees in export revenues. In addition, several west-coast resort complexes were damaged and uncalculated reductions must be anticipated in food production and secondary crops. A massive diversion of domestic capital and foreign aid into recovery projects will slow the island's forward momentum and probably restrict the government's freedom of movement in international affairs. The auspicious moment for renewal of Ramgoolam's electoral mandate will also be indefinitely postponed.

Rising import costs have eaten into the island's usually well-balanced external payments accounts. In his annual report issued in January 1975, Planning and Development Minister Kher Jagatsingh called attention to disequilibrium in the country's growth record. Mauritius is too dependent on sugar production and international market fluctuations, too sensitive to inflationary spurts of liquidity whenever sugar is selling well (particularly painful in 1974), and too inequitable in the distribution of revenues. Without sounding too "socialist," Jagatsingh anticipated greater emphasis on "economic justice" in the 1976-80 development plan.

The narrowness of Mauritius's domestic market restricts import substitution strategies to basic, nonindustrial food crops—for example, vegetables, corn, and potatoes ingeniously planted between cane rows, modest fishing, and dairy development; molasses, rum, ethyl alcohol, becasse (for fuel and fireboard), and other sugar byproducts; ginger and other spices—and some labor-intensive export crops like tea, tobacco, and aloe (for "jute" bags). Most of these efforts are flourishing, thanks partly to external financing from the United Kingdom, the United Nations, and the World Bank's International Development Association (IDA), West Germany, France, and India.

Russian and Japanese assistance in fisheries development should eventually contribute to improved food production and import substitution. The 1974 extension of the controversial 1970 agreement with the USSR commits the Soviets to a joint fishing venture with Mauritius, in addition to research and technical assistance. The island's catch runs at about 3,500 tons per year, one-tenth of what the Japanese take off Mauritius's coasts.

Tea has been grown intensively on only 52 square kilometers of the island's precious land surface, supported by a "soft" loan of $5.2 million from the IDA. South Africa raised its contractual level of purchase from 5 to 7 million pounds of made tea in 1974, when the crop reached a high of 11 million pounds. As in the case of sugar, world shortages have enhanced Mauritian prospects of selling tea in Britain and elsewhere at elevated prices. The South African arrangement is subject to political influence and the habitual Mauritian contradictions in foreign policy. Sales almost collapsed in 1973 after the Mauritian ambassador to the United Nations, as chairman of the General Assembly's African caucus, spoke against accepting the South African delegation's credentials at the General Assembly. South African importers retorted with a boycott of Mauritian tea, which was canceled in November after the two governments agreed to live and let live.

Tobacco production has brought the island to self-sufficiency, and imports of potatoes have now been banned in favor of local production. Less successful experiments have been undertaken with rice, peanuts, soybeans, and livestock raising (especially hogs on Rodrigues).

Export industries represent an attractive answer to the island's need for economic diversification, foreign exchange, and employment opportunities. During the 1960s, about 50 new small-scale industries had been introduced on the island with some success, thanks largely to government incentives and the availability of a literate, low-paid labor force. A far bolder strategy was implemented on November 3, 1970 with the opening of the first of the island's export processing zones (EPZ). These free-trade areas can be certified at any point on the island for overseas manufacturing interests using Mauritius as a

value-additive transshipment point. Once licensed, an EPZ plant
benefits from tax holidays, preferential import and export concessions,
unrestricted repatriation for profits, inexpensive rentals, utilities and
public services, and abundant cheap labor. It can export to commonwealth, European Common Market, and African states under advantages
accorded to "Made in Mauritius" labels—a benefit appreciated by South
African manufacturers otherwise subject to ideological boycott.

The EPZ scheme plays an important role in full-employment
planning, accounting for 80,000 of the 130,000 necessary new jobs
projected for the period 1971-80. Some 14,000 of the EPZ quota are
anticipated by 1975, but by the end of 1974 only 5,000 new positions
had been registered. These were furnished by 41 operating EPZ
enterprises from Japan, Hong Kong, India, Switzerland, South Africa,
and France. Their combined exports of textiles, electronics, watches,
and optical instruments, toys and novelties, food canning, cosmetics,
fertilizers, utensils, bricks, and furniture amounted to $8 million in
1973, or about 5 percent of total export earnings for the year, albeit
apart from sugar.

Despite its modest statistical dimension, the EPZ scheme has
unmistakable symbolic importance in the panorama of diversification
and the display of progressive energies manifested by Mauritius
throughout the industrialized world. The light-manufacturing campaign represents an economic dimension in Mauritius's efforts to
improvise for herself a role of "maritime Switzerland" in an otherwise forbiddingly isolating sea.

The island's development programs have been equally impro-
vised according to imposed circumstances. The entire 1957-62 colonial
program funded by Great Britain had to be reoriented toward reconstruction needs in housing, agriculture, and basic infrastructure
following the two murderous cyclones that struck the island in 1960.
This experience galvanized the antiindependence movement at the time
and reinforced the argument against unprotected foreign policy ventures.[20]

Of the 400 million rupees (approximately $80 million) spent
during the 1960-66 reconstruction and development program, 14 percent went to agriculture and industry, 44 percent to infrastructural
development, 34 percent to social services, and 8 percent to administration and law enforcement. The 1966-70 program took a more
productive emphasis, with 38 percent going to agriculture and industry,
29 percent to infrastructure, 24 percent to social services and 8 percent for administration and law enforcement. British Colonial Development and Welfare Fund aid, representing the lion's share of external
assistance during the 1946-67 period, amounted to 5,876,996 pounds.

After 1967, upon agreement by the Mauritian Government to
keep its public expenditures in budgetary balance, the United Kingdom

agreed to additional aid averaging 4 to 5 million pounds per year. Two interest-free British loans covering the 1971–75 development program brought 10 million pounds in credits for British goods and services and for capital projects.

Britain remains Mauritius's preeminent customer for sugar and still furnishes approximately one-fifth of the island's supplies. Western Europe, South Africa, and Asian rice-exporting nations have taken increasing shares of independent Mauritius's growing imports, although tourism, harbor and port fees, net investment flows, and other intangibles keep international payments in balance. Debt servicing has thus far remained negligible but will rise significantly in the 1980s.

The Western European countries have been active in food aid— as have the United Kingdom, United States, and the World Food Program of the UN's Food and Agricultural Organization. Mauritius's access to EEC markets permitted the new EPZ industries to direct approximately 18 million rupees in manufactured goods to Western Europe during 1973. (There are about 5 rupees to the dollar.) EEC aid included a $6.2 million grant from the European Development Fund for transportation, health, and irrigation projects, and a 7 million rupee grant to the University of Mauritius. France committed a total of 27 million French francs to the 1971–75 development program.

The World Bank and its IDA loan "window" have been important supporters of Port Louis harbor development, including land reclamation projects, as well as rural electrification and irrigation. Several high-level exchanges of visits with New Delhi produced a roster of lively assistance projects in agricultural processing, transportation, technical assistance, and EPZ financing. A 1972 Indian loan of 25 million Mauritian rupees, at 5 percent interest, was applied mainly to agricultural irrigation and communications.

American and Chinese participation remains typically low, although work finally began in 1974 on a new airfield, financed through a 13 million pound loan from Peking. The United States has opened an embassy, negotiated an investment guarantee agreement in 1970, and contributed to small-scale self-help and food assistance programs.

EDUCATION AND UNEMPLOYMENT

Mauritius is judged to be about 70 percent literate. Almost 90 percent of its primary-school-age children are enrolled in public or religious schools, but the record narrows sharply in both quantity and quality of education at the secondary level. An ill-adapted educational system, deplored since the thorough review of its weaknesses in the so-called Titmuss report in 1961,[21] continues, despite some modifications, to turn out hundreds of unemployable school-leavers each year. Only 30 percent pass the Standard VI primary school-leaving exams, and the few trade schools barely dent the ranks of qualified applicants. University of Mauritius places are limited to A-level certificate-holders, and emigration is virtually closed to the unskilled and ill-educated. Thus, a semieducated white-collar Lumpenproletariat tends to congregate in cities, attracted as much by the proverbial illusions of Port Louis as by the battle cries of the so-called radical parties.

A traditionally antirural bias among Creoles militates against "back-to-land" schemes designed to reduce urban unemployment. Perhaps the worst impediments to rational organization of the island's labor force, however, consist in (1) classic tendencies among all social groups to press their youth toward "academic" tracks, which can be successfully completed by only a few and which do as much harm as good to the "failures"; (2) the need to teach bilingually at the primary level—multilingually among the Indo-Mauritians—with little prospect that sixth-year school-leavers will have mastered any language sufficiently to move beyond semiliteracy; and (3) saturation of civil service employment possibilities and low rates of increment and turnover in tourism and other service trades.

At Independence, over 1 percent of the population entered the jobless ranks annually. In 1973, about 20,000 Mauritians reached age 19 each year, with almost half of them competing with earlier school-leavers for clerical jobs. In the long run, improvement in sugar technology, where Mauritius has always been strong, threatens to reduce employment in the industry that employs 40 percent of today's working population. While official statistics hedge the realities, at least 50,000 Mauritians (20 percent of the work force) are probably jobless at any given time, with an equal number seasonally or otherwise underemployed. Another 50,000 are employed in the sugar industry, only 5,000 others in non-sugar-related agriculture, 32,000 in the civil service, about 13,000 in industry (including the EPZs), 14,000 in tourism and other services, and 5,000 in commerce. The prime development goal of 130,000 new jobs in the 1971-80 decade seems as essential as it is unrealistic. A five-year-old Travail pour Tous (Work for Everybody) program sops up some unemployment in public works and other heavy projects, as well as some service trades, but at government expense.

The new state inherited anything but a simple set of social institutions to match its political and economic complexities. An organized labor movement of nearly 50,000 members was sprawled over five national "federations" all more or less affiliated with internationals ranging from Roman Catholic to communist. Attacking a per capita income average that fluctuated from over $300 to $215 in the late 1960s and back to nearly $300 (at inflated currency rates) in 1973, the more radical unions have gradually increased minimum wages in the cane fields (from about $1 per day to about $2.50), in the civil service, town businesses, and the port. It was the student-labor alliance of 1968-69 that ensured the success of the MMM, scourge of the island's landowners and employers. The labor-affiliated cooperative movement, once numbering over 300 cooperatives in agriculture, trade, credit marketing, housing, and other key sectors, now languishes.

Great disparities remain apparent in Mauritian income patterns, however. Although sugar planters and millers are pressed by rising labor and equipment costs, earnings remain profitable in the commercial and professional sectors of the island's cardinal industry. The industrial relations code promised by Ramgoolam to the MMM unions can hardly influence conditions for workers in the EPZs. According to French and Réunionnais sources, "coolie wages" as low as 2.5 and 3 rupees per day are paid women in most EPZ industries, where union representation and strikes are prohibited, and paid leave, maternity leave, family allowances, health care, pensions, and other social benefits are rudimentary or nonexistent. [22]

Inflation has hurt low-income Mauritians as much as anybody. The cost of living for wage-earners doubled between 1971 and 1973, and the index jumped another 48 points between July 1973 and July 1974. Subsidies for basic food imports, which cost 20 million rupees in 1973, multiplied to almost 100 million rupees in 1975, equaling one-fifth of the government budget. Government spokesmen constantly denounce profiteering importers and uncompetitive pricing, but little has been done except to raise wages (43 percent for civil service employees in September 1973) and curb credit.

Mauritius's rural development program, begun in 1973 with an interest-free loan of 20 million rupees from the IDA (covering two-fifths of the cost), undertakes housing, education, social services, marketing, and road improvements in 86 of the island's 400 villages. Using Travail pour Tous labor, the program is regarded by the World Bank as a potential model for rural productivity, population migration, and public services throughout the underdeveloped world.

POPULATION CONTROL

Mauritius has long been regarded as a laboratory for Malthusian demography. Apart from the legendary fecundity of Indo-Mauritian and Creole families and the unavailability of emigration opportunities, a dramatic improvement in public health after World War II brought the rate of population increase over 3 percent by the early 1960s. The virtual elimination of malaria accounted for most of the record, permitting life expectancy to rise from an average of 33 years in 1946 to 60 years by 1960. Mortality fell from 40 per 1,000 population to 10 per 1,000 and, in recent years, to 7.8. At 1960s rates of growth, the population density, already one of the highest for any agricultural territory, threatened to exceed 4,000 per square mile by the end of the century.

A British effort to inculcate family planning practices in 1953 and a liberal contraceptives law failed to take hold on a highly skeptical rural population. Hindu, Muslim, and Creole-Catholic religious leaders were uncooperative, and village women evidently preferred to run the risks of clandestine abortion rather than trust the government to curb their family growth. In 1964, a new approach was launched by the then "autonomous" Ministry of Health, aided by International Planned Parenthood and Action Catholique. A broadside propaganda campaign, using television, posters, educational programs, and religious platforms, and a network of 74 clinic centers encouraged Mauritians to realize the adage that "small family is happy family." The Planned Parenthood clinics handled the entire range of family planning problems, including pre- and postnatal care, inoculations, hygiene, sanitation and diet, and psychological difficulties. Women volunteers canvassed their respective villages to persuade other women to attend the clinics and to consult trained personnel. By 1972, the birth rate was half of its 1960 total, and by 1974, aided partly by emigration of Creoles, the population was increasing on an average of only 1.39 percent annually. Secret abortions were estimated to have been reduced by one-third but still claimed approximately 20,000 fetuses each year (almost equaling the number of live births), with horrendous complications for the aborted mother.[23]

TRANSPORTATION AND TOURISM

Mauritius has been successful and fortunate in respects other than climatic. The capital city's port activity has realized an annual increase of 37 percent in traffic and 70 percent in revenues since the closing of the Suez Canal in 1967. In 1972, a record of 1.7 million tons of cargo passed through the port. To expand and improve facilities at Port Louis, Mauritius received its first commercial World Bank (as opposed to IDA) loan in April 1974; the bank is covering $10 million of the estimated $16 million needed for Phase I harbor development. British commitments to the port have totaled 66.6 million rupees. International authorities expect little diminution of port activity after the canal reopens.

Increased trawler activity and naval visits at the port have also been helpful, despite the political disputes they engender. Iranian warships used Port Louis in 1973, and on a single day in August 1974, British, U.S., and French naval vessels were all to be seen in the harbor.

China's major undertaking on the island, a new airfield at Plaine des Roches, will permit jumbo jets to use Mauritius and also bring the air services nearer the capital city than the present Plaisance Field. Even now, Plaisance sees daily flights to and from Johannesburg, Perth, Sydney, and Melbourne (South African Airways and Qantas), Réunion, Paris, and Djibouti (Air France), and weekly or twice-weekly connections with Lusaka and Blantyre (Qantas), Bombay (Air India and Air Mauritius), Cairo (Lufthansa), Nairobi, Dar es Salaam, and Entebbe (East African Airways, Air Mauritius, and Lufthansa), London (British Overseas Air Corporation, BOAC, and Air Mauritius), Rome (Alitalia), and the Seychelles and the Comoros (BOAC and Air France, respectively). There are three flights weekly to Tananarive (Air France and Alitalia) and three flights by Air Mauritius Piper Navaho to Rodrigues Island.

Britain endowed Mauritius with an excellent road system needed to handle trucking for the sugar industry after the sugar-cane railway was scrapped in 1960. The rivers are too vertical for navigation, but the interior lagoons attract modest boating and plucky fishing by Creole boatsmen.

Tourist traffic profits from an almost full circle of protected coral-sand beaches fringed by casuarinas and other tropical foliage, a warm, dry austral winter marked by splendid rainbows, scaleable mountains, abundant aquatic and terrestrial sports, elegant gardens like Pierre Poivre's marvelous 18th-century Pamplemousses, interesting colonial architecture, museums, exploitable religious ceremonies, waterfalls and rapids, French restaurants, three gambling casinos, colorful East-West population "mixtures," an exotic Port Louis waterfront, and irrepressible apocrypha of buried treasures along the reefs. Promoted by government, airlines, and charter managers, Mauritius's tourist market jumped from 15,500 visitors in 1968 to 37,000 in 1971 and 68,000 in 1973. The 1975 goal is 95,000, but Mauritius will probably settle for 75,000 as air tariffs and other rising costs erode the long-range Scandinavian, German, and British traffic. Réunionnais accounted for nearly one-third of the 68,000 tourists in 1973, and South Africa supplied an almost equal number. Room capacity in Mauritius hotels reached 2,245 in 1974, almost six times the number of rooms available in 1971. Steamy, unspoiled

Rodrigues opened its first airfield in 1973 and its first tourist-class hotel in 1974.

Lacking strong government sanctions, Mauritius's tourist infrastructure has been allowed to develop haphazardly. The island's best assets have become tributary to the mass charter industry, which has furnished a half-dozen major hotel complexes for low-budget standardized tastes. As a result, Mauritius must strive to fill the big hotels at cut rates, with most of the market revenues for prepaid travel, accommodations, and imported luxury items remaining overseas, and a diminishing set of accessible attractions for the more lucrative and discriminating "repeat" trade. Job opportunities in the tourist business have also been disappointing thus far. Travel and hotel managers are recruited abroad, and, out of a target of 18,000 new jobs to be created in the industry by 1980, only about 2,000 have become available to Mauritians. France, the UN Development Program, and the Mauritius Government are cooperating in a training program for tourist personnel opened in 1973. IDA loans have been available for infrastructural development.

MAURITIUS' WORLD

Starting well before Independence, Prime Minister Ramgoolam and his associates envisaged the broadest possible overseas relationships for their small nation. Mauritius has remained busily and flexibly among all continents and most ideologies. And it has weathered great-power disapproval on more than one occasion. Adherence to any agreeable international, regional, or zonal association is implicit in this "open window" strategy. The commonwealth, the UN and all its agencies, the OAU, the EEC, Francophonia, OCAM, the East African Community (since 1965), varieties of international associations of sugar, tea, and tourist suppliers, and untold trade fairs all seem worth the price of the membership card and the air fare for Mauritius. One or another of Mauritius's leaders has dealt cordially with China, India, Egypt, Tanzania, and the African liberation movements, as well as with France, Israel, and South Africa. Contacts with a universe that is entirely "overseas" have seemed essential for the sale of sugar and tea, the attraction of investors and tourists, the location of sources of economic aid and technology, and to bring the world into symbolic proximity. Mauritius counts her benefits far higher than her costs in this inevitably complicated orchestration of external affairs.

A cohesion of Western Indian Ocean islands has been favored rhetorically for decades on Mauritius as elsewhere, but the protagonists seldom find a chance to overcome the real barriers to cooperation between "Britain's sphere" and "overseas France."[24] Cultural exchanges, transportation and communications networks, and tourism have been modest but salutary exceptions. These are due largely to the advantage maintained by the French language throughout the region as well as the profitability of some regional enterprises for French business interests (particularly Air France, the ocean shipping conference, the package tourist entrepreneurs, and communications equipment manufacturers). Some technical discussions take place among the islands on the intricacies of sugar and marketing, vanilla, transportation, and other common interests.

But economic union requires larger-scale regional investment coordination, market sharing, currency and customs unions, reciprocal industrial development concessions, and the like. These elements of a united structure are far more difficult to realize throughout the wide zone occupied by the Seychelles, the Comoros, Madagascar, and Mauritius, let alone Zanzibar, Mozambique, the Maldives, and other prospective participants in regional development. Uneven political status is especially important in the case of Réunion; historical, religious, and cultural differences and mutual suspicions prevail among these non-African, non-Asian, ex-wards of Europe.[25] No island can offer substantial industrial raw materials needed by the others; nor can any island assure markets for the primarily luxury crops (sugar, vegetable and perfume oils, vanilla, cloves, coffee, and the like) that draw the bulk of export revenue for all concerned, while in some instances bringing the islands into unhealthy competition. All except Madagascar are overpopulated, and Madagascar has not welcomed either Asians or Creoles for several decades.

In the past, active leadership from a strong source like Madagascar and with the blessing of France if not both France and Britain might have prodded the smaller units toward cooperative development. But while Madagascar remained on good enough terms with France until 1972, the Malagasy Government proved unenterprising, and, when those relations cooled, France became less interested in Malagasy leadership.

Anticipating independence for the Comoros and the Seychelles in 1975, Mauritius evidently sees prospects for a new dimension to her activist overseas policies. The idea of regional unification was revived in Mauritius during the 1973 OCAM meeting by President Leopold Sedar Senghor of Senegal, whose own experience with regional unity has been less than triumphant. On October 4, 1974, Ramgoolam called for an association of Mauritius, the Comoros, and the Seychelles, to give the islands a single vote in international forums and a chance to coordinate scarce industrial development resources. However suspiciously some neighbors must regard the initiatives of a vigorous comparative "old boy" like Mauritius, Seychelles Chief Minister James Mancham seemed receptive to consultations, and French experts felt that even Réunion might not be excluded from specific points of cooperation with Mauritius.[26]

Ramgoolam's island represents the first effective break from the pattern of systematic dependence on Europe that began to erode in 1970-71. [27] As early as 1965, Ramgoolam told Malagasy President Tsiranana that economic unification of the region was both desirable and necessary; [28] it was one of the rare meetings between the veteran leaders of these two neighbors, and no doubt Tsiranana was not very interested in the matter. A decade later, Mauritius is perhaps prepared to speak with greater authority and even to set the pace.

Mauritius has thus far deployed its modest international resources with remarkable self-assurance. It deals with external powers and interests on a sophisticated level, suggesting the kind of "parity" usually denied to insecure micro-states exposed in strategically festooned oceans. While constantly subject to the winds of conspiracy, Mauritians under Ramgoolam have avoided the paranoia over foreign intrigue that afflicts comparable countries. Occasionally resembling a diplomatic sorcerer's apprentice, the Mauritian style, exemplified by the aged prime minister as well as his younger colleagues and rivals, suggests the broad-gauge freebooting established by the bearded and bewigged personalities of the 18th-century Ile de France.

Whether this self-confident expertise acquired in international self-advocacy can be converted into a force for regional leadership remains to be seen. The record is only exemplary thus far, from the viewpoint of Muaritius's neighbors, not catalytic. And much depends on Mauritius's ability to sustain economic growth and social tranquility at home, under highly questionable circumstances of oceanic meteorology, international trade, and domestic communal volatility. Not to mention the crisis of succession that Ramgoolam's retirement will surely create. The prime minister was able to establish a stable center-moderate power nucleus among Hindus, Muslims, and some Creoles, isolating the MMM and IFB on the left and the PMSD and UDM on the right. But the maintenance of that constellation required constant tinkering, both with the machinery of coalition and the validity of constitutional guarantees. The decline of the potentially powerful PMSD and MMM forces during 1973 and 1974 may not continue. If the center should weaken, and especially if the ethnocentrism of the rival communities is again allowed to dominate party politics, more will have been lost than the dream of Western Indian Ocean unity.

NOTES

1. For historical background see B. F. Mahé de la Bourdonnais, Mémoires des Iles de France et de Bourbon (Paris: Leroux, 1937);

Derek Hollingworth, They Came to Mauritius (London: Oxford, 1965); Auguste Toussaint, History of the Indian Ocean (London: Methuen, 1966); Alix d'Unionville, Les Mascareignes, Vieille France en Mer Indienne (Paris: Albin Michel, 1954); Alan Villiers, Monsoon Seas (New York: McGraw-Hill, 1952); G. A. Ballard, Rulers of the Indian Ocean (Boston: Houghton Mifflin, 1928); Marcel Cabon, Biographie de Ramgoolam (Port Louis: Editions Mauriciennes, 1963).

 2. UNGA resolution 2066 XX, December 16, 1965.

 3. See d'Unionville, op. cit.; F. O. O'Manney, The Shoals of Capricorn (London: Longmans, Green, 1952); Raymond Decary et al., La France de l'Océan Indien (Paris: Société d'Editions Géographiques Maritime et Coloniales, 1952).

 4. See the author's "Mauritius on the Eve," Africa Report (May 1966), pp. 16-24; Burton Benedict, Mauritius: Problems of a Plural Society (New York: Praeger Publishers, for Institute of Race Relations, 1965).

 5. For sociological background, see Benedict, op. cit.; J. E. Meade et al., The Economic and Social Structure of Mauritius; Report to the Governor of Mauritius (London: Methuen, 1961); R. W. Luce, Report of the Government of Mauritius on Employment, Unemployment and Underemployment in the Colony in 1958 . . . (Port Louis: Government Printer, 1958).

 6. Central Office of Information, London, Factel, no. 550, February 28, 1968.

 7. See Luce, op. cit.; Meade, op. cit.; also R. M. Titmuss and B. Abel-Smith, assisted by T. Lynes, Social Politics and Population in Mauritius (London: Methuen, 1961).

 8. See the author's Self-Determination in the Western Indian Ocean (New York: Carnegie Endowment for International Peace, International Conciliation no. 560, November 1966), p. 11.

 9. See UNGA resolution on "Zone of Peace in the Indian Ocean," December 9, 1974; also A. J. Cottrell and R. M. Burrell, eds., The Indian Ocean: Its Political, Economic, and Military Importance (New York: Praeger Publishers, for The Center for Strategic and International Studies, 1972).

 10. Jeune Afrique, no. 564 (October 30, 1971).

 11. Times (London) (Special Report, March 5, 1973).

 12. See Africa Contemporary Record (Exeter, U.K., 1973-74), pp. B226-27.

 13. Jeune Afrique, no. 697 (May 18, 1974).

 14. See Africa Contemporary Record (1973-74), op. cit., p. B229.

 15. See Marchés Tropicaux, October 13, 1974.

 16. Jeune Afrique, no. 697 (May 18, 1974).

17. Douglas Alexander, Holiday in Mauritius: A Guide to the Island (Cape Town: Purnell, 1973).

18. See economic analyses in Financial Times (London), (March 23, 1972); Guardian (London) (March 30, 1974); and numerous Mauritian Government, World Bank, Barclay's Bank DCO, and UN Economic Commission for Africa statistics.

19. T. Balogh and C. N. M. Bennett, Report of the Commission of Inquiry: Sugar Industry (London: Methuen, 1963).

20. The author's Self-Determination, op. cit., pp. 15-24.

21. Titmuss et al., op. cit.

22. Africa Contemporary Record (1973-74), p. B232; see also exchange of letters between A. Fontaine and French Ministry of Overseas Departments and Territories, summarized in Marchés Tropicaux (January 5, and April 13, 1974).

23. See Dr. Escoffier Lambiotte, Le Monde, November 20, 1974.

24. The author's Self-Determination, op. cit., pp. 70-74; see also the author's "New Round for the Western Islands," in Cottrell and Burrell, op. cit., pp. 307-29.

25. The author's Self-Determination, op. cit., pp. 56-62.

26. Report of speech by the Honorable James R. Mancham before UN Committee on Decolonization, May 17, 1974 (Radio Dar es Salaam, June 10, 1974); Jean Charbonneau, Marchés Tropicaux (July 3, 1971).

27. See "New Round . . ." in Cottrell and Burrell, op. cit., pp. 307-29.

28. Nouvelles Malgaches Quotidiennes (Tananarive) (November 10, 1965); the author's Self-Determination, op. cit., p. 58.

GENERAL

Allen, Philip M. "Self-Determination in the Western Indian Ocean."
International Conciliation 560 (November 1966).

"Atoll Trouble." Time Magazine (April 1, 1974).

Baldwin, Hanson. "The Indian Ocean Contest." New York Times
(March 20, 21, and 22, 1970).

Benedict, Burton, ed. Problems of Smaller Territories. London:
Athlone Press, 1967.

Bowles, Chester. "A Considerable Speck." New York Times (May
13, 1974).

Brines, Russell. "Geopolitics in the Indian Ocean." Christian
Science Monitor (October 30, 1974).

Bulpin, T. V. Islands in a Forgotten Sea. Capetown: Books of Africa,
1969.

Burrell, R. M. and A. J. Cottrell. Iran, The Arabian Peninsula,
and the Indian Ocean. New York: National Strategy Information
Center, 1972.

Cooley, John K. "Sino-Soviet Rivalry Flares in Indian Ocean-Red
Sea Area." Christian Science Monitor (September 2, 1970).

Cottrell, Alvin J. and R. M. Burrell. The Indian Ocean: Its
Political, Economic and Military Importance. New York: Praeger
Publishers, 1972.

Decary, Raymond et al. La France de l'Ocean Indien. Paris:
Société d'Editions Géographiques Maritimes et Coloniales, 1952.

Groom, A. J. R. "British Defense Policy under the Conservatives."
Round Table 252 (1973): 483-505.

Les Guides Bleus: Madagascar, Comores, Réunion, Ile Maurice. Paris: Hachette, 1955.

Gwertzman, Bernard. "C.I.A. Chief Doubts Soviet Navy Plans Indian Ocean Build-up." New York Times (August 3, 1974).

Harrigan, A. "Red Star over the Indian Ocean." National Review 23 (April 20, 1971): 421-23.

"The Indian Ocean: Zone of Peace or Sea of Trouble?" Africa Report Special Issue 20, 1 (January-February 1975).

Levine, Richard J. "The Debate over Diego Garcia." Wall Street Journal (April 4, 1974).

Meister, Jurg. "Diego Garcia: Outpost in the Indian Ocean." Swiss Review of World Affairs (April 1974).

Millar, T. B. "The Indian and Pacific Oceans: Some Strategic Considerations." Adelphi Papers #57. London: Institute for Strategic Studies (May 1969).

_____. Soviet Policies in the Indian Ocean Area. Canberra: Australian National University Press, 1972.

_____. "Soviet Policies South and East of Suez." Foreign Affairs 49 (October 1970): 70-80.

Mouton, C. A., ed. Maurice Guide, 1971. Port Louis: Standard Printing Establishment, 1971.

Nicholas, Reginald A. "Indian Ocean Peace Zone Idea Goes Flat." Christian Science Monitor (February 6, 1975).

Ommanney, F. D. The Shoals of Capricorn. New York: Harcourt, 1952.

Pell, Claiborne. "Diego Garcia." U.S. Congressional Record: 93d Senate, Second Session 120, 47 (April 3, 1974).

_____. "Diego Garcia" (Speech on S. 2999). U.S. Congressional Record: 93d Senate, Second Session 120, 62 (May 6, 1974).

Peterson, R. T. "Plea for a Magic Island." Audubon 70 (January, 1968): 50-51.

"Russia Drives East of Suez." Newsweek (January 18, 1971).

"Russia-U.S. Showdown Coming? Behind the Big Power Moves in Indian Ocean." U.S. News (January 24, 1972).

"Russians in the Indian Ocean." Christian Science Monitor (November 16-20, 1970).

Schroeder, Richard C. "Indian Ocean Policy." Editorial Research Reports (March 10, 1970): 189-206.

Sheehan, Neil. "Soviet Is Expanding Navy in Indian Ocean Region." New York Times (October 18, 1970).

Silbert, M.A. "La Décolonisation de l'Ocean Indien (Asie-Afrique) et les Problèmes Qui en Découlent." Mimeographed address given before l'Académie des Sciences d'Outre-mer. Paris: Series 1963.

Spiers, R. I. "U.S. National Security Policy and the Indian Ocean Area." Bulletin of the State Department 65 (August 23, 1971): 199-203.

Stoddard, D. R. "The Conservation of Aldabra." Geographic Journal 134 (December 1968): 471-86.

Stoddard, Theodore L. et al. Area Handbook for the Indian Ocean Territories. Washington, D.C.: Government Printing Office, 1971.

"Suez Canal, Key to Soviet Strategy in Mideast Access to Indian Ocean?" U.S. News (June 22, 1970).

Tara, Vasile, and J. C. Woillet. Madagascar, Mascareignes et Comores. Paris: Société Continentale d'Editions Moderne Illustré, 1969.

Thaler, K. C. "Russia Pushing toward Indian Ocean." China Post (July 22, 1970).

Thomson, George C. Problems of Strategy in the Pacific and Indian Oceans. New York: National Strategy Information Center, 1970.

Toussaint, Auguste. History of the Indian Ocean. Chicago: University of Chicago Press, 1966.

Unna, Warren. "Diego Garcia." New Republic (March 9, 1974).

_____. "Justifying Diego Garcia." New Republic (August 31, 1974).

U.S. Congress. House of Representatives. Committee on Foreign Affairs. Subcommittee on National Security Policy and Scientific Developments. The Indian Ocean: Political and Strategic Future. (Hearings, July 20, 22, 27, and 28, 1971) Washington, D.C.: Government Printing Office, 1971.

Villiers, Alan. The Indian Ocean. London: Museum Press, 1952.

Vivekanandan, B. "Heath Government's Policy for South Asia." India Quarterly 29, 3 (1973): 211-55.

Weintraub, Bernard. "The Value of Diego Garcia." New York Times (June 2, 1974).

Weatherall, Ernest. "Indian Ocean Tapped as Vast Food Supply." Christian Science Monitor (May 2, 1969).

Wilson, Dick. "The Indian Ocean Frontier." Far Eastern Economic Review (September 14, 1967): 517-23.

Witherall, J. ed. Madagascar and Adjacent Islands: A Guide to Official Publications. Washington, D.C.: Government Printing Office, 1965.

Young, E. P. "Soviet Research in the Indian Ocean." Sea Front 14 (January 1968).

MADAGASCAR

Books and Articles

Allen, Philip M. "Madagascar and OCAM: The Insular Approach to Regionalism." Africa Report 11, 1 (January 1966): 13-18.

_____. "Rites of Passage in Madagascar." Africa Report 16 (February 1971).

Cooke, James J. "Madagascar and Zanzibar." African Studies Review. December 1970).

Deschamps, Hubert. Histoire de Madagascar. Paris: Berger-Levrault, 1961.

Gendarme, René. Economie de Madagascar. Paris: Cujas, 1961.

Heseltine, Nigel. Madagascar. New York: Praeger Publishers, 1971.

Kent, Raymond K. From Madagascar to the Malagasy Republic. New York: Praeger Publishers, 1962.

Ramasindraibe, Paul. Le Fokonolona. Tananarive: Impr. de la Mission Catholique, 1962.

Thompson, Virginia, and Richard Adloff. The Malagasy Republic. Stanford, Calif: Stanford University Press, 1965.

Tsiranana, Philibert. Le Cahier Bleu. Tananarive: Impr. Nationale, 1972.

Valette, Jean. Malagasy Foreign Relations in the Nineteenth Century, trans. Shelby Williams. Tananarive: Impr. Nationale, 1964.

Periodicals

Lumière

Madagascar Matin

Nouvelles Malgaches Quotidiennes

La République

Terre Malgache (Agriculture School, University of Madagascar)

REUNION

Books and Articles

Allaire, Jean Claude, and Francoise Allaire. La Réunion. Saint-Denis: Librairie Gérard, no date.

Anon. Petit Atlas de Bourbon. Nantes: Impr. Chautreau, 1962.

Baylongue-Hondaa, A. L'Octroi de Mer à la Réunion (Thesis,
University of Aix-en-Provence, 1972).

Brunet, Auguste. Trois Cent Ans de Colonisation Francais à l'Ile
Bourbon. Paris: Ed. de l'Empire Francais, 1948.

Cercle Eliard Laude. La Réunion, 1969: Une Colonie Francaise.
Paris: Maspero, 1969.

Chabalier, Hervé. "L'Ile aux Esclaves." Le Nouvel Observateur
(March 19, 1973).

Defos, Jean. L'Ile de la Réunion, Etude de Géographie Humaine.
Bordeaux: Institût de Géographie, 1960.

Dubrau, Louis. Les Iles de Capricorne: Maurice, La Réunion,
Madagascar. Brussels: A. De Raches, 1967.

Dujardin, B. Développer la Migration: La Réunion. Saint-Denis:
Ecole Nationale d'Administration, 1970.

Eiglier, Pierre. Problèmes et Perspectives de l'Emploi à la Reunion.
Saint-Denis: Centre Universitaire, 1972.

Gérard, G. Guide Illustré de l'Ile de la Réunion. Nerac, France:
Impr. J. Owen, 1970.

Lavabre, Bernard. La Réunion Touristique. Saint-Denis: Havas, no
date.

LeBlond, Marius. Les Iles Soeurs, ou le Paradis Retrouvé. Paris:
Asalia, 1946.

LeLoutre, Jean-Clause. La Réunion, Département Francais. Paris:
Maspero, 1968.

Mas, J. Droit de Propriété et Paysage Rural de l'Ile Bourbon.
(Thesis, University of Paris, 1971).

Oraison, André. Les Volontaires de l'Aide Technique. Saint-Denis:
Centre Universitaire, 1971.

Orsini, D. J. L'Equipement Sanitaire et Social des Collectivités
Locales à la Réunion. Saint-Denis: Centre Universitaire, 1972.

Parisot, Bernard. "Le Colonat Partiare à la Réunion." Etudes Réunionnaise. Aix-en-Provence, 1965.

Peron, Yves. "La Population des Départements Francais d'Outre-Mer." Population 1 (1966): 99-132.

Ramassamy, Albert. La Réunion Face à l'Avenir. Saint-Denis: Impr. Cazal, 1973.

_____. La Réunion: Les Problèmes Posés par l'Intégration. Saint-Denis, 1973.

Ravat, Yves. La Réunion, Terre Francaise. Port Louis: Regent Press, 1967.

"La Réunion, l'Ile Adoléscente." Le Monde. Special Section (June 6, 1972).

Scherer, André. Histoire de la Réunion. Paris: Presses Universitaire, 1966.

Vailland, Roger. La Réunion. Lausanne: Editions Rencontre, 1964.

Periodicals

Action Réunionnais (weekly)

Bulletin de Statistiques (monthly with frequent supplements) Institut National de la Statistique et des Etudes Economiques (INSEE)

Les Cahiers de la Réunion et de l'Océan Indien (bimonthly) pro-PCR

Cahier du Centre Universitaire de la Réunion (irregular)

Le Combat Nationale (bimonthly) pro-Debré.

Le Créole (weekly)

Cri du Peuple (weekly)

Croix-Sud (weekly)

Le Democrate (weekly) Gaullist

La Gazette de l'Ile (weekly) Gaullist left

Hebdo-Bourbon (weekly) Gaullist left

Info-Nature (triennial) La Société Réunionnaise pour l'Etude et la
    Protection de la Nature

Journal de l'Ile de la Réunion (daily) pro-Gaullist

Nous Créoles (published in Clichy-sous-Bois, France, by emigré
    organization; sympathizes with PCR)

Le Progressiste (weekly) pro-PSR

Le Reveil (weekly)

Statistiques et Indicateurs Economiques (annual) Réunion Department
    Government

Témoignages (daily) PCR

Témoignage Chrétien de la Réunion

COMOROS

Books and Articles

Ballan, Philippe. "Une Problème d'Aujourd'hui: L'Avenir des Iles
    Comores." Cahiers des Ingénieurs Agronomes 211 (December
    1968): 33-36.

Ben Said, Omar. "Cinq Années d'Expérience Communale aux Comores."
    Revue Juridique et Politique, Indépendence et Coopération 2 (April-
    June 1968): 455-62.

Bourde, André. "The Comoro Islands: Problems of a Microcosm."
    Journal of Modern African Studies 3, 1 (May 1965).

Cohen, Jean-Marc. Afrique Noire, Madagascar, Comores: Démo-
    graphie Comparée Paris: INSEE, 1965.

"Comorians Demand Their Independence." The People (Seychelles)
    (November 22, 1972).

Comoros, Territory Government. Rapport Socio-économique sur l'Archipel des Comores: 1970-1971. Moroni, 1973.

Decraene, Philippe. "Les Comores entre l'Autonomie et l'Independance." Le Monde (December 1 and 2, 1972).

_____. "Comoro Archipelago: What Kind of Independence?" Guardian (Manchester) (December 23, 1972).

Delperier, Georges. "Le Territoire d'Outre-mer de l'Archipel des Comores." La Revue de la Police Nationale 91 (September-October 1972).

Dubins, Barbara. "The Comoro Islands: A Bibliographical Essay." African Studies Bulletin (September 1969).

_____. "A Political History of the Comoro Islands: 1795-1886." Ph.D. dissertation, Boston University, 1972.

Essak, Kerim. "Yes! We Want Independence." Daily News (Dar es Salaam) (October 16, 1972).

Fauree, Urbain. L'Archipel aux Sultans Batailleurs. Moroni: Promo al Camar, no date.

_____. Histoire de L'Ile de Mayotte. Moroni, no date.

France, Ministre des Départements et des Territoires d'Outre-mer. Les Comores, Territoire Francais de l'Océan Indien. Paris, 1965.

Gevrey, M. A. Essai sur les Comores. Pondicherry, 1870.

Grosrichard, Francois. "Les Comores: La Richesse Viendra du Ciel." Le Monde (January 27, 1973).

Hoche, Christian. "Comores: A Quel Prix, l'Indépendance?" Le Figaro (January 20-21, 1973).

"Interview with A. Bakari Boina." Africa 21 (May 21, 1973).

Janicot, C. "Les Iles Comores Ouvrent au Tourisme Leur Cadre Grandiose." Connaissance de Monde (March 1962).

Kibasi, Musa. "A Chameleon Called France." Daily News (Dar es Salaam) (December 5, 1972).

Lewis, Flora. "Comoro Islands Choose Freedom from France by a Large Vote." New York Times (December 24, 1974).

Martin, Jean. "L'Archipel des Comores: Quatres Iles à la Croisée des Routes." Revue Francais d'Etudes Politiques Africains (1969).

_____. "Les Notions de Clans, Nobles et Notables, Leur Impact dans la Vie Politique Comoriènne Aujourd'hui." L'Afrique et l'Asie 81 (1968): 39-63.

Ostheimer, John M. "Political Development in Comoros." African Review 3, 3 (1973): 491-506.

Robineau, Cl. "Approche Socio-economique d'Anjouan." Cahier de l'Institūt de Science Economique Appliquée 6 (July 1963): 63-105.

Saint-Alban, Cedric, "Les Partis Politiques Comoriens entre la Modernité et la Tradition." Revue Francais d'Etudes Politiques Africans 94 (October 1973).

Periodicals

Info-Comores (bimonthly of Territory Government)

Promo al Camar (ceased publication April 1972)

Uhuru (underground PASOCO paper)

MALDIVES

Books and Articles

Adeney, Martin. "The Maldives Islands." Venture 22 (March 1970).

Baldwin, Hanson W. "The Indian Ocean Contest." New York Times (March 22, 1972).

Bell, H. C. P. The Maldive Islands. Colombo: Ceylon Government Printer, 1940.

Colombo Plan for Economic Development in South and Southeast Asia. Nineteenth Annual Report of the Consultative Committee: Twenty-Second Meeting, 1972. New Delhi: November, 1972 (and other Annual Reports).

Farmer, B. H. "Maldive Islands: Physical and Social Geography." In The Far East and Australia. London: Europa Publications, 1969, pp. 257-59.

De Font Galland, Guy, "Maldives: Real Delight for Tourists," Christian Science Monitor (January 29, 1974).

"Former DoD Officials Say Atoll to Be a Major Base." China Post (March 16, 1974).

"Freedom for Maldives Threatens Base." Guardian (Manchester) (July 27, 1965).

"Gan and the Maldives." Guardian (Manchester) (October 30, 1969).

Hockley, T. W. The Two Thousand Islands. London: Witherby, 1935.

Hussain, Adnan. The Maldive Islands Today. Colombo, Sri Lanka: Maldives Information Department Office, no date.

"The Islands of Not Having." Time (May 17, 1971).

"Isolated Maldive Islands Now Letting the World In," New York Times (April 9, 1972).

Maldive Embassy. Briefly Introducing the Maldive Islands. Washington, D.C., no date.

"Maldives Mayhem." Guardian (Manchester) (March 15, 1972).

"Maldives No Loss to UK." Guardian (Manchester) (March 11, 1975).

"Maldives Prime Minister Banished to Atoll." Times (London) (March 11, 1975).

"A Nasty Spot of Bother in the Maldives." Sunday Times (London) (December 6, 1970).

"Sick Islands in the Sun." Sunday Times (London) (March 12, 1972).

United Kingdom. Text of Treaty between Great Britain and the Maldives over Lease of Gan. London: Her Majesty's Stationery Office, July 1965.

United Nations Development Programme. Assistance Report by Government of Maldives 1972-6 to UNDP General Council. June 1973.

_____. Interim Report by Administrator of UNDP on Special Measures to Help Least Developed Nations. 17th session. January 1974.

_____. Report of a Mission to the Maldive Islands (1966).

U.S. Department of State. Republic of Maldives. Background Note. Washington, D.C.: Government Printing Office, 1971.

Villiers, Alan. "The Marvelous Maldive Islands." National Geographic (June 1957).

SEYCHELLES

Books and Articles

Barclay's Bank International. Seychelles: Economic Survey. London: Williams Lea, 1972.

Belling, Lawrence N. Seychelles: Islands of Love. Boulogne: Editions Delroise, 1971.

Benedict, Burton. "Dependency and Development in the Seychelles." Social Science Quarterly (Summer 1963).

_____. People of the Seychelles. London: Her Majesty's Stationery Office, 1966.

Bradley, John T. The History of Seychelles. Victoria: Clarion Press, 1940.

Great Britain, British Information Service. Seychelles (Fact Sheets on the Commonwealth). New York, June 1970.

_____. Central Office of Information. Mauritius and Seychelles. London, 1964.

_____. Foreign and Commonwealth Office. Report on the Seychelles Constitutional Conference. Cmnd Paper #4338 (March 9-13, 1970).

_____. Treaty Series. Exchange of Notes with United States Concerning U.S. Tracking Station on Mahé. Cmnd Paper #3232 (1967).

Hurd, H. R. Seychelles: Report on Taxation in the Colony. Victoria, 1959.

Keynes, Quentin. "Seychelles Tropic Isles of Eden." National Geographic 116, 5 (November, 1959): 670-95.

Lionnet, Guy. The Seychelles. Newton Abbot, Devon, England: David and Charles, 1972.

Marston, D. W. "Seychelles." Travel 133 (March 1970): 48-53.

Matthews, D. O. Report on the Tourist Industry of Seychelles and Future Development of that Industry. Victoria: Government Printer, no date.

Proctor, John. Conservation in the Seychelles. Victoria: Government Printer, 1970.

Rowe, J. W. F. The Economy of the Seychelles and Its Future Development. Victoria: Government Printer, 1959.

Sauer, Jonathan D. Plants and Man on the Seychelles Coast. Madison: University of Wisconsin Press, 1967.

"The Seychelles: Down with Coconuts." Time (September 25, 1965).

Seychelles Government. Conservation Policy in the Seychelles. Victoria: Government Printer, 1971.

_____. Development Plan for the Period 1969-1972. Victoria: Government Printer, 1969.

_____. Records of the Legislative Assembly. Victoria: Government Printer, annual.

_____. Residential Development in the Seychelles. Victoria: Government Printer, 1970.

_____. Tourism Development in the Seychelles. Victoria: Government Printer, 1971.

Smith, W. E. "Outermost Paradise." Holiday 44 (August 1968): 20-25.

Thomas, Athol. Forgotten Eden. London: Longmans, 1968.

U.S. Department of State. Colony of the Seychelles. Background Note. Washington, D.C.: Government Printing Office, 1969.

Veevers-Corter, Wendy. Island Home. London: Hale, 1971.

Walker, H. J. "Economic and Social Change in the Seychelles." Geographical Review, Geographical Record 57, 3 (July 1967): 429-31.

Waugh, Alec. Where the Clock Strikes Twice. New York: Farrar, Strauss and Young, 1951.

Webb, A. W. T. Story of Seychelles. Victoria: October 1965.

_____. Population Census of the Seychelles Colony. Victoria, 1960.

Periodicals

L'Echo des Iles (bimonthly, Catholic Church)

Journal of the Seychelles Society (annual)

Le Nouveau Seychellois (bimonthly)

The People (weekly, SPUP)

The Seychelles Annual (ceased publication)

Seychelles Culture (monthly of Francophone community)

Seychelles Bulletin (daily run by government)

Seychelles Weekly (weekly, SDP)

Le Seychellois (daily of Seychelles Taxpayers' and Producers' Association)

Books and Articles

Allen, Philip M. "Mauritius on the Eve." Africa Report 5 (May 1966): 16-24.

Alexander, Douglas. Holiday in Mauritius: A Guide to the Island. Cape Town: Purnell, 1973.

Barclay's Bank. Mauritius: An Economic Survey. Port Louis: 1969.

_____. DCO. Mauritius: An Economic Survey. Oxford: Institute of Commonwealth Studies, 1964.

Benedict, Burton. "Education without Opportunity." Human Relations 9 (1958): 315-29.

_____. "Factionalism in Mauritian Villages." British Journal of Sociology 8, 4 (1957): 328-42.

_____. Indians in the Plural Society. London: Her Majesty's Stationery Office, 1961.

_____. "Mauritius at the Crossroads." British Journal of Sociology 12, 14 (1961): 387-91.

_____. Mauritius: Problems of a Plural Society. New York: Praeger Publishers, 1965.

_____. "Stratification in Plural Societies." American Anthropologist 64 (1962): 1235-46.

Brookfield, H. C. "Mauritius: Demographic Upsurge and Prospect." Population Studies 112, 2 (1957): 102-22.

_____. "Population Distribution in Mauritius." Journal of Tropical Geography 13 (1959): 1-22.

Cabon, Marcel. Biographie de Ramgoolam. Port Louis: Editions Mauriciennes, 1963.

Desmond, Annabelle, and Judy K. Morris. "The Story of Mauritius from the Dodos to the Storks." Population Bulletin 18, 5 (1962): 93-114.

Egli, David. "Mauritius, Where Foreign Aid Meets the Demographic Monster." Ceres 3, 1 (January-February 1970): 42-45.

Food and Agricultural Organization. Mauritius: Land and Water Resources Survey. New York: United Nations, July 1966.

Great Britain, British Information Service. Mauritius. New York, 1966.

_____. Central Office of Information, Mauritius and Seychelles. London: Her Majesty's Stationery Office, 1964.

Hahn, Lorna, with Robert Edison. Mauritius: A Study and Annotated Bibliography. Washington, D.C.: American University, 1969.

Hollingworth, Derek. They Came to Mauritius. London: Oxford University Press, 1965.

Leapman, M. "Tragedy in Mauritius." New Statesman (May 21, 1965).

Lelyveld, Joseph. "Racially Torn Mauritius Seeks National Unity." New York Times (March 19, 1968).

Luce, R. W. Report to the Government of Mauritius on Employment, Unemployment and Underemployment in the Colony in 1958 . . . Port Louis: Government Printer, 1958.

Malim, Michael. Island of the Swan. London: Longmans, 1952.

"Mauritius: Into the Vacuum." Time (June 15, 1970).

Meade, J. E. The Economic and Social Structure of Mauritius. London: Methuen, 1961.

Mohr, Charles. "In Mauritius: A Search for Unity." New York Times (December 26, 1970).

Naipaul, V. S. The Overcrowded Barracoon. London: André Deutsch, 1972.

Ommanney, F. D. "Fading Lustre: Mauritius." Geographical Magazine 26 (1954): 496-98.

Scott, Sir Robert. "Long Walk to Self-Government." Times (London) (March 12, 1968).

Simmons, Adele Smith.   Mauritius: The Politics of Pluralism.
    Ph.D. dissertation, University of Oxford, 1969.

De St. Jorre, John. "An Impoverished Independence: The Lonely
    Problems of Mauritius." Round Table 58 (April 1968): 217-19.

Titmuss, Richard M., B. Abel-Smith, and Tony Lynes. Social
    Policies and Population Growth in Mauritius. London: Methuen,
    1961.

U.S. Department of State. Mauritius. Background Note. Washington,
    D.C.: Government Printing Office, 1970.

Periodicals

Advance (pro-Ramgoolam)

L'Aube

Le Cernéen (pro-Duval)

L'Express

Inforama (vehicle for government releases)

Le Mauricien (pro-Duval)

Mauritius Times

Le Militant (MMM paper, banned)

The Nation (Labour Party)

The Star (the Muslim community's paper)

Sunday Express

La Vie Catholique

Weekend

ABOUT THE EDITOR AND THE CONTRIBUTORS

JOHN M. OSTHEIMER, educated at Yale University, is the author of Nigerian Politics (1973) and several articles. He teaches Political Science at Northern Arizona University.

MARTIN ADENEY is on the staff of the Guardian newspaper in London. He has written and broadcast extensively about South Asian affairs and in 1968-69 was attached to the Colombo Plan Bureau as a feature writer. He is the author of "Passage to Opportunity," a Colombo Plan booklet about some of the Plan's projects. He visited the Maldives in 1969.

PHILIP M. ALLEN, with a doctorate from Emory University, has served in the State Department, is the author of Self-Determination in the Western Indian Ocean (1966), The Traveller's Africa (1973), and many articles. He teaches at Johnson State College in Vermont.

WILLIAM K. CARR, of Washington, D.C. was one of the authors of Area Handbook for the Indian Ocean Territories (1971), has a doctorate in anthropology-linguistics, is the author of many articles, and has access to U.S. Government sources for Indian Ocean policy.

THE INDIAN OCEAN: ITS POLITICAL, ECONOMIC,
AND MILITARY IMPORTANCE

> edited by Alvin J. Cottrell
> and R. M. Burrell

MICRONESIA AND U.S. PACIFIC STRATEGY:
A Blueprint for the 1980s

> James H. Webb, Jr.

SOUTHEAST ASIA UNDER THE NEW BALANCE
OF POWER*

> edited by Sudershan Chawla,
> Melvin Gurtov, and Alain-
> Gerard Marsot

*Also available in paperback as a PSS Student Edition.